Relating to Self-harm and

Relating to Self-harm and Suicide presents original studies and research from contemporary psychoanalysts, therapists and academics focusing on the psychoanalytic understanding of suicide and self-harm, and how this can be applied to clinical work and policy.

This powerful critique of current thinking suggests that suicide and self-harm must be understood as having meaning within interpersonal and intrapsychic relationships, offering a new and more hopeful dimension for prevention and recovery. Divided into three parts, the book includes:

- a theoretical overview
- examples of psychoanalytic practice with self-harming and suicidal patients
- applications of psychoanalytic thinking to suicide and self-harm prevention.

Relating to Self-harm and Suicide will be helpful to psychoanalytic therapists, analysts and mental health professionals wanting to integrate psychoanalytic ideas into their work with self-harmers and the suicidal. This text will also be of use to academics and professionals involved in suicide prevention.

Stephen Briggs is Professor and Director of the Centre for Social Work Research in the University of East London and Vice Dean in the Adolescent Department of the Tavistock Clinic. He has worked as a clinician, teacher and researcher in the Tavistock's Adolescent Department since 1991 and has written widely on infancy, adolescence and suicide.

Alessandra Lemma is a Consultant Clinical Psychologist working in the Adolescent Department of Tavistock and Portman NHS Foundation Trust where she is also the Head of Psychology. She teaches widely and has a particular interest in trauma and body image disturbances. She trained as a psychoanalyst and is a member of the British Psychoanalytical Society.

William Crouch is a Clinical Psychologist in the Adolescent Department, Tavistock and Portman NHS Foundation Trust, with a training post in psychoanalytic psychotherapy. He has worked with young people in community mental health teams and in-patient units; he has set up a mental health service in an inner city Youth Offending Team.

Relating to Self-harm and Suicide

Psychoanalytic Perspectives on Practice, Theory and Prevention

Edited by Stephen Briggs, Alessandra Lemma and William Crouch

Routledge
Taylor & Francis Group

LONDON AND NEW YORK

First published 2008 by Routledge
27 Church Road, Hove, East Sussex BN3 2FA

Simultaneously published in the USA and Canada
by Routledge
711 Third Avenue, New York, NY 10017, USA

Routledge is an imprint of the Taylor & Francis Group, an Informa business

Typeset in Times by Garfield Morgan, Swansea, West Glamorgan
Paperback cover design by Design Deluxe, Bath

This publication has been produced with paper manufactured to strict environmental standards and with pulp derived from sustainable forests.

British Library Cataloguing in Publication Data
A catalogue record for this book is available from the British Library

Library of Congress Cataloging-in-Publication Data
Relating to self-harm and suicide : psychoanalytic perspectives on practice, theory, and prevention / edited by Stephen Briggs, Alessandra Lemma, and William Crouch.
        p. ; cm.
    "The book is based on and developed out of the discussions that took place at the Second International Suicidality and Psychoanalysis Congress"– Introd.
    Includes bibliographical references and index.
    ISBN 978-0-415-42256-7 (hbk) – ISBN 978-0-415-42257-4 (pbk.)
1. Suicide. 2. Parasuicide. 3. Suicidal behavior. 4. Psychoanalysis. I. Briggs, Stephen. II. Lemma, Alessandra. III. Crouch, William, 1969– IV. International Congress on Psychoanalysis and Suicide (2nd : 2006 : London, England)
    [DNLM: 1. Suicide–psychology. 2. Psychoanalysis. 3. Psychoanalytic Therapy. 4. Suicide–prevention & control. WM 165 R382 2008]
    RC569.R44 2008
    616.85'8445–dc22
                                                                            2007038787

ISBN 978-0-415-42256-7 (hbk)
ISBN 978-0-415-42257-4 (pbk)

To the memory of our colleague
Clare Doherty

Contents

List of contributors

Robin Anderson is a Training Analyst in adult, child and adolescent analysis at the British Psychoanalytical Society. He was also a Consultant Child and Adolescent Psychiatrist in the Adolescent Department of the Tavistock Clinic until 2003, where he was also Chair of the Department until 2000. He now concentrates on teaching and working in private psychoanalytic practice. He has published papers on both child and adolescent and adult psychoanalysis and psychotherapy, and numerous book chapters, and has also edited two books, including *Facing It Out: Clinical Perspectives on Adolescent Disturbance*, with Anna Dartington. He has particular interest in early object relationships and the way in which they manifest themselves in later life, especially during adolescence. He has applied this in working with suicidal young people.

David Bell is a Consultant Psychiatrist in Psychotherapy at the Tavistock Clinic, where he is Director of a Specialist Unit (the Fitzjohn's Unit) for assessment and treatment of Personality Disorder. He is Chairman of the Scientific Committee of the British Psychoanalytical Society, where he is also a Training and Supervising Psychoanalyst. He is Director and Principal Lecturer on the course 'The Development of Psychoanalytic Concepts' at the Tavistock Clinic. He has lectured and published widely on the psychoanalytic approach to serious psychiatric disorder, Freud scholarship, the work of Klein and Bion, psychoanalysis and culture. His publications include editing *Psychoanalysis and Culture: A Kleinian Perspective* (Tavistock Clinic Series, Tavistock/Duckworth 1998; reprinted Karnac 2005) and *Paranoia* (Icon Press 2002).

Stephen Briggs is Professor and Director of the Centre for Social Work Research in the University of East London/Tavistock Clinic, and Vice Dean in the Adolescent Department of the Tavistock Clinic. He has worked as a clinician, teacher and researcher in the Tavistock's Adolescent Department since 1991. He has written widely on infancy, adolescence and suicide. His books include *Growth and Risk in Infancy* (Jessica Kingsley 1997) and *Working with Adolescents: A Contemporary*

Psychodynamic Approach (Palgrave 2002) and he is Joint Editor of the *Journal of Social Work Practice*. He was Chair of the Organising Committee of the 2nd Psychoanalysis and Suicidality Congress, hosted by the Tavistock and Portman NHS Foundation Trust and held in London in 2006.

Donald Campbell is a member, training analyst and former President of the British Psychoanalytical Society. He worked for thirty years at the Portman Clinic in London where he also served as Chairman. He is the past Secretary General of the International Psychoanalytic Association. He has published on the subjects of suicide, violence, perversion, child sexual abuse and adolescence.

William Crouch is a Clinical Psychologist in the Adolescent Department, Tavistock and Portman NHS Foundation Trust, with a training post in psychoanalytic psychotherapy. He has worked with young people in community mental health teams and in-patient units; he has set up a mental health service in an inner city Youth Offending Team. As well as working as a clinician he has taught and conducted research in many areas of child development. He has a particular interest in self-harm by young people. He has written two papers including 'Deliberate self harm at an adolescent unit: a qualitative investigation', *Clinical Child Psychology and Psychiatry* 9(2): 185–204.

Elmar Etzersdorfer is the medical director of the Furtbachkrankenhaus, Hospital for Psychiatry and Psychotherapy, in Stuttgart, Germany. He is a psychiatrist and psychoanalyst (Viennese Psychoanalytical Society, German Psychoanalytical Association, International Psychoanalytical Association) and Chairman of the German Association for Suicide Prevention. He has published on different aspects of suicidological behaviour, including psychoanalytic and epidemiological, and the influences of media reporting on suicidal behaviour.

Georg Fiedler is a psychologist, teacher and Deputy Director of the Centre for Therapy and Studies of Suicidal Behaviour (TZS) at University Hospital Hamburg-Eppendorf. He is a National Representative of the International Association for Suicide Prevention (IASP), a member of the WHO/EURO Network on Suicide Prevention and Research, Secretary of the National Suicide Prevention Program for Germany, a member of the Board of the German Association for Suicide Prevention, and Secretary of the German Academy for Suicide Prevention.

Benigna Gerisch is a psychoanalyst (DPV/IPA), diplomaed-psychologist, psychotherapist, psychological psychotherapist and family therapist. She has worked as a psychotherapist and scientific member in the Centre for Therapy and Studies of Suicidal Behaviour (TZS) at University Hospital

Hamburg-Eppendorf since 1990, and as a psychoanalyst in private practice. She is an Associate Member of the European Editorial Board of the International Journal of Psychoanalysis. She has written on suicidality and gender differences, as well as psychoanalytical studies on suicidality in novels, films and in theatre. Her publications include *Suicidality Among Women – Myth and Reality: A Critical Analysis* (Edition Diskord 1998) and *The Suicidal Woman – Psychoanalytical Hypotheses on their Development* (Vandenhoeck & Ruprecht 2003). In 2000 she was the winner of the scientific award for young people given by the DPV for a study of explanatory patterns for the psychoanalytical understanding of suicidality in women.

Mark J Goldblatt works as a psychiatrist and psychoanalyst in Boston, Massachusetts. He is on the faculty of the Boston Psychoanalytic Society and Institute and is an Assistant Clinical Professor of Psychiatry at Harvard Medical School. He is a Clinical Associate at McLean Hospital and on the faculty of the Center for Psychoanalytic Studies at Massachusetts General Hospital. He teaches and supervises on suicide and psychodynamic therapy and also treats patients in private practice. He has written about many topics, including co-editing with Terry Maltsberger *Essential Papers on Suicide* (NYU Press 1996).

Paul Götze is a specialist in neurology, psychiatry, psychosomatic medicine, psychotherapy and psychoanalysis. He is a Professor at the Clinic for Psychiatry and Psychotherapy, a Founder and Head of the Centre for Therapy and Studies of Suicidal Behaviour (TZS) at University Hospital Hamburg-Eppendorf in Germany, and President of the German Academy of Suicide Prevention. Paul also teaches psychotherapy and psychoanalysis at the Michael Balint Institute and the Adolf Ernst Meyer Institute. His fields of research include short-term psychotherapy, psychodynamic aspects of psychosomatic and psychiatric disorders, especially transference and countertransference and suicidality, cultural history, philosophy, psychoanalytical understanding and therapy.

Robert Hale. Following a five-year research project into suicide at St Mary's Hospital, Robert Hale was appointed as a consultant in the Portman Clinic in 1980. His interests have included the different ways in which individuals abuse their bodies and the bodies of others. His current clinical interest is in paedophilia. In the past he has been Dean of Postgraduate Studies at the Tavistock Clinic and latterly Director of the Portman Clinic.

Ann Heyno is a student counsellor, Head of the Counselling and Advice Service and Director of Student Support Services at the University of Westminster. She taught counselling at Birkbeck (including on the MSc) for nineteen years, including ten years as Course Organiser for the

Diploma in Student Counselling. She is currently joint-chair of HUCS (Heads of University Counselling Services) and represented HUCS on the RaPSS (Responses and Prevention in Student Suicide) Advisory Group. She is also a member of AMOSSHE (Association of Managers of Student Services in Higher Education). Her publications include 'Cycles in the mind: clinical technique and the educational cycle', in *Clinical Counselling in Further and Higher Education* (Routledge 1999), 'Helping the unemployed professional', with Roland Pearson (Wiley 1988), and 'Student counselling; the wailing wall or a force for change?', in *Advocacy, Counselling and Mediation in Casework* (Jessica Kingsley 1988).

François Ladame is a psychiatrist and psychoanalyst and Professor of Psychiatry in the Faculty of Medicine, University of Geneva. He is also Head of the Units for Adolescents and Young Adults within the Department of Psychiatry, Geneva University Hospitals. He is a Training Analyst of the Swiss Psychoanalytical Society, Co-chair of the Forum on Adolescent Psychoanalysis of the European Psychoanalytical Federation, and former President of the Swiss Psychoanalytical Society. François has published numerous books alone or with other authors, several of which have been translated into Italian or English, around thirty chapters in books and over a hundred scientific papers.

Alessandra Lemma is a consultant clinical psychologist working in the Adolescent Department of the Tavistock and Portman NHS Foundation Trust where she is also the Head of Psychology. She teaches widely and has a particular interest in trauma and body image disturbances. She trained as a psychoanalyst and is a member of the British Psychoanalytical Society. She is an Honorary Senior Lecturer at University College London. She has published several books: *Starving to Live: The Paradox of Anorexia Nervosa* (Central Publishing 1994), *Invitation to Psychodynamic Psychology* (Whurr 1995), *Introduction to Psychopathology* (Sage 1996), *Humour on the Couch* (Whurr 2000), *Introduction to the Practice of Psychoanalytic Psychotherapy* (Wiley 2003), *The Perversion of Loss: Psychoanalytic Perspectives on Trauma* (ed. with S. Levy; Whurr 2004), and *Envy and Gratitude: Contemporary Perspectives* (ed. with P. Roth; in preparation; IPA Publications). She was on the Organising Committee of the 2nd Psychoanalysis and Suicidality Congress, hosted by the Tavistock and Portman NHS Foundation Trust and held in London in 2006.

Reinhard Lindner is a neurologist, psychiatrist, psychodynamic psychotherapist and specialist in psychosomatic medicine. He is a member of the Centre for Therapy and Studies of Suicidal Behaviour (TZS) at University Hospital Hamburg-Eppendorf and a teaching psychotherapist. His specific areas of interest lie in gender and age-specific suicidality, qualitative psychotherapy research and suicide prevention.

Jeanne Magagna qualified as a child, adult and family psychotherapist from the Tavistock Clinic in London. She is a consultant psychotherapist at Ellern Mede Centre for Eating Disorders and is also the Head of Psychotherapy Services at Great Ormond Street Hospital for Children in London. She is the Joint Coordinator and Vice-President of the Centro Studi Martha Harris Tavistock Model Child Psychotherapy Trainings in Florence, Venice and Palermo in Italy. She also acts as a consultant to the organizers and staff group of Family Futures Consortium, an adoption and fostering treatment centre in London. Her publications are mainly in the area of eating disorders, psychoses and infant observation. She is the joint editor of *Psychotherapy with Families* and editor of *Universals of Psychoanalysis*. Her publications are included in the popular books *Closely Observed Infants* (ed. L. Miller *et al.*), *Surviving Space* (ed. A. Briggs), *Eating Disorders in Children and Adolescents* (ed. R. Bryant-Waugh and B. Lask) and *The Generosity of Acceptance, Vol. 2* (ed. G. Williams).

John T. Maltsberger is a member of the faculty at the Boston Psycho-analytic Institute and an Associate Clinical Professor of Psychiatry at Harvard Medical School. In over thirty years of study of suicide and psychoanalysis he has written many papers including (with Dan Buie) 'The devices of suicide' (*International Review of Psychoanalysis*, 1980), (with Mark Goldblatt) *Essential Papers on Suicide* (New York University Press 1996) and 'The descent into suicide' (*International Journal of Psychoanalysis*, 2004).

Frank Matakas was born in Cologne, Germany and went to medical school in Cologne and Hamburg. He qualified in neuropathology at the Free University of Berlin, and has done research work in neuropathology and published on cerebral blood flow and its computer simulation. He qualified in psychiatry and psychoanalysis in Cologne. Since 1981 he has been head of a psychiatric hospital in Cologne, and has published on depression, schizophrenia and the specific therapeutic processes in a day hospital.

Carine Minne is a consultant psychiatrist in forensic psychotherapy and a psychoanalyst. She trained in forensic psychiatry and psychotherapy and has been based at the Portman Clinic and Broadmoor Hospital since 1999. She has developed long-term continuity of psychotherapy treatment for certain forensic psychiatry patients as they move through progressively lower secure settings and back into the community. Her particular area of interest is in treating young people with severe personality disorders who have been extremely violent, and providing a psycho-analytic aspect to the overall multi-disciplinary treatment plan. She is also the Training Programme Director for the five-year dual accreditation

Specialist Registrar training held between the Portman Clinic and the Three Bridges Medium Secure Unit, and she is a member of the National Training and Development Strategy for forensic psychotherapy. She is currently writing a book with Dr Leslie Sohn on forensic psychoanalytic issues.

Israel Orbach is a professor of psychology at Bar-Ilan University in Israel. He received his PhD in psychology from Yeshiva University in New York and was trained at Albert Einstein School of Medicine. For the past thirty years he has been engaged in teaching, research and psychotherapy. His main interest is in suicidal behaviour at all ages. He founded, with others, the Israeli Association for Suicide Prevention and served as its first president. He is the recipient of the American Association of Suicidology Dublin award (2002) and of the International Association of Suicide Prevention award (2003), both for distinguished contribution to the understanding of suicide.

Martin Seager is Consultant Psychologist and Head of Psychology in Redbridge Psychological Services and an adult psychotherapist. Previously he was Head of South Essex Psychology Service. He teaches on the Clinical Psychology Doctoral programmes at the University of East London and Essex University/Tavistock & Portman NHS Foundation Trust. He has written widely in mental health and psychology journals, is mental health advisor for Radio Essex and convenor of a national working party assessing universal psychological care principles and standards in the NHS.

Maggie Turp is a psychoanalytic psychotherapist and supervisor in private practice and a chartered psychologist. Her academic career has included lectureships at the University of Reading and at Birkbeck College, London. She is the author of a number of journal papers and two books, *Psychosomatic Health: The Body and the Word* (Palgrave 2001) and *Hidden Self-Harm: Narratives from Psychotherapy* (Jessica Kingsley 2003).

Foreword

Peter Fonagy

Suicide is responsible for a staggering 1.5 per cent of the total global burden of disease. It represents 20 million years of lost healthy life attributable to either premature death or permanent disability. It is one of those rare disorders where prevalence does not follow the usual lines of socioeconomic determinism. The risk of dying from suicide for whites is more than double that for blacks (Hoyert *et al*. 2006). The highest rates of suicide are in Eastern Europe where ten countries have suicide rates in excess of 27 per 100,000 population. This compares to a rate of 10–12 in other Western countries, including the United States (Centers for Disease Control and Prevention 2005). Of course these figures shrink almost into insignificance when compared to the rate of suicide attempts, which is around half a per cent a year, and suicidal ideation which is 3.3 per cent (Kessler *et al*. 2005). The size of the human tragedy associated with suicide is immense. Even in economic terms it has been estimated that in the United States alone suicidality is associated with nearly $12 billion lost income (Goldsmith *et al*. 2002). In the UK, each day two children or adolescents take their own lives, and each year 16,000 make an attempt at suicide. In UK inner-city areas suicidal ideation is reported in over 40 per cent of the population.

What do we know about the causes of suicide? Most formulations distinguish between factors that predispose and those that trigger (Mann 2002). In most Western countries suicide is strongly associated with psychiatric disorder, particularly mood disorders, which are associated with over half of suicides. Stressful life events are also correlates but clearly this is not the whole picture. Physical illness, age and gender are also strongly related to suicidal risk, as are factors such as substance misuse, the availability of lethal means, media models of suicidal acts, a sense of hopelessness and pessimism, impulsivity and attitudes to suicide (Mann 2002). A particularly striking fact about suicide is how closely related it is to being offered and receiving care. Eighty-three per cent of suicides have had contact with a doctor within a year of their death and 66 per cent within the last month of their life (Andersen *et al*. 2000; Luoma *et al*. 2002). This highlights the ambivalence inherent in the suicidal act, the pull from the individual who wishes to terminate their life to engage others, particularly care providers, in their struggle. It is a pull that we all feel in the counter-transference when we are asked to adopt the role of the person who stands in between the intention to end existence and the physical body that will perpetrate that act.

A major meta-analysis of suicide prevention strategies (Mann *et al.* 2005) identified that educating doctors about suicide and restricting access to lethal means (e.g. in prescribing) are effective methods to prevent the problem. These interventions are generally focused on educating primary care physicians about the detection and treatment of depression. In terms of treatment interventions, it is important to note that of the 90 per cent of suicides that are associated with psychiatric disorder, more than 80 per cent are untreated at the time of the individual's death (Henriksson *et al.* 2001). This might suggest that antidepressant medications have a great deal to offer. However, meta-analyses of randomized controlled trials have generally not detected benefit for suicide or suicide attempts in trials of antidepressants for psychiatric disorder (Fergusson *et al.* 2005; Gunnell *et al.* 2005; Khan *et al.* 2003). There is some epidemiological evidence that higher prescription rates correlate with decreasing suicide rates, but such evidence is hard to interpret (Gibbons *et al.* 2005; Hall *et al.* 2003). This correlation is not invariably found (Guaiana *et al.* 2005). The risk of ecological fallacy, inferring causality from group correlations, raises appropriate questions about this line of argument. In fact, at least in a paediatric and adolescent population, there have been considerable concerns about SSRIs increasing the risk of suicide in young people (Whittington *et al.* 2004). In any case, there are promising results from psychological therapy which suggest that at least prevention of the repetition of suicidal behaviour may be achieved by a range of therapeutic interventions. Needless to say, there is reasonable evidence for cognitive therapy (Brown *et al.* 2005) and problem-solving therapy (Hawton *et al.* 2002), but in this instance there is also evidence for psychodynamic psychotherapy from Elspeth Guthrie's group (Guthrie *et al.* 2001) and our own work with borderline personality disorder (Bateman and Fonagy forthcoming). In our study we found that suicide rates remained significantly lower in borderline patients treated with a mentalization-based approach than in a treatment-as-usual group over a period of six years following the end of therapy. It seems that psychotherapy alone or in combination with antidepressants is an effective treatment for suicide attempts and for preventing new attempts after a suicide attempt has taken place.

As this brief overview suggests, there are good bases for advancing our understanding of suicide attempts from a psychoanalytic standpoint. This massive emotional and economic burden, which falls not just on the sufferer but also on family members and healthcare providers, can be prevented or at least the risk can be reduced. Psychoanalysis, the most sophisticated discipline devoted to the study of subjective experience, has much to tell us about the internal world of those who choose to end their lives rather than struggle on. The epidemiological associations, including the strikingly high prevalence of mental disorder in suicide, cannot be of much help because they point to common factors that have extremely high background prevalence. In epidemiological surveys one in ten of us are possibly depressed and maybe as many as one in five have or have had some kind of mental disorder. Suicide is a much more specific risk but is also likely to be a final common pathway which is not going to have a single cause. In drawing conclusions from studying the internal worlds of our suicidal patients we must be careful to avoid the temptation of being persuaded by the plausibility of associations that we find and jumping to conclusions. After all, what we observe in our patients could as easily be a consequence of a previous attempt at suicide or a sequel to an event that may be linked to suicide rather than its cause. In particular, we must try to avoid at all costs generalizing from a few cases to a complex problem in a heterogeneous population. It is improbable that suicide in Japan has the same meaning as suicide in the UK, and it could be that all that these two acts have in common is the premature ending of a human life. Psycho-analysis has a massive amount to contribute in developing a subtle and nuanced picture of the individual with suicidal ideation. Out of that detailed picture, both screening techniques and prevention strategies will emerge which go way beyond the specific individuals whom psychoanalysis has a realistic chance of reaching.

This volume beautifully summarizes some of the most insightful psycho-analytic perspectives on a problem that is indeed a representation of the denial of life and an endorsement of hopelessness and final pessimism. It is a testament to the intensive training we undertake that psychoanalytic clinicians can retain a capacity to think, even when confronted with the bleakness of suicidal ideation and the professional pressures that this invariably brings. It is the openness of psychoanalysts to this experience that marks us out and that may indeed be most helpful for others in studying this volume. For those who are not psychoanalysts but are inter-ested in the internal world of the person who seeks an end to their life, this volume will surely open new windows of insight. For those who are already committed to a psychoanalytic orientation, the sophistication and subtlety of the ideas in this volume will reaffirm their commitment with patients whom it is all too easy to follow in losing faith and hope.

References

Andersen, U.A., Andersen, M., Rosholm, J.U. and Gram, L.F. (2000) 'Contacts to the health care system prior to suicide: a comprehensive analysis using registers for general and psychiatric hospital admissions, contacts to general practitioners and practising specialists and drug prescriptions', *Acta Psychiatrica Scandinavica*, 102(2): 126–134.

Bateman, A. and Fonagy, P. (submitted) 'Eight-year follow-up of patients treated for borderline personality disorder: mentalization based treatment versus treatment as usual', *American Journal of Psychiatry*.

Brown, G.K., Ten Have, T., Henriques, G.R., Xie, S.X., Hollander, J.E. and Beck, A.T. (2005) 'Cognitive therapy for the prevention of suicide attempts: a randomized controlled trial', *Journal of the American Medical Association* 294(5): 563–570.

Centers for Disease Control and Prevention (2005) National Center for Health Statistics: self-inflicted injury/suicide web page. Available at www.cdc.gov/nchs/fastats/suicide.htm.

Fergusson, D., Doucette, S., Glass, K.C., Shapiro, S., Healy, D., Hebert, P., *et al.* (2005) 'Association between suicide attempts and selective serotonin reuptake inhibitors: systematic review of randomised controlled trials', *British Medical Journal* 330(7488): 396.

Gibbons, R.D., Hur, K., Bhaumik, D.K. and Mann, J.J. (2005) 'The relationship between antidepressant medication use and rate of suicide', *Archives of General Psychiatry* 62(2): 165–172.

Goldsmith, S.K., Pellmar, T.C., Kleinman, A.M. and Bunney, W.E. (2002) *Reducing Suicide: A National Imperative*, Washington, DC: National Academies Press.

Guaiana, G., Andretta, M., Corbari, L., Mirandola, M., Sorio, A., D'Avanzo, B., *et al.* (2005) 'Antidepressant drug consumption and public health indicators in Italy, 1955 to 2000', *Journal of Clinical Psychiatry* 66(6): 750–755.

Gunnell, D., Saperia, J. and Ashby, D. (2005) 'Selective serotonin reuptake inhibitors (SSRIs) and suicide in adults: meta-analysis of drug company data from placebo controlled, randomised controlled trials submitted to the MHRA's safety review', *British Medical Journal* 330(7488): 385.

Guthrie, E., Kapur, N., Mackway-Jones, K., Chew-Graham, C., Moorey, J., Mendel, E., *et al.* (2001) 'Randomised controlled trial of brief psychological intervention after deliberate self poisoning', *British Medical Journal* 323(7305): 135–138.

Hall, W.D., Mant, A., Mitchell, P.B., Rendle, V.A., Hickie, I.B. and McManus, P. (2003) 'Association between antidepressant prescribing and suicide in Australia, 1991–2000: trend analysis', *British Medical Journal* 326(7397): 1008.

Hawton, K., Townsend, E., Arensman, E., *et al.* (2002) 'Psychosocial versus pharmacological treatments for deliberate self harm', *Cochrane Database Systematic Review*.

Henriksson, S., Boethius, G. and Isacsson, G. (2001) 'Suicides are seldom prescribed antidepressants: findings from a prospective prescription database in Jamtland county, Sweden, 1985–95', *Acta Psychiatrica Scandinavica* 103(4): 301–306.

Hoyert, D.L., Heron, M., Murphy, S.L. and Kung, H.C. (2006) *Deaths: Final Data for 2003. National Vital Statistics Reports; April 19 2006.* Hyattsville, MD: National Center for Health Statistics, 54(13).

Kessler, R.C., Berglund, P., Borges, G., Nock, M. and Wang, P.S. (2005) 'Trends in suicide ideation, plans, gestures, and attempts in the United States, 1990–1992 to 2001–2003', *Journal of the Americal Medical Association* 293(20): 2487–2495.

Khan, A., Khan, S., Kolts, R. and Brown, W.A. (2003) 'Suicide rates in clinical trials of SSRIs, other antidepressants, and placebo: analysis of FDA reports', *American Journal of Psychiatry* 160(4): 790–792.

Luoma, J.B., Martin, C.E. and Pearson, J.L. (2002) 'Contact with mental health and primary care providers before suicide: a review of the evidence', *American Journal of Psychiatry* 159(6): 909–916.

Mann, J.J. (2002) 'A current perspective of suicide and attempted suicide', *Annals of International Medicine* 136(4): 302–311.

Mann, J.J., Apter, A., Bertolote, J., Beautrais, A., Currier, D., Haas, A., *et al.* (2005) 'Suicide prevention strategies: a systematic review', *Journal of the American Medical Association* 294(16): 2064–2074.

Whittington, C.J., Kendall, T., Fonagy, P., Cottrell, D., Cotgrove, A. and Boddington, E. (2004) 'Selective serotonin reuptake inhibitors in childhood depression: systematic review of published versus unpublished data', *Lancet* 363(9418): 1341–1345.

Preface

Nicholas Temple

Suicide flies in the face of human hope and violently attacks relationships. It is at once the most difficult thing of all to bear and almost impossible to understand. This wide-ranging book brings together psychoanalytic approaches to understanding the origin of suicidal wishes, the treatment of suicidal patients and the prevention of suicide. It explores the dangerous unconscious forces set up in the relationship between the suicidal patient and those who are trying to help, which are so difficult to manage.

The chapters grew from the papers and dialogue that took place at the 2nd International Suicidality and Psychoanalysis Congress held in London in April 2006, which brought together contrasting psychoanalytic views, including those of Klein, Freud, Bion and Glasser. The book explores the important issue of suicide and depression and takes Freud's paper 'Mourning and melancholia' (1917) as its starting point. Freud emphasized the revengeful and self-destructive states of mind in melancholia turning against the self in hatred.

The nature of suicidal wishes and fantasies and their significance in the individual's primary relationships are explored. The complex nature of the internal world of the suicidal patient is discussed, including the importance of revenge as a motive for suicide. The idea of the killing of the self is involved with the wish to kill off those figures who are experienced as neglectful or persecutory and deserving of punishment. The authors describe the close association between murderous wishes and suicide as self-murder.

Melanie Klein's ideas about splitting and projective identification provide a basis for understanding how a suicidal patient may split good from bad in the internal world, locating the bad in the body which is to be destroyed, with the fantasy of obliterating the bad and leaving the good intact, as if the self-murder in suicide could get rid of the bad objects and preserve the good. Cases of multiple shooting followed by suicide emphasize this.

The book tackles what can be done from a psychoanalytical perspective. It is a challenge to standard approaches which tend to avoid the powerful feelings brought about by suicide in anybody who tries to help the suicidal patient. The negative therapeutic reaction illustrates the danger of suicide occurring at a time when the patient is recovering and primitive guilt pulls them back towards suicide.

The authors emphasize the very difficult feelings brought about in the countertransference to suicidal patients, not only in the terrible experience of loss, when the suicidal adolescent aims to rob his parents of their most treasured possession, but also the danger of countertransference feelings that can repeat the neglect by unconsciously failing to challenge the suicidal risk by allowing the patient to act out in small ways which allow the suicidal fantasy to go unnoticed.

This book is important because it offers a complex and in-depth approach to coping with suicidal patients by understanding them better, helping them with effective psychoanalytical treatment and applying psychoanalytical ideas to identify protective factors in suicide prevention.

Dr Nicholas Temple FRCPsych
Consultant Psychiatrist in Psychotherapy
Chief Executive, Tavistock and Portman NHS Foundation Trust

Acknowledgements

We are grateful first of all to all the speakers and delegates of the Second International Suicidality and Psychoanalysis Congress, organized by the Tavistock and Portman NHS Trust and held in London between 30 March and 2 April 2006. The inspiring quality of the papers presented and the discussions that took place was the major stimulus for this book. We would also like to acknowledge the support of the Tavistock Conference Unit, Alireza Afshari and Victoria Harrison for the organization of the Congress.

We are grateful to the editor and publisher of *Psychoanalytic Psychotherapy* for allowing us to include David Bell's chapter and to John Gordon and Gabriel Kirtchuk for allowing us to include Carine Minne's chapter.

We wish to particularly thank Catherine Lemberger for the work she has devoted to assisting us, in the production of this book and the Congress, and our colleagues, on the organization committee for the Congress, Liz Webb and Jeannie Milligan, whose support was crucial both for the Congress and for the early stages of editing this book. We thank Jonathan Buhagiar for helping in the final stages of producing the manuscript.

Introduction

Stephen Briggs, William Crouch and Alessandra Lemma

> Suicide is an act with meaning and has a purpose, both manifest and unconscious. It takes place in the context of a dyadic relationship, or rather its failure, and the suffering is experienced by the survivors, or rather, part survivors of the suicide attempt.

The quotation is from Robert Hale's first chapter of this book. It sets the scene and defines the territory. From a psychoanalytic perspective, suicide must be understood as relational, emotional, having meaning and impacting powerfully on others. In this book, we aim to explore psychoanalytic approaches to understanding, treating and preventing suicide, to present international and contemporary perspectives on current psychoanalytic thinking and practice, and to elucidate the contribution that this makes – and could make in the future – to contemporary approaches to suicide prevention.

The book is based on and developed out of the discussions that took place at the Second International Suicidality and Psychoanalysis Congress which we had the privilege to host in London in March/April 2006. These discussions were energetic and stimulating. They impressed on us, first, that there are some significant new developments within psychoanalytic thinking about suicide, in theory and practice, and, second, that the dialogue between contemporary practice and policy for suicide prevention and psychoanalytic approaches provides a lively critique of current mainstream approaches and offers a different dimension for understanding prevention. These two strands of thought – and debate that took place around them – motivated the production of this book and are at the heart of it. Accordingly the book consists in the main of chapters written by participants who made key contributions to the Congress.

Structure of the book

The book has been organized into three sections. In the first of these there are seven chapters which provide a theoretical overview. In each of these

chapters there is a significant discussion of an important theoretical position. Although all the contributors are psychoanalytic in their orientation,
they do not necessarily always share the same analytic tradition. We regard
such theoretical pluralism as important generally and essential when trying
to understand an overdetermined act like suicide. In the second section of
the book, five chapters include detailed accounts of psychoanalytic practice
with suicidal patients (in psychoanalysis and psychoanalytic psychotherapy). The third section consists of six chapters which demonstrate application of psychoanalytic thinking to suicide prevention.

It is central to the psychoanalytic method, and the way that theory is
generated from practice, that theory and practice are closely connected; thus
in all three sections, and in all chapters, there is an intermingling of theory
and practice. Therefore chapters in Parts 2 and 3 also develop theoretical
points and discussions, and the chapters in Part 1 are rich in practice
examples. The chapters, though arranged in these three sections, can be
cross-referenced to other important criteria; these include the method or
setting in which the work takes place (in-patient, out-patient, hospital,
private practice), the age and developmental stage of the group of patients/
clients, the theoretical tradition in which the author of each chapter writes,
and the language group she or he represents. This introduction will highlight
some of the main themes within each of the three sections and point out
some of the key cross-referencing points.

Suicide prevention: practice and policy

Suicide prevention has become a major issue for social policy worldwide.
Organizations at international, national and local levels have developed
approaches and strategies for reducing the suicide rate. It is imperative that
any approach to understanding suicide and working with suicidal and self-
harming people is connected with the larger picture of policy. A common
theme in the development of suicide prevention policies is to apply research
that identifies risk factors and high risk groups.

Preventing and reducing suicidal behaviour presents a conundrum.
Although we can identify high risk groups, find ways of reducing access to
the means for committing suicide, and realize that many if not most
suicides are 'preventable', there is a considerable gap between the larger
picture, generated by epidemiological research that identifies risk factors,
and the experience on the ground for practitioners working in mental health
and other settings in which there is no sure means of predicting suicidal
risk. As one eminent authority has put it:

> There are no consensually agreed on or valid, reliable risk assessment
> scales or other instruments that have standardized or simplified the task
> of assessment. There is no agreed on strategy for intervening in the life

and death decision of the suicidal mind or for treating the suicidal character.

(Berman *et al.* 2006: 7)

In the absence of consensus, there is a requirement for robust models of theory and practice. In this book we explore two key themes relevant to this requirement: first, how suicidality is understood from a psychoanalytic point of view, and, second, how this approach may provide a distinctive dimension to the task of suicide prevention. All the chapters contribute to our evolving understanding of the important role for the psychoanalytic perspective and what new questions it raises.

Developments in psychoanalytic theory

The contributors to this volume recognize a common heritage in Freud's (1917) discussion of suicide in his paper, 'Mourning and melancholia'. This paper, which 'overtowers everything else pertinent to suicide in the psycho-analytic literature' (Maltsberger and Goldblatt 1996: 5) is the starting point for thinking about suicidal relatedness. From Freud's formulation of the suicidal act arising from the reaction to the loss of an ambivalently loved and hated object, with whom the self has identified, the nature of suicidality as a problem of *relatedness* becomes a possible and necessary area for study. Freud was in fact often preoccupied with suicidality, and the range of his full contribution to understanding suicide has been understated (Briggs 2006), but 'Mourning and melancholia' has been the point of departure for the psychoanalytic study of suicide in different countries throughout the world. Freud's formulation of suicide, which we emphasize as starting a fruitful exploration of suicidal dynamics, lies in understanding the *constellation* of suicidal relatedness; this is far more than the simple 'aggression turned against the self' which Goldblatt (Chapter 8) points out has become a cliché. The most detailed discussion of 'Mourning and melancholia' in this book can be found in David Bell's chapter (Chapter 4).

Subsequent theoretical developments have been located in divergent traditions, showing marked differences of emphasis in different linguistic areas (Perelberg 1999). By including contributions from these different linguistic areas – North American, German, French, Israeli and British – and from the different main theoretical strands, we are able to identify here the emergence of layered overlapping of interdependent thinking between these separate traditions and developments. From this we can identify key themes and emphases.

Suicide has been understood psychoanalytically as primarily relational, involving dyadic relatedness. This position is derived from Freud's (1923) discussion in 'The Ego and the Id' of the conflict between ego and superego in certain pathological states, particularly melancholia. From an object relations perspective, the dyadic conflict involves conflicts between different internalized aspects of others, and poses, for the clinician, the key question 'Who is hurting or killing whom?' (Bell, Chapter 4). The clinician's need to understand different constellations of suicidal dynamics within this under-pinning dyadic conflict has contributed to the development of models of suicidal relatedness. In North America, Maltsberger and Buie (1980) began to identify distinctive 'suicide fantasies', that is, patterns of unconscious relational dynamics that power suicidal behaviour. The notion of suicide fantasy has been developed in the UK by Hale (Chapter 1) and Campbell (Chapter 2). Though there are now a number of such typologies, Hale particularly describes these to include fantasies of merger (or reunion/rebirth), punishment, revenge, elimination (assassination) and dicing with death. The essence of the dynamics of suicide fantasies is that an impossible 'no-win' conflict exists. Glasser's (1979) 'core complex', used by both Campbell and Hale in their formulations of suicide fantasies, captures the dilemma for those patients for whom neither separateness nor intimacy are possible; the former stirs terror of abandonment and the latter engulfment. In such cases suicide appears to be a 'solution', and one which is based on an unrealistic appraisal of the dynamic impact of suicide on the self.

This links with a train of thought about suicidal dynamics that tran-scends localities of place and theoretical tradition, namely, that suicide takes place in a psychotic moment or state of mind. Time and again in the various contributions to this book we see that this notion is returned to and re-explored. In various ways, our writers describe the impact on suicide of a psychotic part of the personality (Anderson, Chapter 5), a primitive psy-chotic superego which demands omnipotence, not knowledge (Bell, Chapter 4), and the delusion of surviving the suicide (Hale and Campbell, Chapters 1 and 2). Maltsberger (Chapter 3) introduces the theme of suicide as a traumatic state of disintegration, in which, totally overwhelmed by over-powering emotions, the active attack on the body has a calming effect. It is the impairment of reality testing that evidences the transient psychotic moment. The fear of break-up of the self and total disintegration consti-tutes for the suicidal person a possibility far worse than suicide. Ladame (Chapter 6) similarly discusses the 'psychotic moment' in which reality testing does not function; in a state of panic and being traumatically over-whelmed a suicide bid appears to be the only solution. Orbach (Chapter 7) draws partly on Maltsberger to discuss how the impact of mental pain and a sense of emotional flooding is significant in bringing about suicidal states of mind.

This theme is linked closely with the idea that suicide constitutes a traumatic experience. In this book there is considerable attention paid to understanding and elaborating the theme of suicide as trauma. In Maltsberger's thinking, it is the internal state of disintegration that constitutes a traumatic experience. Ladame's discussion is based on the view that a suicidal crisis is a psychic trauma, in which the psychic apparatus is disabled, temporarily frozen through the rupturing effect of a suicidal act. Magagna (Chapter 9) points out that the parallel between the effects of suicide and trauma was first commented on by Edwin Shneidman (Shneidman *et al.* 1976), and she discusses the state of psychic numbness experienced by people after a suicidal act. The clinical and practice implications of this line of thought are significant and broad-ranging and will be discussed later in this introduction.

A further line of theoretical development is the discussion of depression and the application of ways of differentiating different kinds of depression underpinning suicidal dynamics. This considerably extends Freud's understanding of 'melancholia'. Although most people who commit suicide are depressed, most depressed people are not suicidal, and some who commit suicide are not classifiable as depressed. Orbach (Chapter 7), drawing on Shneidman's work, suggests that the psychiatric category of depression is irrelevant for understanding suicide. Rather, Orbach stresses that it is the inner state of mind that needs to be understood. Other authors consider the differentiation of different qualities of 'depression' to be helpful in this regard. Matakas and Rohrbach (Chapter 13) distinguish between different responses to the symptoms of depression. One group they find refuse to let others meet their regressed needs, and another group do not themselves accept such needs. Bell, using a Kleinian framework, distinguishes between depressive pain – in which the aim is to make reparation and in which concern for self and other is apparent – and clinical depression, which is driven by persecutory anxiety and a suicidal state, which is accusatory and pervaded by a sense of irrevocably damaged objects.

The theme of the underlying destructive relatedness to self and others is further developed by Goldblatt (Chapter 8), through careful clinical descriptions of hostility. Anderson (Chapter 5) contextualizes the stirring up of uncontained primitive parts of the self in the context of the developmental stresses of adolescence, and Etzersdorfer (Chapter 12) and Magagna (Chapter 9) both discuss such hostility as attacking links between objects, life and liveliness. Etzersdorfer relates this to the death instinct and Magagna emphasizes the attack on the good internal object.

A number of authors discuss destructive relatedness to the body. Hale refers to suicide as the attempt to 'kill the self's body' (Chapter 1). This theme is explored in relation to relating to the body in adolescent development (Anderson, Chapter 5), hatred of the body (Orbach, Chapter 7) and gendered experience (Gerisch, Chapter 10). Gerisch links the gender-specific experience of the body with the clinical detail of how women who are suicidal encounter both core complex anxieties – the fear of intimacy and the fear of separateness. Experiences of intimacy and separateness are felt in and through the body and relatedness to it.

How does the psychoanalytic approach help to prevent suicide?

Psychoanalytic contributions to suicide prevention are located in three domains: the contribution of clinical psychoanalytic work in psychoanalysis and psychoanalytic psychotherapy; applications of psychoanalytic thinking to work undertaken by workers in various public, private and voluntary settings in the mental health field; and, third, applications to understanding broader practice and policy issues including organizational dynamics. All three of these strands are represented in this book.

Psychoanalytic clinical practice

The psychoanalytic treatment of suicidal patients represents a significant contribution to the reduction of suicidality. Through analysis and psycho-therapy the underlying relational and emotional factors that cause suicidal behaviour can be identified, understood and worked through. One of the significant developments in the psychotherapeutic treatment of suicide is that psychoanalytic clinicians are beginning to write more about clinical experiences of work with suicidal patients. This focuses on the elucidation of a particular theme in relation to an experience of a particular patient and analysis or psychotherapy. It has the merit of providing detailed discussions of what transpires between patient and analyst or therapist; how the qualities of relatedness develop in the treatment and how the analyst or therapist makes sense of these experiences through reflecting on and analysing the transference and countertransference. These clinical accounts recognize suicide as an important clinical consideration in its own right – that is, not simply a 'symptom' – and this increases the value of this kind of writing for understanding the treatment of suicidal patients. The tone of realism is also important to note. These clinical chapters demonstrate reflective discussion of the vicissitudes of treatment, alongside a balanced appraisal of the process and outcomes. Specifically, in this respect, psycho-analytic writers have recently been able to discuss the impact and meaning of suicide attempts undertaken by patients within treatment. This adds to the realism of the accounts and enhances understanding of the particular kinds of relatedness that develop, including the pressures analysts and therapists face when working with the potential for suicidal and other forms of acting out.

Central to these clinical discussions is the focus on transference and countertransference. Campbell (Chapter 2) focuses on the role of the father transference in a pre-suicide state, particularly where the father is felt to be absent or ineffective. Campbell explores the meaning of the transference and countertransference in relation to a patient's pre-suicide state and suicide attempt. This very challenging area of work invites an exploration of the adaptations that may be required both at the level of theoretical understanding and at the level of analytic technique in different settings when working with suicidal patients. Some key themes can be identified.

Goldblatt (Chapter 8) introduces a way of working in which special therapeutic accommodations are used to enable building the therapeutic alliance. He points out that these accommodations tend to demand sacrifices from the therapist, and they are necessary because the extraordinary needs of such patients cannot be met by 'normal' techniques, particularly when dealing with the patient's hostility where it cannot be accessed through more 'classical' interpretations. Through a detailed account of his work with one patient, Goldblatt suggests that, with some patients, interpreting the hostility would be experienced concretely as an attack, and not providing some between-session contact, as was the case with this patient, would be experienced as abandoning. Of course, there are different and firmly held views about the way that the analytic setting is handled. Others would argue that it is the psychotic or more perverse part of the patient that attacks the setting and draws the therapist into changing it. These important technical questions deserve more open debate.

Second, several authors examine the need to extend the boundaries of psychoanalytic work, either through developing new understanding or through working with new groups of patients, in challenging settings. Minne (Chapter 11) comes into this category in describing work within a high security hospital. She defines the treatment aims with people who have committed violent crimes as treading between enabling awareness and understanding, which is essential to prevent further violent crimes, and at the same time also attending to the potentially catastrophic and suicidal effects of undoing the defensive purpose of not knowing.

Gerisch (Chapter 10) adds to the literature on gender and suicide. Gender is a key variable in suicide: men complete suicide more frequently but women make more attempts. Discussing analytic work with a woman, she suggests that the shared gender between mother and daughter presents a particular vulnerability to suicidal behaviours because it increases the risk that the body acts as the central organizing structure of unconscious intersubjective processes in the mother–daughter dyad. Etzersdorfer (Chapter 12) offers a counterpoint through discussing a disturbed man whose suicidality is seen as a defence against fears of a psychotic breakdown. Suicidal threats are a constant theme in the treatment, a threat both to the treatment and the patient's life. The patient rarely directly talks about suicidal thoughts but they appear in the material as projected into others. Magagna (Chapter 9), working in a hospital setting, provides an innovative framework for assessing and understanding suicidality in young people, and, in a series of examples, links the wish to die through anorexia with quicker methods to identify patterns of relationships underlying suicide or self-harm.

Applications to prevention and postvention

In the third section of this book there are two particular themes. The first of these is an exploration of the application of a psychoanalytic approach to work in different settings and with different groups of people. This includes Lindner and colleagues' discussion of suicidality in later life (Chapter 15), Heyno's exploration of working in a student counselling setting (Chapter 14), and Turp's discussion, from the perspective of a psychotherapist, of working with 'hidden' self-harm (Chapter 16). This is conceptualized as the need to identify significant lapses in self-care that go beyond 'normal' risk taking.

The assessment of risks at different levels is an important theme with regard to the second aim of this section, which is to explore the relationship between psychoanalytic thinking and suicide prevention policy. There is increasing recognition that suicidal people can be treated unkindly, sometimes cruelly – not necessarily consciously – by professionals in mainstream services (NICE 2004). People with histories of suicide can have negative experiences of accessing services and feel themselves stigmatized by these contacts. In this book, an understanding of unconscious processes operating within organizations provides a framework for understanding these experiences, for individuals within organizations and in terms of organizational cultures.

Bell (Chapter 4) – in a commentary that is referred to by a number of other authors in this book – discusses how, under the emotional pressure of working with suicidality, organizations can become omnipotent, losing the boundary between care for the suicidal and taking total responsibility (and blame). This is particularly relevant in 'risk aversive' cultures, in health services and other sectors where suicidality is present. Heyno's discussion (Chapter 14) shows how educational organizations can become 'infected by' and identify with the fantasy of eliminating experiences of pain, and adverse, stigmatizing publicity. Briggs (Chapter 18) discusses the effects of suicide on individuals and organizations, pointing out the impact of primitive or abnormal superego function on stigmatizing interactions.

Seager (Chapter 17) explores concepts of risk and safety in health organizations in the UK. He critiques conscious and unconscious failures of containment, often operating at an unconscious level, and found particularly at points of transition and discharge. He suggests that there needs to be a change at a policy level, where psychoanalytic thinking could be used to think more about concepts of 'psychological safety'. In Maytree, a respite centre for the suicidal, in London, where the emphasis is on containment, a different and more benign culture is produced, which is not 'risk aversive' or omnipotent (Briggs *et al.* 2007).

One of the powerful and consistent themes in the book is that suicide prevention would be enhanced by recognition of the meaning and impact of psychic trauma, both on those who make suicide attempts and on those – family, friends, and professionals – who are affected by suicidal behaviour. At many points in the book it is recognized and evidenced that a significant proportion of patients who attempt suicide have experienced traumatic events at some stage in their lives. These experiences lead to specific and recognizable patterns of relatedness. If these are the focus of attention for professionals, the approach to suicidal people can follow principles of containment rather than enactment and repetition of traumatizing – and stigmatizing – dynamics. This leads to the re-evaluation of service provision and the premises on which this is based.

Recognizing and understanding the importance of the effects of psychic trauma, as discussed above, lead to realignment of services, and a reorientation of the ways in which they are delivered. Ladame (Chapter 6) and Matakas and Rohrbach (Chapter 13) give examples of the development of in-patient services based on a recognition of the meaning of trauma and depression. Ladame's model of treatment prioritizes the need for containment following the psychic trauma of a suicide attempt. In his view, the appropriate kind of containment can only be achieved in time-limited and focused in-patient settings. Matakas shows how suicide rates in a psychiatric hospital fell once the treatment method was changed to recognize the need to relieve the depressed person of responsibilities that were experienced as overwhelming, and thus to allow regression.

Also considering work in a hospital setting, Magagna (Chapter 9) argues against the traditional distinction between physical and emotional care for young people who have attempted suicide or have life-threatening eating disorders. Rather than relegate psychotherapeutic work, which would aid understanding, until after the physical regime has reached its goals, she believes that this should be a priority. The implication for work in these and other settings is the priority of recognizing the emotional impact of this kind of work and structuring ways in which staff can process it. Settings which provide staff with supervision through 'work discussion' groups dealing with the experience of working with disturbance have been shown to be effective in educational and psychiatric settings (Lemma 2000; Warman and Jackson 2007).

This overview of the themes developed in this collection testifies to the ways that the psychoanalytic approach enriches understanding and interventions. It also emphasizes the complexity of the painful and sometimes terrifying states of mind that can contribute to suicidality. For those professionals working in this area the countertransference can be hard to bear. The pressure towards enactment is considerable and sometimes inevitable. There are no easy solutions. It is, however, evident that all the authors who have contributed strive to 'keep thinking' even when under this kind of extreme pressure and that this makes an important contribution both to understanding suicidality and preventing it. The importance of the psychoanalytic approach to suicide and self-harm lies in its capacity to conceptualize relatedness, and the unconscious processes that affect suicidal people and those in personal and professional contact with them. This approach extends understanding and provides ways of intervening which promote prevention.

References

Berman, A., Jobes, D. and Silverman, M. (2006) *Adolescent Suicide: Assessment and Intervention*, 2nd edn, Washington, DC: American Psychological Association.

Briggs, S. (2006) '"Consenting to its own destruction. . . ." A reassessment of Freud's development of a theory of suicide', *Psychoanalytic Review* 93, 4: 541–564.

Briggs, S., Webb, L. and Buhagiar, J. (2007) 'Maytree, a respite centre for the suicidal: an evaluation', *Crisis; The Journal of Crisis Intervention and Suicide Prevention* 28, 3: 140–147.

Freud, S. (1917) 'Mourning and melancholia', in J. Strachey (ed.) *The Standard Edition of the Works of Sigmund Freud, XIV* (pp. 237–258), London: Hogarth.

Freud, S. (1923) 'The Ego and the Id', in J. Strachey (ed.) *The Standard Edition of the Works of Sigmund Freud, XIV* (pp. 1–66), London: Hogarth.

Glasser, M. (1979) 'Some aspects of the role of aggression in the perversions', in I. Rosen (ed.) *The Pathology and Treatment of Sexual Deviations*, Oxford: Oxford University Press.

Lemma, A. (2000) 'Containing the containers: the effects of a psychodynamically informed training and casework discussion groups on burnout in psychiatric nurses', unpublished doctoral thesis, Surrey University.

Maltsberger, J.T. and Buie, D.H. (1980) 'The devices of suicide', *International Review of Psychoanalysis* 7: 61–72.

Maltsberger, J.T. and Goldblatt, M.J. (1996) *Essential Papers on Suicide*, New York and London: New York University Press.

NICE (2004) Self-harm: the short-term physical and psychological management and secondary prevention of self-harm in primary and secondary care. http://guidance.nice.org.uk/CG16

Perelberg, R. (ed.) (1999) 'Psychoanalytic understanding of violence and suicide: a review of the literature and some new formulations', in J. Perleberg *Psychoanalytic Unerstanding of Violence and Suicide*, London: Routledge/New Library of Psychoanalysis.

Shneidman, E.S., Farberow, N.L. and Litman, R.E. (eds) (1976) *The Psychology of Suicide*, New York: Science House.

Warman, A. and Jackson, E. (2007) 'Recruiting and retaining children and families' social workers: the potential of work discussion groups', *Journal of Social Work Practice* 21, 1: 135–148.

Part 1

Developments in theory

Chapter 1

Psychoanalysis and suicide: process and typology

Robert Hale

This chapter presents what I consider to be some of the basic dynamics of suicide. Much of it is taken from a paper written with Donald Campbell in 1991 (Campbell and Hale 1991), but it also borrows from authors in *Essential Papers on Suicide* by Maltsberger and Goldblatt (1996). It is, then, a mixture of my own and other people's ideas. The work on which it is based took place over twenty-five years ago when I was working at St Mary's Hospital. For five years I saw only people who had attempted suicide. I had an office on the Acute Medical Admissions ward and saw well over 500 people who had been admitted following a suicide attempt. Some of these people went on to psychotherapy with me or a colleague, and a very small number entered psychoanalysis. Some twenty-two years later, two colleagues (Jenkins *et al.* 2002) followed up a cohort of 240 consecutive admissions following a suicide attempt. Not surprisingly, given previous studies, a much higher proportion of them ended up killing themselves than would be expected by chance, but surprisingly the rate of death by suicide did not fall significantly over the years. The conclusion, then, is that suicide remains a lifelong option which can be employed at times of crisis.

It is worth recording a note of caution in relation to much psychiatric research on suicide. A recent review on American figures by Luoma and colleagues (2002) revealed that of those people who killed themselves, only 33 per cent had been in contact with secondary psychiatric services in the previous year, but 75 per cent had been in contact with their GP. In the month prior to death 20 per cent had been in contact with mental health services, whereas 50 per cent had consulted their GP. It is impossible to say whether this indicates that the majority of those killing themselves are not mentally ill or do not recognise it, or, alternatively, do not see any purpose in consulting psychiatric services. However, figures would suggest that we might be looking in the wrong place since most psychiatric research concentrates on those in contact with secondary psychiatric services and ignores the vast majority who are not. Therefore prevention strategies might be better focused on education and support of general practitioners and counsellors in general practice settings.

Psychoanalytic interest in suicide dates from the 1910 symposium *On Suicide* in which Wilhelm Stekel wrote the most basic and crucial statement on suicide: 'I am inclined to feel that the principle of talion plays the decisive role here. No one kills himself who has never wanted to kill, or at least wished the death of another' (Friedman 1967: 87). He went on to explore the nature of the relationship between the suicidal young person and his or her parent:

> The child wants to rob his parents of their greatest and most precious possession: his own life. The child knows that thereby he will inflict the greatest pain. Thus the punishment the child imposes upon himself is simultaneously a punishment he imposes on the instigators of his suffering.
>
> (Friedman 1967: 87)

On the other side of Europe, in England, the poet A.E. Housman (1939/1995) wrote the following lines in the same year:

> Good creatures, do you love your lives
>   And have you ears for sense?
> Here is a knife like other knives,
>   That cost me eighteen pence.
>
> I need but stick it in my heart
>   And down will come the sky,
> And earth's foundations will depart
>   And all you folk will die.

From these authors we learn immediately that suicide is an act with meaning and has a purpose, both manifest and unconscious. It takes place in the context of a dyadic relationship, or rather its failure, and the suffering is experienced by the survivors, or rather, part survivors, of the suicide attempt.

It will already be seen that I do not draw a distinction between suicide and attempted suicide as do many descriptive psychiatrists. This is because I understand suicidal acts along a spectrum: fundamentally the wish to kill the body is present in all suicidal acts, as is the wish to survive. The fantasies which drive the suicidal act are multiple, complex and over-determined. They frequently contain internal contradictions, the most obvious being the wish to live and the wish to die. A patient who was himself a statistician took 199 aspirins. When asked why he did not take the two-hundredth, he replied, 'It fell on the floor – I thought it would have germs on it.' My working definition of the suicidal act is the conscious or unconscious intention at the time of the act to kill the self's body. This should be contrasted with acts of self-mutilation in which the intention is not to kill but to torture the body.

Suicide is a form of acting out. Freud (1914) originally used the term to describe the phenomenon of a patient, whilst in psychoanalytic treatment, carrying out an action that in symbolic form represents an unconscious wish or fantasy, which cannot be experienced or expressed in any other way within the treatment. Over the years the term has been broadened to describe a general character trait in which a person is given to relieving any intrapsychic tension by physical action.

Acting out is the substitute for remembering a traumatic childhood experience, and unconsciously aims to reverse that early trauma. The patient is spared the painful memory of the trauma, and via his action masters in the present the early experience he originally suffered passively. The actors in the current situation are seen for what they are now rather than for what they represent from the past. Furthermore, the internal drama passes directly from unconscious impulse to action, shortcutting both conscious thought and feeling. The crucial element is that the conflict is resolved, albeit temporarily, by the use of the patient's body, often in a destructive or erotised way.

The person will implicate and involve others in this enactment. The others may be innocent bystanders, or have their own unconscious reasons for entering and playing a continuing role in the patient's scenario. The patient thus creates the characters and conflicts of his past in the people of his present, forcing them (by the use of projection and projective identification) to experience feelings which his consciousness cannot contain. He gains temporary relief, but as the players in the patient's play disentangle themselves from their appointed roles, projections break down, and what has been projected returns to the patient. Because he knows no other solution by which he can escape his inner conflicts, the patient is forced to create anew the same scenario in a different setting. This is the essence of what Freud (1920) referred to as 'the repetition compulsion'. In suicide, the unconscious fantasy often revolves around settling old scores from unfinished and unacknowledged battles of childhood. These are memories that reside in that part of the patient's mind of which he is unaware, and of which he has no understanding. Freud described these memories as 'ghosts' which compulsively haunt the patient: 'That which cannot be understood inevitably reappears; like an unlaid ghost that cannot rest until the mystery has been solved and the spell broken' (1901: 122).

Our way into this mystery is by viewing acting out as equivalent to a symptom. In a symptom a fantasy finds symbolic expression in psychological phenomena (or in the case of a psychosomatic symptom, in physical illness); in acting out it is the action which is the symbol of the unconscious conflict. As with the symptom, the exact form of the action is precisely and specifically fashioned by the unconscious fantasies and conflicts. A close examination of the external facts of a suicidal act and the analysis of their symbolic meaning are the clearest pathways to the fantasies which have driven it.

I want now to consider the three sets of personality constellations that underlie a propensity towards suicidal behaviour, and then to describe the final common pathway of the descent into suicide with the fantasies which drive this movement. A recent paper by Apter (2004) confirms the limitations of sole reliance upon assessment of psychiatric disorder in determining suicidal risks. Apter cites the frequent association between suicidal states and mental disorder, commenting, 'However, these diagnostic indicators have low specificity, do not aid greatly the prediction of suicidal behaviour within diagnostic categories such as depression and do not shed light on the aetiology of suicidal behaviour' (2004: 24). Apter hypothesises that there are three sets of personality constellations that may underlie a propensity towards suicidal behaviour:

1   Narcissism, perfectionism and the inability to tolerate failure and imperfection, combined with an underlying schizoid personality structure that does not allow the individual to ask for help and denies him the comforts of intimacy. In most cases these seem to be lifelong personality patterns not related to stress or periods of depression. Apter describes these people as using achievement as a kind of pseudo-mastery substitute for a lack of real interpersonal closeness in the form of a suicidal act. Shame and humiliation are triggers for suicidal acts in this group of people.

2   Impulsive and aggressive characteristics combined with an over-sensitivity to minor life events. This sensitivity often leads to angry and anxious reactions with secondary depression. These people tend to use defences such as regression, splitting, dissociation and displacement. They have often suffered childhood physical and sexual abuse and there is often a history of alcohol or substance abuse in adult life. Apter (2004) links these characteristics to an underlying disturbance of serotonin metabolism, which he suggests is genetic in origin. However, given the high incidence of childhood traumatic events in this group of patients, and with the increasing knowledge of the biological consequences of child abuse, it seems possible that the biochemical abnormalities are at least to an extent determined by childhood trauma. In adult life these people are seen as impulsive, at times aggressive, with a low tolerance of frustration. They are often categorised as having borderline personality disorder.

3   In those persons whose suicidal behaviour is driven by hopelessness often related to an underlying depressive state, Apter suggests that this hopelessness results from mental illness, such as affective disorder, schizophrenia or anxiety disorder, using the paradigm underlying

mental illness to account for the suicidal behaviour. Clearly this is the case when one encounters an individual who has longstanding bipolar disorder (recurrent manic depression or recurrent depression) or a recurring schizophrenic illness. However, in my experience, in the majority of cases, the depressive state is a reaction to life circumstances and represents unconscious anger turned towards the self.

Core complex relationship

The starting point for suicide is the core complex relationship, as described by Glasser (1979), which refers to a way of relating to the 'significant other'. For the person who engages in this sort of relationship there are two equal and opposite terrors: first, that of closeness, because with it comes the fear of being engulfed by the other person, and thus of losing one's own identity; and second, that of being left and thus abandoned to starve by the other. Whilst this is an almost ubiquitous phenomenon, what identifies the core complex individual is first the intensity of the feelings, and second the means by which they control their partner. In 'normal' individuals, the signals for an appropriate degree of togetherness or separation are affectionate or collaborative; in the core complex individual the distance is maintained by communications or acts of cruelty and coercion.

Betrayal and the pre-suicidal state

Inevitably something will happen which is perceived by the suicidal individual as a betrayal of trust, usually an act of abandonment, and the individual enters the pre-suicidal state described by Ringel (1976). This is the 'accident about to happen' state in which the suicidal fantasies are becoming conscious, and preparations for the suicidal act are made. The pre-suicidal state may last hours or days, but eventually there will be a final trigger which will destroy all ego controls, and the individual's mind fragments into a state of confusion.

The trigger

A trigger to violence may take any of three forms, and precipitate the final breakdown into a destructive attack, either suicidal or violent:

1   An actual physical attack, however small, which crosses the body boundary. In the process of an extended argument, one workmate pushed his fingers into the ribs of Mr A to make his point more forcefully. In response, Mr A broke his mate's jaw.
2   A physical gesture may be experienced as an attack or as rejection. The commonest gesture must be a V-sign, but it can be a denigrating

look, or a turning away, or a rejection, like shutting the door in someone's face.
3   Words which have an intrusive, dismissing and sexualised character, which are felt as a physical assault or dismissal.

All three things have in common, first, that they are experienced as an assault or as a rejection, and, second, that the recipient/'victim' cannot assess them objectively so that they are felt to be overwhelming. It is thus the internal meaning of the trigger that matters. What is explosive to one person may be innocuous to another. What is catastrophic at one time may be irrelevant at another.

Confusion

Two observations substantiate the importance of confusion as an element in violent suicidal acts. First, in general hospitals the commonest cause of violence is a toxic confusional state in which an innocuous stimulus is perceived as threatening – delirium tremens is a good example. Second, about 35 per cent of suicides and a very large number of acts of violence occur after alcohol has been ingested. It is commonly suggested that 'alcohol dissolves the superego' and with it the conscience and a prohibition against violence. I would also suggest that intoxication impairs the ability of the ego to discriminate between threatening and non-threatening forces whether from outside or within. As a result, terrifying conjunctions of thoughts can occur which the ego in a confusional state is unable to keep separate or realistically evaluate.

Confusion has two elements. First, the conjunction of two previously separated ideas, probably unconscious, coming together into consciousness may be so unacceptable that they are attacked and fragmented into chaotic disorder. Second, this chaos is in itself terrifying for it represents the total loss of control that we all fear – that is, going mad. Thus, when more sophisticated ego defences fail, more primitive 'reflective' physical defences are employed to get rid of unacceptable thoughts and feeling states. The body barrier is crossed.

Body barrier

The term 'body barrier' describes the resistance that exists in everybody to translating the now conscious fantasy of violence into physical action. The state of confusion described above reduces this resistance. However, if this resistance has been once overcome it becomes increasingly easy to adopt a physical pathway for discharging the intrapsychic tension. This explains in part the repetitive nature of self-destructive acts.

The stages of the suicidal process which is the final common pathway to suicide can be represented graphically as in Figure 1.1.

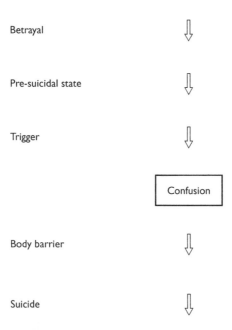

Betrayal

Pre-suicidal state

Trigger

Confusion

Body barrier

Suicide

Figure 1.1 Core complex relationship

The fantasies driving suicide

The suicide fantasies, which elaborate the relationship between the 'surviving self' and the body, take at least five forms, which I will now describe briefly. Although one type of fantasy may dominate consciously, suicide fantasies are interdependent and at an unconscious level not mutually exclusive. Within the patient, each fantasy is organised around a wish to gratify pre-genital impulses, which are predominantly sadomasochistic or oral-incorporative in nature.

First, an almost universal suicidal fantasy is the *revenge fantasy*. The revenge fantasy centres on the impact that the suicide makes on others. Here, a conscious link to a real object is maintained more strongly than in other suicide fantasies. The often conscious thought in the revenge fantasy is 'They will be sorry'. The implicit message is that the parents have raised a child who hates himself because they did not love him enough.

A second fantasy, the *self-punishment fantasy*, is dominated by guilt, frequently associated with masturbation which aims to gratify, in fantasy, incestuous wishes, and an erotisation of pain and death. Here, the surviving self is gratified by its sadistic treatment of its own body rather than that of others, as occurs in a revenge fantasy. Masochistic impulses are satisfied as well, in the self's identification with the helpless, passive, submissive body.

The third fantasy is the *assassination fantasy*, in which the individual experiences his or her body as a source of madness which seems confusing, alien and threatening. By killing their body that is driving them mad, the self in their suicidal fantasies 'survives'. In this fantasy the suicide is conceived of as killing the assassin body before it kills me, the self. Suicide is then enacted in self-defence.

The fourth fantasy is the *dicing with death fantasy*. In this the individual is leaving the outcome of their suicidal act to fate. They are handing over the responsibility for their life to an outside agent.

The fifth fantasy, which underpins all other fantasies, is the *merging fantasy*. The suicidal act expresses the wish to fuse with an omnipotent mother: 'By becoming one with her, the suicidal patient hopes to taste again the omnipotent, timeless, mindless peace of his baby origins, far from the wearisome, hostile inner presence of his miserable adulthood' (Maltsberger and Buie 1980/1996: 409).

Conclusion

Suicide is a complex and subtle process. In this chapter I have outlined various stages in this process that help us to understand the particular state of mind of the suicidal individual and how this makes it possible for suicidal acts to occur.

I would like to finish with an excerpt from an account written by a patient after she completed treatment. It is quoted with her knowledge and permission.

> It was the failure of another relationship – one in a series – at 22 years old which precipitated a serious attempt to kill myself by swallowing 70 aspirins, a carefully premeditated step, when I had moved beyond persistent depression into despair. I differentiate the two in the hope that anyone reading this, whether professionals or individuals similarly afflicted, will understand that suicide is a process in which intervention – and hence prevention – is always possible, but timing is crucial.
>
> Suicidal thoughts, as at other traumatic periods of perceived abandonment, obsessed me after this particular break-up, and I carefully bought two bottles of aspirins at separate shops to avoid suspicion and hid them. At this stage, as until almost the final day of the attempt, my feelings were ambivalent: I wanted to die and I wanted desperately to be rescued, so that even after buying the aspirins, I continued to make plans for my next university term.

However, I remained in a state of alternating active grief, with a terrifying sense of solitude and a paralysing lethargy. As it was during a vacation, the usual props of study and university friends were withdrawn, and my mother was unavailable as ever, impatient or actively hostile to my moods (which were presumably threatening or incomprehensible to her). The trigger for my attempt was an incident in which she snapped at the sight of me in tears: 'You shouldn't think so much' – shorthand for 'feel so much'.[1]

I don't think I can adequately describe the sense of utter rejection and loneliness this gave me, the vista of a closed circle in which my emotions were overpowering me (as if I were being attacked from within), and yet I was commanded to ignore them – a psychic impossibility.

On the evening of this day I returned from a futile meeting with the boyfriend who had left me repeatedly, and banged my head against the house wall, as if that could rid me of the unendurable pain I felt, or at least replace it with a bearable physical pain. All the clichés used to evoke extraordinary states now took on a living force: I was literally out of my mind, beside myself with grief, and beneath this a complex, impotent anger and sense of betrayal at my parents' abandonment at crucial times over many years. I did not recognise this anger at the time, nor in a sense was I able to experience it properly (live it), even as it was crippling me. With hindsight, I can say that I needed to access the sources of all these powerful, flowing emotions and engage with them, but I had to have a guide, a support to do so.

The day after what felt like a final rejection, I was so frightened by my state that I begged my younger sister, who was still attending school, to come home early if possible, because I was terrified of being alone. When both she and my parents had gone, I was left alone in the house and was overwhelmed with anguish again – at this stage I was still fighting an impulse not simply to kill myself, but to 'destroy' myself – to be rid of all feeling. This stage of living, active struggle was succeeded by a terrible passivity and near-calm; I ceased to hope or battle; I felt a complete inevitability. It was as if I were entering the acute stage of an illness, the culmination of the strange alternating state I had been in for weeks: intense painful feeling alternating with a hopelessness and extreme lethargy.

Once I had given in I felt a certain relief. I wanted oblivion and imagined death would be peaceful – a permanent sleep. When I actually began to take the aspirins, it was more difficult than I expected. I had to force them down and that was lonely and frightening. Even at this stage, at some level I think I wanted to be interrupted, found. The calm followed again. I curled up on the floor and waited to lose consciousness. After several hours I was still awake. I began to feel very ill and afraid, and it was as if another, rational, part of me now took over. I rang the sister I was closest to and told her what I had done. She took immediate control, ringing an ambulance and rushing home to be with me. I was taken to a hospital where my stomach was pumped. I spent a strange hallucinatory night, unable to sleep, with my ears ringing with tinnitus from the aspirins. I passed in and out of waking dreams between bouts of sickness.

What I remember most of that night is the practical kindness of the black nurse on night duty who must have been cursing an extra, 'self-inflicted' patient. She said very little to me, but her manner was humane. I fell asleep sometime in the early morning, and woke later to find three young doctors looking down at me. They asked me a few questions which I could not really answer, but seemed, above all, bemused. Later a woman hospital psychiatrist came to see me, and she effectively fed me a superficial diagnosis along the lines of 'It was a silly accident, wasn't it?' to which I weakly agreed, from awkwardness, confusion and exhaustion, probably also to distance myself. The whole experience, and perhaps its physicality, had provided a temporary exorcism. Underneath my feelings remained.

Shortly after this very brief conversation I was discharged home. Both my parents and I were bewildered and wary with each other, but this time my mother took action and arranged for me to see a psychoanalyst recommended to her by a colleague. My meeting with him marked the first time anyone tried seriously to understand what I had been going through. My feelings resurfaced frighteningly during our meeting, but a lifeline had been created, even though he was not able to take me on as a patient, since I wanted (or this may have simply been assumed by my parents – I don't remember) to return to university.

My analyst suggested I seek counseling at university while I continued my course, but I felt unable and unwilling to do this for a variety of reasons: I felt as if I were being sent away again by the one person who had shown understanding, and also I had a superstitious feeling that I should be unable to complete my course if I were also undergoing counseling (I think I was partly right because it involves such a powerful journey and I wasn't strong enough at that point). And the family embargo on emotional revelation remained internalized. I finally returned to my analyst some years later and began this delayed journey.

I worry writing this, that my suicide attempt – for all the rational filter that analysts and 12 years' distance have given it – will still seem incomprehensible to outsiders. My experience of those years is both remote and still raw to myself. Approaching even its edge has been overwhelming. At times I have to stop writing. Also the more I try to explain, the more I have a strange and horrible feeling that I will not be understood. This goes deep and is related to my parents' rebuttals and refusals.

I don't know that I can finish the account well. By 'well' I mean clearly, so that the complex truth of what happened is conveyed. But, even as a professional writer, I find it impossible. I am so frightened of somehow tidying, smoothing things over, falsifying, but most of all I am frightened of being misunderstood – still – of this account being 'rejected', going unheard, being discounted or disconfirmed. Because those were all the things which happened to me as a child and teenager within the family, which were reactivated by any external rejection and which ended in my suicide attempt. Although it is truer to speak of it as my 'suicide', as I began to later, because it was a kind of death and then, very slowly, over years of psychoanalysis, a kind of rebirth.

It has taken many years to understand what I have tried to convey of the feelings which led to suicide, both within a long, careful process of psycho-analysis and afterwards. I am still absolutely certain that without the most skilled, patient professional help I might not have survived or, at best, would have lurched from intermittent crisis to crisis. This help was not available at the hospital where I was taken and this is one reason I wanted to write my account, so that others will fare better than I initially did. I was privileged to see an excellent, empathic analyst, and particularly lucky because the 'match' was somehow right for me – or at least I was made to feel it was, simply by being met at the centre of my hurt.

The process (of analysis) I underwent was both basic and profound; basic in that I developed a primary and secure sense of self that I lacked before (I think of it as the pieces knitting together to form a solid core – I'm far from immune to emotional storms, whether others' or my own, but now I can weather them). The analysis was profound in that the process still informs my life today. I not only understand some of the forces which shaped me, but have a much greater understanding or intuition of those which shaped my parents' and even my grandparents' lives. I continue to explore these, and events have come to light which have enlarged my understanding further.

One of my sisters also embarked on psychotherapy later, perhaps in part because my experience had paved the way a little. And I think my analysis had a subtle effect on the whole family.

Perhaps, most importantly, I am now a mother myself, something I could never have dreamt of, *conceived*, prior to my analysis, and that has been immensely reparative.

I think now that my suicide, which might only have been destructive – to others as well as myself – became instead creative of a new life. My journey continues and I hope that others can be helped by having the right kind of intervention early enough, but that depends on many things: primarily a much greater education about mental health issues, the creation of new specialist services, and effective publicity, particularly for young people.

Note

1 Tantamount to a 'don't be as/where you are' – translated to a psychic instruction: 'don't be' (unless you can be otherwise).

References

Apter, A. (2004) 'Personality constellations in suicidal behaviour', *Imago* xi, 1: 5–27.

Campbell, D. and Hale, R. (1991) 'Suicidal acts', in J. Holmes (ed.) *Textbook of Psychotherapy in Psychiatric Practice* (pp. 287–306), London: Churchill Livingstone.

Freud, S. (1909) 'Analysis of a phobia in a five-year-old boy', in J. Strachey (ed.) *The Standard Edition of the Works of Sigmund Freud, X* (pp. 1–149), London: Hogarth.

Freud, S. (1914) 'Remembering, repeating and working-through', in J. Strachey (ed.) *The Standard Edition of the Works of Sigmund Freud, XII* (pp. 145–156), London: Hogarth.

Freud, S. (1920) 'Beyond the pleasure principle', in J. Strachey (ed.) *The Standard Edition of the Works of Sigmund Freud, XVIII* (pp. 1–64), London: Hogarth.

Friedman, P. (ed.) (1967) *On Suicide*, New York: International Universities Press.

Glasser, M. (1979) 'Some aspects of the role of aggression in the perversions', in I. Rosen (ed.) *The Pathology and Treatment of Sexual Deviations*, Oxford: Oxford University Press.

Housman, A.E. (1939/1995) *Collected Poems*, London: Penguin Books.

Jenkins, G.R., Hale, R., Papanastassiou, M., Crawford, M.J. and Tyrer, P. (2002) 'Suicide rate 22 years after parasuicide: cohort study', *British Medical Journal* 25: 1155.

Luoma, J.B., Martin, C.E. and Pearson, J.L. (2002) 'Contact with mental health and primary care providers before suicide: a review of the evidence', *American Journal of Psychiatry* 159: 909–916.

Maltsberger, J.G. and Buie, D.H. (1980/1996) 'The devices of suicide; revenge, riddance and rebirth', *International Review of Psycho-Analysis* 7: 61–72; reprinted in J.G. Maltsberger and M. Goldblatt (eds) (1996) *Essential Papers on Suicide* (ch. 25, pp. 397–417), New York: New York University Press.

Maltsberger, J.G. and Goldblatt, M. (1996) *Essential Papers on Suicide*, New York: New York University Press.

Ringel, E. (1976) 'The presuicidal syndrome', *Suicide and Life-Threatening Behaviour* 6: 131–140.

Chapter 2

The father transference during a pre-suicide state

Donald Campbell

Introduction

The transference with a suicidal patient will always be unique for that patient and therapist. In fact, it is probably more accurate to say that the therapist is likely to be the object of multiple transferences and counter-transferences, together or singly, during their treatment of a suicidal patient. However, this chapter will not focus on the transference dynamics that arise over the course of the psychotherapeutic treatment of a suicidal patient. Instead, it will consider the nature of the transference object during a particular time in treatment, the period just prior to a suicide attempt, which I refer to as the pre-suicide state. Clinical material from the analysis of a patient during a pre-suicide state will be presented to indicate the nature and psychic importance of a transference to the father during that time.

The pre-suicide state and the suicide fantasy

An individual enters a pre-suicide state whenever the normal self-preservative instinct is overcome and their body becomes expendable. A person may have suicidal thoughts or feel suicidal for varying lengths of time, but once the body has been rejected a suicide attempt may be made at any time (Campbell 1995).

During a pre-suicide state the patient is influenced, in varying degrees, by a suicide fantasy which reflects the self's relation to its body and others. The fantasy may or may not become conscious, but at the time of execution it has the power of a delusional conviction and has distorted reality. The suicide fantasy is the motive force. Killing the body fulfils the fantasy (Campbell and Hale 1991).

Maltsberger and Buie (1980) observed a process of splitting and denial in suicidal individuals, which was confirmed by my patients who reported that when they tried to kill themselves they expected their body to die. However, they also believed that another part of them would continue to live in a conscious body-less state, otherwise unaffected by the death of their body.

Although killing the body was a conscious aim, it was, in fact, a means to an end. The end was the pleasurable survival of an essential part of the self (which I will refer to as the 'surviving self') that would survive in another dimension (Maltsberger and Buie 1980). This survival was dependent upon the destruction of the body.

The various suicide fantasies of my patients, which elaborated the relationship between the surviving self and the expendable body, were underpinned by a wish for the surviving self to merge with an idealised mother image. However, these patients felt themselves to be in a double bind. The real mothering object was perceived as ungiving, dangerous and untrustworthy. While being preoccupied with the wish to merge with an idealised mother, they became anxious about being engulfed by the object if they should succeed in merging, or being abandoned to starve if they should be unsuccessful in getting into the object (Glasser 1979).

The suicide fantasy represented a solution to the conflict between the wish to merge with mother, on the one hand, and the subsequent primitive anxieties about annihilation of the self, on the other. By projecting the hated, engulfing or abandoning primal mother onto the body and then killing the body, the surviving self is free to fuse with the split-off idealised, desexualised, omnipotently gratifying mother represented by states of oceanic bliss, dreamless eternal sleep, a permanent sense of peace, becoming one with the universe, or achieving a state of nothingness (Maltsberger and Buie 1980).

Just as there was a split between the good surviving self and the bad body, there was also a split between the hated, engulfing or abandoning primal mother, now identified with the body, and the idealised mother with whom the surviving self would fuse once the bad mother/body had been eliminated.

The role of the father during a pre-suicide state

During the analyses of my suicidal patients it became apparent that they experienced their fathers as either withdrawn or actively rejecting them, and having failed to reclaim their wives. Furthermore, each patient had felt their father had left them with a severe anxiety about surviving with a disturbed mother. The fantasy, which emerged as a solution to the pathological relationship between mother and child, was revived during the pre-suicide state. The father's role was often obscured by the patient's relationship with the mother, which dominated the suicide fantasy, and by the father's absence or ineffectiveness. However, it was during the pre-suicide state that the father's failure *to stake a claim* on his child left the child with no alternative to the pathological mother–child relationship. A parent's *staking a claim* on their child is not meant in a legalistic, narcissistic or possessive way, but rather refers to acting upon a belief that the parent has something special to give their child that differs from what the parent of the opposite sex can give, and which recognises the uniqueness and independence of their child, its joys and sufferings, its strengths and vulnerabilities.

One consequence of the constraint imposed by the pre-oedipal father's intervention in the mother–infant dyad is that it sets limits on the wish for a timeless relationship with mother where there are no interruptions, no limitations on duration – where the child, in fantasy, controls access to mother (Campbell 1995). The pre-oedipal father represents the world outside the exclusivity of the mother–infant relationship, for example the realities of time and place. In the pre-suicide state my patients experienced the frequency (five-times-a-week analytic sessions) and the beginning and ending of sessions as representative of father's constraint regarding time. At other times in analysis these phenomena were often experienced quite differently. However, during pre-suicide states, lateness, absences and difficulty in leaving sessions appeared as defiance of the reality of time and an enactment of the experience of a father who was unable to provide an alternative to the wish to merge with mother in a timeless state.

Mr Adams's suicide attempt

Mr Adams had made two suicide attempts before starting his analysis with me. Early in our contact he showed me scar tissue where he had slashed his wrists. He also regularly and frequently gambled, which I thought represented a manic solution to his feelings of helplessness, impotence and despair. I understood the self-defeating, self-impoverishing aspect of his gambling behaviour as Mr Adams dicing with death, particularly after his mother's suicide attempt increased his anxiety about his own survival. I was worried about the self-destructive component of his gambling. As his wish to triumph over the odds intensified, I took up his pattern of losing money as a way of demonstrating his mother's failure, that is, leaving him bereft and without resources. His failures also invited his mother to rescue him and it was clear he wanted me to do the same. These interpretations appeared to have an effect; Mr Adams stopped gambling. Furthermore, his attitude became more positive and he began investing again in his work and family.

At this point, Mr Adams interrupted his analysis in an optimistic frame of mind to go to Edinburgh, his home town, to try to generate business for his neglected company. However, once there, business did not go well and he could not face his old friends.

One Sunday afternoon he felt lonely and suicidal and called his wife in London, hoping she would express sympathy and come to join him. Instead, Mrs Adams complained about his using suicide to blackmail her. She couldn't stand his threats any more and told him to get on with it if he was going to kill himself.

At first Mr Adams felt shattered, hurt, rejected and totally alone. However, once he decided to kill himself he felt great relief and calm. He took seventy 10 mg tablets of Valium and lay down, feeling at peace. As the pills took effect he felt he was drifting off into another dimension. There was a sense of oneness, a merging into another kind of existence. He was found by accident and rushed to hospital. (Although Valium, even in a large overdose, is not pharmacologically lethal, a fact of which Mr Adams was unaware, it is the lethality of the intent that is psychically important.)

I was shocked when I heard the news. I felt that I had missed something and had let Mr Adams down.

What follows is what I learned from Mr Adams after his suicide attempt, what I learned by thinking again about what Mr Adams had told me before the attempt, and what I learned when I compared this experience with that of other suicidal patients.

Material from Mr Adams's analysis

Mr Adams was a 'mummy's boy', who was alternately indulged and abandoned according to the whims of his narcissistic mother. He felt rejected by his father who was seldom at home and appeared to favour his older brother. Mr Adams wanted to join in the family business after A levels and was hurt when father sent him off to university in Glasgow. His father died of cancer shortly after Mr Adams returned to Edinburgh with his degree. At the age of 30, while under severe stress at work, Mr Adams took an overdose of Valium. A year later, on the brink of a business failure, he took another overdose and cut his wrists.

When he was 40, Mr Adams came to see me looking dishevelled and unshaven after he had gambled away his money – half a million pounds. He looked and sounded melancholic – feeling impoverished (as he was in reality), slighted and unjustly treated. He told me that when he went to a casino he often started with a little money but soon won thousands, only to lose it all at the end of the night. His older brother had taken over his financial affairs, blocked all of his bank accounts, left him with a weekly allowance and gone off to Australia for a holiday. Mr Adams said that he felt suicidal and then made a slip, saying 'father' instead of 'brother' had left him and gone off to Australia. When I called his attention to his slip he referred to his suicidal thoughts and added, 'it all started with my father's death'.

After Mr Adams's father died, his mother confided only in him that she would one day commit suicide. In passing he said that his mother also confided to him that she had 'killed' her own mother with a drug overdose after she had a paralysing stroke. After associating to his fear that his wife might leave him, Mr Adams added that he didn't understand why he always avoided his mother.

One month after Mr Adams started five-times-weekly analysis, his mother made a serious but unsuccessful suicide attempt at home in Edinburgh. Mr Adams wasn't surprised. 'I didn't go to see her because my brother is there. I'm glad he's upset and had to come back from Melbourne. I stayed in bed all day yesterday.' Mr Adams justified his coldness by referring to his family's very rational attitude to death. Without recognising the failure of this defence, he described his father as 'paranoid, full of fear and panic during his last week. His face at the funeral home was distorted and ugly. I tried to push his lips into a calm expression. My mother is always calm.'

The next day he was furious that his brother had advised him not to sell his shares to settle his debts, but to keep them and gamble that they would increase in value. I linked his rage at being put at risk to satisfy his brother's wish for excitement with his mother's secret which had put him at risk as the passive, guilty accomplice, waiting for a predicted self-murder. I then took up what I thought was his fear that I would put him at risk by not taking seriously his earlier attempts to kill himself.

In the sessions Mr Adams regularly complained that I did not give him advice and suggestions. I interpreted this behaviour in the transference in terms of his view of me as distant and withdrawn and his efforts to get compensation for what his mother failed to give him by actively demanding more from me. This was often followed by transient regressed states featuring rambling and mumbled conversation and narcissistic withdrawal into drowsiness, which I interpreted as Mr Adams's identification with his narcissistic mother. This appeared to be what Pearl King (1978) refers to as a reverse transference – that is, the patient relating to the analyst in such a way as to give the analyst the experience of the patient as a child by relating to the analyst as the parent had done. My interpretations seemed to have a positive effect and there were obvious signs of improvement in Mr Adams's appearance. It was at this point that Mr Adams went off on his business trip.

Countertransference during a pre-suicide state

The assessment of Mr Adams's suicide attempt began with the fact that I was shocked when I heard the news. By focusing on the period before the suicide attempt and understanding my response to it, I hoped to shed some light on why I was caught by surprise. But first I will outline my view of the countertransference and the role of the father during a pre-suicide state.

Sandler's (1976) concept of the analyst's role response provided a useful framework for considering the analyst's reaction. Sandler draws attention to the patient's unconscious attempts to provoke the analyst to behave in such a way as to confirm the patient's illusory (transference) image of the analyst. The analyst may hold his 'affective response' (King 1978) to this prodding in his consciousness and make use of it to understand the transference. Failure to hold responses and the enactment of them in behaviour, attitude or remark represents the analyst's unconscious role response.

Sandler suggests that:

> Very often the irrational response of the analyst, which his professional conscience leads him to see entirely as a blind spot of his own, may sometimes be usefully regarded as a compromise-formation between his own tendencies and his reflexive acceptance of the role which the patient is forcing on him.
>
> (1976: 46)

Sandler views this type of countertransference reaction as a piece of behaviour or an attitude that results from the overlap of the patient's pathology and the analyst's. Consequently, the professional is only likely to become aware of his role in a countertransference interaction by observing his own feelings and behaviour after the fact, after he has responded. Nevertheless, by viewing his countertransference behaviour as related to the patient, and thinking of it as a compromise between his own tendencies or propensities and the role relationship that the patient is unconsciously seeking to elicit, the analyst can deepen his understanding of the transference and his part in the patient's suicide scenario.

It became apparent that an essential ingredient of the pre-suicide state is the patient's attempt to involve the analyst in an active way in the suicide scenario. Straker (1958) pointed out: 'A decisive factor in the successful suicide attempt appears to be the implied consent or unconscious collusion between the patient and the person most involved in the psychic struggle.' The unconscious collusion is buried in the analyst's countertransference.

Asch (1980) has demonstrated the vulnerability that the therapist of the suicidal patient has to being provoked into negative countertransference attitudes, which are experienced by the patient as collusion in the suicidal fantasy. This collusion confirms for the patient the analyst's active participation in a regressive sadomasochistic fusion, places the analyst in the role of the executioner, and gives the patient justification for retaliation via a suicide attempt.

The sadomasochistic dynamic may also manifest itself in the subtle and superficially benign form of the patient's feeling of being at peace, which contributes to increased self-assurance and confidence (Laufer and Laufer 1984). Depressive affects, anxieties and conflicts are no longer communicated. This narcissistic withdrawal cuts the therapist off from moods and behaviour, which would normally elicit an empathic response of alarm or worry and may result in the sudden loss of subjective emotional concern for the patient (Tahka 1978).

In a narcissistic regression, which dominated my suicidal patients during the pre-suicide state, there is the prospect of imminently fulfilling a merging suicide fantasy. As far as these patients were concerned, they were already at peace because they had crossed a rational barrier of self-preservation, identified the assassin/mother with their body, and had no doubts about killing it.

The professional, burdened with anxieties about his or her patient's life, or exhausted by the patient's relentless attack on hope, or angry about being blackmailed (often before a holiday break from treatment), may be tempted to retaliate by giving up on his or her patient, or may use the patient's sense of peace to justify relaxing his therapeutic vigilance. In the case of Mr Adams, external signs of decreased stress and improvement in the patient were used to defend against the analyst's unconscious wishes to retaliate by letting go of the suicide risk.

The father and the pre-suicide state

The questions for the analyst remained, "Who was I in the transference? Who was the object evoked by Mr Adams and enacted by me?' It was clear from Mr Adams that he felt distant and alienated from his father. The absence of his father in Mr Adams's material was consistent with their relationship. I understood that my failure to perceive and respond interpretatively to Mr Adams's suicide risk confirmed, in Mr Adams's mind, my role as the distant, uninvolved father. Mr Adams gave the impression that his father had failed his son during an early phase of development.

In normal development, both pre-oedipal parents represent to the child the world outside the exclusivity of the mother–infant relationship, for example the realities of time and place and objects. Let us consider the role that the 'good-enough' pre-oedipal father plays as friendly rival with both his child and his wife, in offering each of them a dyadic relationship that is parallel to and competes with the mother–child unit.

In 'good-enough' fathers the pleasure of procreation and the birth of their child is accompanied by feelings of envy and exclusion from the mother–child relationship as well as adjustment to a secondary role with the child. Initially, fathers can defend against this change by supporting the mother and making use of passive feminine aspects of their makeup to identify with the mother. However, a more active, masculine identification will emerge in the father's relationship with his child and wife. On the one hand, the attractive and attracting father stakes a claim on his child and, with mother's help, enables the child to move from the exclusivity of the infant–mother relationship into an inclusive position as part of a pre-oedipal triad.

Father's gender role identity and parental oedipal impulses influence the idiosyncratic nature of the claim he makes on his child. For instance, his conscious and unconscious fantasies and anxieties about female sexuality will affect the way he relates to his daughter from the beginning. She may be 'daddy's little girl'. Gender-influenced relating will also play a part in the way a father helps his son dis-identify from mother (Greenson 1968) and father's view of the way his wife relates to his male offspring. The father may even be conscious of not wanting his wife to 'feminise' his son. Whatever form this process of claiming his child takes, and there will always be infinite variations influenced by mixtures of projections and reality, the child will become aware that he or she occupies a place in father's mind that is separate and distinct from mother.

The child also becomes aware of a place for mother in father's mind and a place for father in mother's mind. Father reclaims his wife by seducing her back to him and rekindling her adult sexuality. The father who reclaims his wife and engages his child on his own terms protects them both from lingering overlong in a 'fusional' or symbiotic state and facilitates the separation and individuation process (Mahler and Gosliner 1955).

Freud (1931) recognised the little girl's attachment to her father as a refuge from her first attachment to mother. Loewald (1951) referred to the child's positive, pre-oedipal relationship with the father who stands for a paternal veto against the engulfing and overpowering womb that threatens to undermine the ego's orientation to reality and its efforts to establish boundaries between self and other.

The father's twofold response supports the child's right to an independent existence that is separate from mother while providing the toddler with a means of coping with its longing for her. Abelin (1978) postulates that around 18 months this process results in an early triangulation in which the toddler identifies with the rival father's wish for mother to form a mental representation of a self that is separate and longing for mother. The good-enough father provides a model for identification as well as an alternative relationship to the child's regressive wishes to return to a 'fusional' state with mother with subsequent anxieties about engulfment.

In the analysis of suicidal patients it often becomes apparent that they perceived their fathers as either withdrawn or actively rejecting them, and as having failed to reclaim their wives. Other suicidal patients that I saw had also felt abandoned to their anxiety about surviving as a differentiated self when left with a disturbed mother.

The patients' suicide fantasies articulated in the present represented internalised early pathological relationships between mother and child and father. The pre-oedipal father's role was often obscured by the patient's relationship with the mother, which dominated the suicide fantasy, and by the father's absence or ineffectiveness. However, it was during the pre-suicide state that the internalised father's failure to intervene in the pathological mother–child relationship became most critical. It was clear that Mr Adams intended to kill his body while maintaining the fantasy that part of him would survive. After taking the overdose, Mr Adams felt calm, as he had described his mother, and told me that he expected to pass into 'another dimension' and wondered what it would be like.

There was evidence of the co-existence of other suicide fantasies. Mr Adams's suicide attempt was influenced by his identification with his suicidal mother. For instance, while talking about his suicide attempt he made a slip saying his mother was 40 – his age. It also emerged in his analysis that Mr Adams hoped that his suicide would serve as revenge against both his parents.

Mr Adams's suicide fantasy was organised around a sadomasochistic relationship with his mother whose shared secret had tortured him by making him an accomplice in a homicide (the overdose that she had administered to her mother) and her own planned suicide. His mother's unsuccessful attempt on her life increased his guilt because he had ignored her explicit warnings that she would kill herself. His fear that she would kill him increased as well. He slipped in telling the analyst of his mother's suicide attempt, saying 'My mother tried to kill myself'.

Mr Adams felt his father did not relate to him in his own right. For instance, father could not support his son's wish to join him in the family business. Mr Adams associated from feeling suicidal to being left by his father, and then recalled that his suicidal fantasies started with his father's death. However, Mr Adams felt abandoned to his mother by his father long before his father's death. Father and brother had paired off while he was left with mother. Without his father as an alternative object with whom to identify, Mr Adams was left in a masochistic tie to a murderous mother.

Mr Adams relied upon splitting of the self and the object to survive his mother's suicide attempt, which he experienced as an attack on his life. The resulting suicide fantasy during the pre-suicide state had two components: an unconscious fantasy and a delusional conviction. Mr Adams's unconscious fantasy that identified his body with a bad mother initially came into the analysis as non-verbal communications in his neglect and mistreatment of his body. After his suicide attempt this identification was put into words by Mr Adams: 'Mother couldn't care for her body and she couldn't care for mine. How could I care for myself?' Getting rid of his bad mother, now identified with the object of his suicidal attack – his body – would make it possible for his split-off surviving self to merge with the split-off idealised mother – the nameless 'other dimension'.

There was a breakthrough of his unconscious identification of his body with his mother and his sadistic revenge against the bad mother, represented by his wife, when he made a slip: 'I can't say to my wife "I want to kill yourself".' The fantasy of merging with an idealised mother (which was on his mind when he took the pills) became a delusional conviction during the pre-suicide state.

Mr Adams's slip of the tongue, 'My mother tried to kill myself', represented a breakthrough of a preconscious awareness of mother's sadistic attack on him via her suicide attempt and formed the basis of his identification with the aggressor. In proceeding with his suicide plan, Mr Adams turned passive into active, and shifted from a masochistic to a sadistic role, in order to extract revenge. Mr Adams's depression lifted as he planned the details of his execution, which included collecting Valium tablets, returning to his birthplace, and deceiving others about his intentions by appearing more sociable and optimistic. He stopped gambling. In sessions he talked about his earlier suicide attempts as well as his mother's attempt on her life.

At this critical point in the analysis I saw myself, in retrospect, as a guard going to sleep at his post. In this case, the decisive factor in precipitating the suicide attempt was the relaxation of vigilance regarding the suicide risk, a lessening of empathic contact with Mr Adams, and an enactment of his father's withdrawal and failure to stake a claim for his child's right to a relationship with him by not protecting Mr Adams's analytic time and place with me.

Later, in his analysis, it became clear that fantasies enacted in his gambling had been displaced on to his suicide fantasy, including the belief that he would omnipotently triumph over the loss of his father and be chosen by fate/mother. The pre-suicide stage, like gambling, is a manic flight from judgement into narcissism.

Mr Adams was unconsciously in the grip of a repetition compulsion and had tested me to see if I would repeat his earlier experience with his father. My response to Mr Adams's behaviour (e.g. an apparent improvement and the undetected meaning of a narcissistic withdrawal) coincided with his breaking of the analytic structure (by cancelling sessions), which I failed to prevent. This failure was experienced by the patient as a failure to maintain the reality of our analytic relationship, that is, the realities of time and place, thereby leaving the patient without an alternative to the timeless merging fantasy of his suicide scenario. Mr Adams left the analyst to return to his mother. I had failed to analyse the merging fantasy that was gratified in this way and the destructiveness inherent in it.

The therapist of a patient who is in a pre-suicide state of mind is likely to be faced with a decision about whether to admit their patient to hospital or to continue working with their patient outside hospital. This decision should be based on the viability of the treatment at that time, an assessment of the patient's capacity to contain an impulse to act out between sessions, and the reliability of a sensitive network of family, friends, and/or professionals. There is always the possibility that the suicidal patient will experience not being referred by their therapist to hospital as confirmation that the therapist does not care enough to look after them in this way. On the other hand, the suicidal patient who has been referred to hospital may feel that their therapist has been defeated by them, or that their therapist has given up on them, and has abandoned their therapeutic work.

This empathic failure was experienced by Mr Adams as an enactment in the transference of the neglectful pre-oedipal father who sanctioned his younger son's return to a seductive and 'murderous' mother. In this way, I unwittingly entered into and played a role in Mr Adams's suicide fantasy. Although Mr Adams's suicide fantasies were the outcomes of a pathological bond with his mother, during the pre-suicide state his relationship with his father, particularly father's failure to protect him from his mother, functioned as the sanction of the suicidal act.

Some types of transferences during work with suicidal patients

While working with suicidal patients the clinician may be subject to a variety of transferences that influence the development of the father transference during the pre-suicide state, such as the omnipotent mother, the rescuer, the saviour, the executioner and the failure.

Suicidal patients frequently try to draw the therapist into taking responsibility for their living or dying, a representation of the infant's earliest dependence upon its mother. Consequently, as Herbert Hendin (1981) noted, therapists are cast in or tempted to play the role of saviour. The therapist as the father in the transference is often cast in this role following the disillusionment with the mother. In my view, this only serves to set up the therapist to unwittingly play the role of executioner.

It is not uncommon for suicidal patients to hold apparently contradictory images of suicide as fulfilment of rebirth and reunion fantasies and revenge at the same time. By splitting the bad, dangerous part of the parent onto the patient's body, a benign idealised aspect of the parent is preserved for a reunion in death. In the transference, the patient experiences the therapist as sanctioning, or responsible for, the murderous attack on their body, thereby assuaging a persecuting super-ego that would punish destructiveness. It is the patient's suicide that punishes the therapist for being a 'bad parent' who wanted their child dead. When the transference is to a therapist who fails to prevent a suicide, the patient has projected feelings of helplessness and despair about themselves and, particularly with adolescents, their anxiety about ever being able to develop an adult self with an independent sexual identity (Laufer and Laufer 1984).

Conclusion

It has not been my intention to talk about transferences that emerge in the course of working with a suicidal patient, but rather to focus on a particular type of transference to the father, which I believe is particularly critical during the pre-suicide state. In the analysis of Mr Adams various transferences emerged, but as he moved toward a suicidal act, which would, in his mind, unite him with his mother, he made a last-minute appeal to a father who could offer an alternative to this regressive move. I don't know if this pattern emerges in every analysis of a suicidal patient, but I have seen it in other suicidal patients I have treated.

The analysis of a pre-suicide state based on material from before and after Mr Adams's suicide attempt illuminated the father transference, which had been enacted in my countertransference and the cancelled sessions. The transference was to a father who failed to claim his child for himself, who abandoned him to a smothering, 'murderous' mother, and who did not offer an alternative to an exclusive mother–child fusion. The father had not stood in the way of a regressive pull to a sadomasochistic relationship with mother, which formed the core of the suicide fantasy. The patient reversed his experience of being abandoned by his father by leaving his analyst to join his mother – in death.

References

Abelin, E. (1978) 'The role of the father in the pre-oedipal years', *Journal of the American Psychoanalytic Association* 26: 143–161.

Asch, S. (1980) 'Suicide and the hidden executioner', *International Review of Psycho-Analysis*, 7: 51–60.

Campbell, D. (1995) 'The role of the father in a pre-suicide state' *International Journal of Psycho-Analysis* 76: 315–323.

Campbell, D. and Hale, R. (1991) 'Suicidal acts', in J. Holmes (ed.) *Textbook of Psychotherapy in Psychiatric Practice* (pp. 287–306), London: Churchill Livingstone.

Freud, S. (1931) 'Female sexuality', in J. Strachey (ed.) *The Standard Edition of the Works of Sigmund Freud, XXI* (pp. 223–245), London: Hogarth.

Glasser, M. (1979) 'Some aspects of the role of aggression in the perversions', in I. Rosen (ed.) *The Pathology and Treatment of Sexual Deviations*, Oxford: Oxford University Press.

Greenson, R. (1968) 'Dis-identifying from mother', *International Journal of Psycho-Analysis* 49: 370–374.

Hendin, H. (1981) 'Psychotherapy and suicide', *American Journal of Psychotherapy* 35: 469–480; and also in J.T. Maltsberger and M.J. Goldblatt (eds) (1996) *Essential Papers on Suicide* (pp. 427–435), New York and London: New York University Press.

King, P. (1978) 'Affective response of the analyst to the patient's communications', *International Journal of Psycho-Analysis* 59: 329–334.

Laufer, M. and Laufer, M.E. (1984) *Adolescence and Developmental Breakdown*, New Haven and London: Yale University Press.

Loewald, H.W. (1951) 'Ego and reality', *International Journal of Psycho-Analysis* 32: 10–18.

Mahler, M.S. and Gosliner, B.J. (1955) 'On symbiotic child psychosis – genetic, dynamic and restitutive aspects', *Psychoanalytic Study of the Child* 10: 195–212.

Maltsberger, J.G. and Buie, D.H. (1980) 'The devices of suicide', *International Review of Psycho-Analysis* 7: 61–72.

Sandler, J. (1976) 'Countertransference and role-responsiveness', *International Review of Psycho-Analysis* 3: 43–78.

Stekel, W. ([1910] 1967) 'Symposium on suicide', in P. Friedman (ed.) *On Suicide* (pp. 33–141), New York: International Universities Press.

Straker, M. (1958) 'Clinical observations of suicide', *Canadian Madical Association Journal* 79: 473–479.

Tahka, V.A. (1978) '"On some narcissistic aspects of self-destructive behaviour and their influence on its predictability", psychopathology of direct and indirect self destruction', *Psyciatra Fennica, Supplementum*: 59–62.

Chapter 3

Self break-up and the descent into suicide

John T. Maltsberger

In this chapter it is my aim to show that the destructive force of over-powering affect acting on a friable self is of critical importance to understanding suicide. Elsewhere (Maltsberger 2004), I have provided a detailed discussion of the ways in which the self, through misfortunes of development, is fissured, and prone to break apart when stressed. The self, a substructure of the ego, may in some circumstances go to pieces. I propose that this is commonly the case in suicide. Edward Glover (1888-1972), a distinguished London psychoanalyst, gave a paper on suicidal mechanisms at the 1927 Innsbruck Congress. In his talk he tried to show that suicide, 'although primarily the result of destructive forces directed through the super-ego, could not come about without a regression of the ego to primitive animistic levels and the adoption of primitive autoplastic methods of dealing with tension based on the processes of primary identification' (Glover 1930: 121).

Suicide and self break-up

Suicide occurs in states when affect cannot be moderated. Floods of anguish, rage, aloneness, self-loathing sweep through the mind. That they cannot be controlled and that they are excruciatingly painful is traumatic, and traumatic anxiety is aroused. This experience, far from that of signal anxiety, is not created by the ego, but by overwhelming internal stimuli that are beyond its mastery. It is experienced passively and helplessly, as if arising from outside the self, an intolerable deluge. Dynamically, traumatic anxiety is the same thing as primary anxiety, and, as Freud (1926) suggested, it is, if persistent and intense, ego-destructive. It was Edward Bibring (1953) who showed that prolonged experiences of helplessness in the face of intolerable emotional suffering can damage the ego, lead to withdrawal of the inner influences that ordinarily protect it, and expose it to the full spate of aggression directed at it from the superego. The helpless self, at the mercy of an unremitting anguishing attack, gives way to hopelessness, and may then begin to break up.

Let us step aside at this juncture to see how this appears clinically. Imagine a patient who for developmental reasons cannot moderate affect well, a patient whose narcissistic integrity depends to an unusual degree on support from outside himself, perhaps from other persons, or perhaps from some work he values highly. Further imagine that life strikes this patient a blow, perhaps out of the blue, or because the patient has done something to get himself into trouble. In a word, the patient experiences a precipitating event. Affects are aroused, affects of great intensity, very painful affects. He feels enraged, anguished, alone, desperate, and cannot endure it. Casting around for relief, the patient tries to engage others to help him, but often does so in ways that repel potential sources of support, so that emotional distancing increases. There may be hints of suicide and feeling-driven outbursts – outbursts of words or behaviour that are out of character and frighten the patient even more. The patient may take to drink, or to drugs. Social and work adaptations begin to fail. At this stage the patient's self-integrity is breaking up, regression is threatened, and to escape from an intolerable affective trap, there may be a suicide attempt.

Self-representations

Now let us return to what is happening with the self. The psychoanalytic construction of the representational world by Sandler and Rosenblatt (1962) opens to our view the unfolding drama of suicidal break-up. They offer us a metaphorical theatre of the patient's inner world, the great proscenium of mental life, wherein living portraits of the self are seen to move, to feel, to remember, to interact, and to have their being, along with similar portraits of objects. Not only does conscious imagination play itself out there; the inner world theatre is also the stage whereon our dreams are enacted. These living portraits of self and others, the actors on that stage, Sandler and Rosenblatt called self and object representations.

The self-representation is built up over a lifetime, but it remains fluid as experience and learning alter its organization. Withdrawal of self-regard, or flooding with aggression directed from a critical superego, can lead to disorganization of the self-representation. Self breakdown in suicidal crises is reflected in the events of the inner world.

Suicidal patients in breaking apart their mental and their body selves commonly objectify their bodies, thereby enabling self attack (Maltsberger 1993). When the self-representation disarticulates and the portion of it which represents the body takes on the characteristics of an object representation, the way is open for attacking the body as though it were something or someone else, not the self. The body, in the language of Melanie Klein, takes on a 'not-me' quality (Klein 1957). When this happens, the patient can adopt a paranoid attitude toward his own disowned flesh, and may attempt to rid himself of it, experiencing his body as a persecutory enemy. The body, or parts of it, feel as though they belong to someone else. The body, now an enemy, may feel like something that can be expelled because it is hurtful and threatening. This is the device to which Freud in 'Mourning and melancholia' (1917) referred when he described the ego's falling under the shadow of an internalized object, rendering it vulnerable to the attack of the superego. Structural cohesion of the self-representation is lost, and the positive narcissistic colouring of the body-representation is abandoned (Orgel 1974).

Aggression, disassociation and derealization

Theoretically the integrity of the representational world, the self-representation, and the body image, as well as the integrity of the super-ordinate ego–superego system, depend on the neutralization of aggression over the course of development. Too much unneutralized aggression in the ego–superego system invites ego regression and self break-up.

Introjects excessively charged with unneutralized aggression (sometimes called 'hostile' or 'sadistic' introjects when they take on representational qualities) are discussed in the psychoanalytic literature as playing a part in suicidal phenomena (Maltsberger and Buie 1980). These introjects tend to operate in a fluid way, sometimes loosely attaching themselves to the super-ego system, sometimes becoming affiliated with the body portion of the self-representation, and sometimes seeming to have an independent position in the mind. When attached to the superego, such introjects promote self-directed cruelty, criticism, and self-destructive attitudes. When influenc-ing the body-self, they invite feelings of self-alienation and self-revulsion, including a disposition to self-attack. When affiliated with neither superego nor self-representation, they tend to take up a life of their own as hostile inner presences. We see them at work among the personae of multiple personality disorder. They may be projected out onto others – that is, when they affiliate themselves to object representations, they give rise to fears of persecution from without (Asch 1980).

Instability between the self and object representations invites dissociative experiences. In fact, phenomena such as derealization and depersonaliza-tion can be understood as evidence that the integrity of the representational world is loosening. Dissociation may be subtle and not always evident to us – the patient may actually feel quite composed and behave in a deliberate, organized way.

A 22-year-old law student who had been in a depressive anguish for some days decided to kill himself. As soon as the decision was made he experi-enced a sudden calming of mind, and reported that for the first time in weeks he felt competent and collected. Coolly driving to a high bridge he jumped off, feeling detached from himself, observing what was happening with the admiration of an onlooker. As soon as he began to fall, the dissociation broke, and he began to scream in terror.

Laufer and colleagues (Laufer and Laufer 1984; Laufer 1989, 1995) take the position that, at least in adolescents who attempt to commit suicide, the alteration of consciousness that accompanies the act represents such a failure of reality testing that the attempt should be understood as a transient psychotic episode. Calming occurs as the intolerable passive suffering of the patient is turned into the activity of attack on the patient's body, which is experienced as alien to the core self, and, as the seat of intolerable sexual and other painful feelings, an enemy which must be destroyed in self-defence.

Let me be clear about the term 'transient psychotic episode'. It gave rise to some confusion when used at a previous conference in Hamburg.[1] Psychotic as used here does not necessarily denote any of the specific diagnoses listed in such standard nomenclatures as the American Psychiatric Association's Diagnostic and Statistical Manual, or the ICD, though episodes of this kind may occur in the indexed diagnoses, such as major depressive episodes. By 'psychotic' I refer to a mental state in which the 'thoughts, affective response, ability to recognize reality, and ability to communicate and relate to others are sufficiently impaired to interfere grossly with the capacity to deal with reality' (Sadock 2000). No hallucinations are ordinarily found in these states, and to the extent that the patients are deluded, the false convictions under which they labour are not likely to be long in duration. They are typically affect-driven. Such states are often accompanied by depersonalization and other dissociative phenomena, in the sense that suicidal mental and behavioural processes are separated from the rest of the person's psychic activity. Suicidal ideas and plans are apt to be separated from the emotional tone (anguish and anxiety) which expectably might accompany them.

Self-object confusion occurs in states other than dissociated ones. Suicide in psychotic patients – here I refer to classical affective psychoses but especially in schizophrenia – can take place as the patient strives to rid himself of an interior enemy, interior in the sense that the enemy is located in a part of the self which has been split off and is then treated as an alien object. Some of these patients are trying to kill off hallucinated persecutors which they localize in their bodies before attacking them there. Others have delusions that their heads or other body parts are infested with an alien enemy that can be destroyed by body attack.

A 23-year-old psychotic patient committed suicide while in hospital. She addressed the following note to her psychiatrist who, before reading it, had not been aware that the patient was deluded:

> These last few days were a deathlike existence. I am so tired I just want to sleep. My mind, oh, my mind, it's sick. I feel as if I am sinking and I

can't call for any help but death. I don't seem to feel as though I want to die. It's like another person telling me what to do. I feel as though my mind isn't connected to my body, and it seems to refer to me as in 'you,' as in, 'Die, you fool, die.' I feel as though there are two of me, and the killer is winning. When my death comes, it won't be suicide. It's that someone has murdered me. While I am writing this letter, it's like the other part is laughing at me and calling me a fool for writing this nonsense, but it's how I feel, I know it must sound confusing to you, but this is the only way I can express myself. I wish I could have told you many of my confused feelings, but I feel as though you won't understand and believe me and then the other part takes over and goes into therapy for me. I want to destroy that part of me, but I cannot seem to separate myself in therapy to do it, while it's trying to kill me, I'll kill myself and take it with me. . . . I took those pills before, it was to kill the other part of me, but I really won't die, I'll just wake up and things will be different. That's how I feel tonight, that I'm not really going to die, and the other one is and I don't know how to explain that to you. I seem to be contradicting myself, but I am writing as I feel. . . . I have used the term Robot to you, it's like someone is hurt up in my head and is using my eyes as windows and controlling me and my actions. . . . If you think I'm looking for pity through this, you're crazy, because it won't do me any good, for where I'm going I need pity like I need another problem. Well that's it, so have a good laugh. It's on me.

Borderline patients often speak of feeling 'empty' inside. Therapists generally understand such statements metaphorically, but on a number of occasions I have encountered suicidal patients who quite concretely believed there were anatomically empty spaces in the thorax or abdomen. Self-attack is well known among borderline patients, who frequently describe their bodies as not real. One suicidal borderline patient felt that someone from the outside had foisted her body on her, that it was a sinister counterfeit of her true body. From such observations as these we have ample evidence that patients objectify their body-selves and confuse them with representations of hostile others. We also may recall that borderline patients often develop confusions in the transference, so that they are unable to tell where they leave off and their therapists begin. These patients often disavow their own feelings, especially hateful ones, attributing them to their therapists, and cannot distinguish affective boundaries.

Conclusions

In concluding I shall provide a summary of events that characterize that ego regression, and some of Glover's primitive autoplastic methods of dealing with the accompanying tension.

1   Because of defects in ego development the patient is left with a vulner-
    able self, ill equipped to manage the intense affects that may follow
    upon misfortunes – i.e. precipitating events. One may think of the self
    as cracked, or fissured, vulnerable to fracture, especially in repre-
    sentational functioning.
2   When intense affective flooding overcomes the self, a state of help-
    lessness ensues that cannot be tolerated. The anxiety that arises is
    traumatic and signals impending break-up of the self.
3   Helplessness in the face of desperate, anguished suffering gives rise to
    hopelessness. The protective positive affective coloration of the self-
    representation, and of the body-representation in particular, is
    withdrawn.
4   The self, or the ego, is left unprotected as raw aggression, emerging
    through the superego, is directed at the self.
5   The integrity of the self-representation breaks up. Split-off parts of the
    self-representation are experienced as objects, or parts of objects.
6   Reality testing is abandoned. Survival seems possible if the fragmented
    self can rid itself of the menacing objectified parts that have become
    affiliated with destructive introjects.
7   Suicidal self-attack occurs as a grandiose measure for escaping the
    intolerable suffering of traumatic, primary anxiety that accompanies
    self break-up.

I opened by quoting what Edward Glover said at the Innsbruck Congress
in 1927: that suicide implies 'a regression of the ego to primitive animistic
levels and the adoption of primitive autoplastic methods of dealing with
tension based on the processes of primary identification'. When caught in
an intolerable affect trap from which no escape seems possible, with the self
losing its integration and breaking apart, reality testing fails and primitive,
magical solutions for getting out and getting away suggest themselves to the
desperate patient. A drowning man in a panic will grasp at whatever spar or
flotsam is within reach, and so it is here. Suicide suggests itself as a means
for escape and for rescue, and the patient, unable to tell fact from fancy, or
parts of the disintegrating self from others, will try anything to get away.

Note

1 The first Psychoanalysis and Suicidality Conference hosted by the University of
  Hamburg-Eppendorf, August 2001.

References

Asch, S. (1980) 'Suicide, and the hidden executioner', *International Review of
  Psychoanalysis* 7: 51–60.

Bibring, E. (1953) 'The mechanism of depression', in P. Greenacre (ed.) *Affective Disorders* (pp. 13–48), New York: International Universities Press.

Freud, S. (1917) 'Mourning and melancholia', in J. Strachey (ed.) *The Standard Edition of the Works of Sigmund Freud, XIV* (pp. 237–258), London: Hogarth.

Freud, S. (1926) 'Inhibitions, symptoms, and anxiety', in J. Strachey (ed.) *The Standard Edition of the Works of Sigmund Freud, XX* (pp. 75–175), London: Hogarth.

Glover, E. (1930) 'Grades of ego-differentiation', in *On the Early Development of Mind* (pp. 112–129), London: Imago Publishing Co., 1956.

Klein, M. (1957) *Envy and Gratitude and Other Works*, New York: Basic Books.

Laufer, M. (1989) *Developmental Breakdown and Psychoanalytic Treatment in Adolescence: Clinical Studies*, New Haven and London: Yale University Press.

Laufer, M. (ed.) (1995) *The Suicidal Adolescent*, London: Karnac.

Laufer, M. and Laufer, E. (1984) *Adolescence and Developmental Breakdown*, London: Karnac.

Maltsberger, J.T. (1993) 'Confusions of the body, the self, and others in suicidal states', in A. Leenaars (ed.) *Suicidology: Essays in Honor of Edwin S. Shneidman* (pp. 148–171), Northvale, NJ: Jason Aronson.

Maltsberger, J.T. (2004) 'The descent into suicide', *International Journal of Psychoanalysis* 85, 3: 653–668.

Maltsberger, J.T. and Buie, D.H. (1980) 'The devices of suicide: revenge, riddance, and rebirth', *International Review of Psychoanalysis* 7: 61–72.

Orgel, S. (1974) 'Fusion with the victim and suicide', *International Journal of Psychoanalysis* 55: 531–538.

Sadock, B.J. (2000) 'Signs and symptoms in psychiatry', in B.J. Sadock and V.A Sadock (eds) *Kaplan and Sadock's Comprehensive Textbook of Psychiatry* (pp. 681–682), Philadelphia: Lippincott, Williams, and Wilkins.

Sandler, J. and Rosenblatt, B. (1962) 'The concept of the representational world', *Psychoanalytic Study of the Child* 17: 128–145.

Chapter 4

Who is killing what or whom?

Some notes on the internal phenomenology of suicide[1]

David Bell

> The ego can kill itself only if . . . it can treat itself as an object.
>
> (Freud 1917: 252)

Introduction

The psychiatric literature on suicide tends to give emphasis to the demographic and social aspects. We know that completed suicide is commoner in men than in women, whereas for attempted suicide the relation is reversed. Social isolation and the loss of important supporting structures which give meaning to life (such as employment and family bonds) are very important risk factors for suicide. Coming nearer the individual, we know that there is a clear link between depression and suicide, although there is a tendency for this to be rather overstated. It is likely that a very significant number of completed suicides and attempted suicides occur in the context of personality disorder, where, as a result of the high degree of dissociation, depressive affect is minimal. From a psychoanalytic perspective, the distinction between personality disorder and illness is in any case less clear.[2]

Case illustration

Ms A, a middle-aged woman, had suffered a very significant bereavement about two years before I saw her for a consultation. She was going about her life in an apparently calm and ordinary manner, showing little outward expression of depression. She was from time to time beset by a wish, as intense as it was sudden, to hang herself. As she put it, 'I could be walking down the stairs having taken a break from my work to make some tea and would suddenly say to myself "Go and hang yourself".' She kept a noose in the basement. In this case, as in many others, dissociation is a far more sinister sign than overt misery and depression.

This case brings to mind a further general feature in assessing suicide risk, namely the method that is envisaged for carrying out the act.

Thoughts of overdose for example are usually less sinister than thoughts of self-hanging or gassing.[3] The relevant feature here is, perhaps, the intensity of the internal violence that the planned method reveals.

I now put aside these general considerations, not because I believe them to be unimportant, but because they are all of limited help in understanding, assessing and managing the individual case. The above factors lack any clear sense, either of the internality of the potential suicide or of the relationship between this internality and the immediate context, particularly with reference to the most important relationships. All suicidal acts take place in the context of human relationships, real and imagined.

Freud's 'Mourning and melancholia'

It was consideration of those mental processes that underlie self-destruction that led Freud to a formed theory of the internal world. In 1910, the Vienna Psychoanalytic Society held a symposium on suicide and it was during that symposium that Stekel made his far-reaching remark, 'No-one kills himself who has never wanted to kill another, or at least wished the death of another' (Stekel 1910, quoted in Campbell 1999). Freud remarked at this same symposium that suicide would not be understood until more was known about the intricate processes of mourning and melancholia. 'Mourning and melancholia', the paper Freud published in 1917, marked a watershed in the development of psychoanalytic theory. It was the beginning of a theory of the internal world peopled by primitive internal figures, the foundations of a theory of identification, and was also one of the crucial steps made in the development of the concept of the superego – and all of these are of course relevant to our theme. For the moment, however, I would like to examine in more detail the process of 'turning against the self in hatred', which is central to Freud's paper.

Freud noted that in melancholic states the patient berated himself with various criticisms, accusations of worthlessness, weakness, etc. He suggested that, if one listened carefully to these various recriminations, one could see that they often fitted not the patient himself, but someone else whom 'the patient loves, has loved or should love' (Freud 1917: 248). This object of the patient's affections has been lost; but instead of giving up the object, the patient has dealt with his loss by incorporating the lost object into himself, identifying with it (that is, becoming the lost object). The ego, now identified with the lost object, is now the target of all the hatred accusation that belonged originally to the object:

> The shadow of the object fell upon the ego and the latter would henceforth be judged by a special agency, as though it were an object, the forsaken object. In this way an object-loss was transformed into an ego-loss and the conflict between the ego and the loved person into a

cleavage between the critical activity of the ego and the ego as altered
through identification.

(Freud 1917: 249)

The critical agency later became the superego, and its activities were
revealed as not just critical but archaic, cruel and murderous. Although
Freud here appears to be referring to an actual loss of a current external
figure, it subsequently became clear that in melancholia it is all previous
losses that are activated, the losses we all have had to bear as part of
development – at root, the loss of the primary object, ordinarily the
mother, and all that she represents. The point, however, that I wish to stress
here is that, underlying all suicides and similar acts of self-destruction, there
is an attack upon the self, that is, a self identified with a hated object. The
act is an attack upon an object and simultaneously a punishment of the self
for all its sadistic and cruel attacks upon the object.

Klein's contribution

An understanding of the complexity of the internal world and the importance of states of internal persecution in mental life is central to the work of
Melanie Klein. She showed how the inner world is built up through a
complex interplay of processes of projection and introjection, which I now
summarise.

Fundamental to development is the establishment, internally, of a good
object which can be felt to support, to sustain the self in the face of the
various anxiety situations that characterise development. In order to preserve the good object it is necessary for the infantile mind to create various
splits, but most critical is that between his own loving and aggressive
impulses. The world so formed is divided between idealised 'good' objects,
which are maintained internally, and 'bad' ones, which are felt as persecuting and are projected externally. The more intense the infant's own
sadistic feelings, the more terrifying the external 'bad' object and the more
intense the idealisation of the 'good' object which is felt to offer a perfect
world with absence of frustration, anxiety or any mental pain. In this
situation there is a lack of capacity to experience loss as the absence of a
good object. Instead, the place where there might have been awareness of
the absence of a good object is replaced by the presence of an object felt to
be bad and responsible for all the painful feelings of loss and frustration.

Klein used the term 'projective identification' (Klein 1952) to describe a
process, dominant in these early primitive situations, whereby internal
objects and feelings are projected into objects which then become identified
with that which has been projected onto them. This phase of development,
dominated by these splitting and projective mechanisms, Klein described as
the 'paranoid/schizoid position'. It is this inner situation that dominates in

all severe psychopathology and particularly so in acts of self-destruction where, as I will describe further, attempts are made to rid the self of all bad objects which have become identified with parts of the body, or even the whole self, and through so doing finally unite with an object felt to be perfect and ideal.

As infantile development proceeds, the lessening of the splitting and projective processes brings a move towards integration, a process described by Klein as the move towards the depressive position. The new integration of the object brings awareness that cruel impulses have been directed towards an object that is not 'just bad' but complex, not good or bad but good and bad; and this recognition brings very painful feelings of remorse and guilt, which in turn are the foundation for the capacity to be aware of an object which, although absent, remains good. This brings feelings of pining for the lost object and a mourning of its loss. The toleration of the psychic pain attendant on these processes can be borne only on the basis of the acquisition of a secure good object which provides the necessary internal support.

Klein thus described two fundamental positions, or ways of being in the world. The achievement of the depressive position is not a once-and-for-all phenomenon but is re-negotiated again and again throughout life. Each developmental challenge, or traumatic situation (such as those brought by the losses that are inevitable in life), brings the two possibilities: regression to illness or further integration. Klein thought that serious depressive illness took its point of origin as the individual's incapacity to manage the psychic pain characteristic of the depressive position. It is important here to emphasise that the depressive position as defined by Klein is completely distinct from depressive illness. From the perspective offered here, depressive illness or melancholia arises from the incapacity to manage depressive pain and is characterised by primitive schizoid processes.[4]

It is commonly observed that patients suffering from depressive illness become dangerously suicidal when they are in fact recovering, and this observation is quite consistent with the above account. Improvement, the move towards integration, brings the patient into touch with a persecuting guilt which it is difficult to bear. For some, this results in suicidal impulses which act as the only way of ridding the mind of the pain.

I will now describe some inner situations characteristic of suicide. This will be followed by some case illustrations of how an understanding of the inner world of the suicidal patient can influence the general management of the situation.

The inner situation of suicide

There are very few things in psychiatry that can be said with certainty, and one of them is this. Suicide attempts never take place for the stated reason.

At most, the cause given is the trigger and, relatively speaking, only a superficial explanation. To say, for example, that an adolescent took an overdose because he failed his exams leaves open the question of why failing an exam results in a wish to destroy the self. A patient I knew took an overdose in adolescence, in the context of impending exams, and 'exam stress' was the explanation recorded. He received no help. Later in life, in his late forties, as a patient in analysis, he was able to explain that whilst studying for his exams he was overwhelmed by the need compulsively to masturbate. His semen had left a stain that he could not eradicate, and he had become terrified that his mother would 'find him out'. Why such a discovery terrified him, and the link between this and the conscious and less conscious fantasies that accompanied his masturbation, became clear subsequently. But, for the present purpose, this case serves to illustrate the point that what the patient recalls consciously is usually more a rationalisation than an explanation. These patients are often terrified of recognising serious mental disturbance in themselves, let alone of giving any publicity to this situation. This terror overrides the anxiety that arises from the awareness of the threat to their lives and so results in a minimisation of its seriousness.

Underlying all suicide attempts there are phantasies[5] concerning the self and the relation to the body which are usually, though not always, deeply unconscious. In addition, from a phenomenological perspective many suicide attempts occur in the context of beliefs in indestructibility. I can think of patients, for example, for whom the experience of repetitive resuscitation provided support for this omnipotence. From an internal point of view, one might say, in some of these cases, a finally successful suicide, given the delusional belief in indestructibility, may be regarded as accidental.

Deep splits in the inner world between a part of the self in relation with an idealised object, and a part of the self felt to be bad and subject to terrifying inner cruel attacks, are characteristic of most suicidal patients. The idealisation serves to protect the good object from the self's own murderous wishes. The bad parts of the self may become identified with part, or even all, of the body.

I will now describe in more detail some different situations which will serve to illustrate some of the 'internal phenomenologies' that underlie many suicides.

In certain patients there is a profound intolerance of frustration. Any awareness of needs or desires unsatisfied precipitates serious mental difficulties. The possibility of the awareness of absence, in line with the model described above, is replaced by the feeling of a persecuting presence often experienced as existing in the body. The body provides a particularly apt vehicle, in that it is the body that brings awareness of needs and desires (such as for food, sexual contact), namely awareness of reality. Hatred of this awareness, which is critically linked to intolerance of frustration, can result in attacks on the body, with the underlying phantasy that by getting rid of the body, or part of it, the patient can be rid of his desires and live on in an 'ideal' world without ever having to bear again the frustration of desires unsatisfied. It is a case of 'shooting the messenger', the body, because the message that it brings, awareness of painful aspects of reality, cannot be borne.

A further aspect of these phantasies becomes apparent if one asks the question 'What sort of situation in life approximates to never having to bear a need unsatisfied?' The answer is, of course, the intra-uterine situation, or at least our phantasies of it. In separating himself from his hated body, the suicide may also believe that he is re-uniting himself with an idealised maternal object, never to be separated again.

The body that is attacked may represent the hated primary object, in other words an internal mother. Again there is a deep split in the mind between good and bad objects. The envied, hated mother who is attacked in phantasy is kept separate from an ideal mother felt to support life. This situation is particularly important in adolescence (see Laufer 1995). For example, the pubertal changes in a girl's body make it increasingly difficult to locate hated sexual aspects of herself in an object, mother, that is felt to be external. Such an adolescent may experience the eruption within herself of a sexual body as evidence that she is being taken over by a hated mother. It is of interest, in this context, to recall that many who are contemplating suicide say they are prevented from carrying out the act for fear of the terrible pain it would cause to the actual parents. This, in some cases, reflects a kind of insight, in that the wish to carry through the act is partly motivated by the desire to inflict this pain on the primary objects.

In all these situations, 'good' objects are projected outside the self, and their importance should never be underestimated. A patient may say, for example, that she cannot commit suicide as long as her pet dog is alive. The dog here represents all the good objects which need to be kept alive and protected from the murderous feelings that dominate the mind.

Klein (1935) pointed out that

> while in committing suicide the ego intends to murder its bad objects, in my view at the same time it also aims at saving its loved objects, internal and external . . . the phantasies aim at preserving the good objects and that part of the ego identified with good objects and also destroying that part of the ego which is identified with the bad objects.
>
> (Klein 1935: 276)

The point here is that, however mad it might seem, some acts of suicide are aimed at preserving what is good. It is as if the self, feeling unable to resist the pull towards terrifying destructiveness, in despair kills itself to save the world. But it must also be true that being lured into the belief that destruction of the self is the only way of saving the good objects, might itself also be fuelled by the deadliest forces in the mind.

Some suicidal patients – and this is typical of severe melancholia – are continuously internally persecuted by an archaic and vengeful superego from which there is no escape (a psychic claustrophobia). Its punishing quality is merciless. It inflates quite ordinary faults and failures, turning them into crimes that must be punished. In this situation, suicide, a submission to the internal tormentors, may be felt as a final release. The skin itself may be felt to be the prison within which these torments take place. Cutting the skin is here associated with a feeling of relief, the self having become identified with the blood escaping. However, this relief may be overtaken by perverse excitement, resulting in a frenzy of mutilating attacks. These processes also create a vicious circle in that the evidence of damage done to the objects that have become identified with parts of the body, gives fuel to further internal recriminations. It is for such reason that some patients will go to great lengths to obtain plastic surgery to cover up their scars, which, however, can never provide what is asked of it, namely perfect, that is magical, repair of all evidence of the damage inflicted, being erased from the body and so from the mind.

Finally, I would like to address those situations where the suicidal or self-destructive act is carried out in the service of projection. Here the patient, through the act, seeks to invade an object, projecting into it the guilt and rage he feels he has suffered at another's behest. Sometimes the object of this attack is someone who has actually behaved in a cruel and tormenting way, but more often the object's only crime is to have faced the subject with unbearable 'facts of life', such as the fact that he cannot control the other. Usually in such cases, the subject feels that having projected the guilt, rage and other intolerable feelings into his object through the suicidal act, he can live on, finally free of these feelings. As Alvarez has pithily put it:

> a man may take his life because he feels the destructive elements in him cannot be borne: so he sheds them at the expense of guilt and confusion of his survivors . . . but what is left he hopes is a purified idealised image of himself that lives on . . . suicide is simply the most brutal way of making sure you won't be forgotten.[6]

(1974: 129)

In some cases, this process is further driven by an excitement born not only of the sense of being finally rid of these bad destructive elements but also of a certain feeling of triumph over the object, believing that the object will inescapably be punished for ever.

Those mental health workers who are on the receiving end of this act are left in no doubt as to the invasive power of these projective processes, not only to overwhelm one's belief in having the capacity to help that particular patient, but any patient, or even one's belief in oneself as a worthwhile human being.

Many patients describe a feeling of complete calm and peacefulness once they have resolved to kill themselves. Sylvia Plath (see Alvarez 1974) tidied up the house, putting everything in order, before she gassed herself. Tidying up confirms that the inner mess and confusion have finally resolved, and should not be mistaken for the exercising of a balanced rational judgement. This apparent tranquillity is the outward sign that the suicide has already entered the delusional world in which he feels himself to be free of all the inner persecution.

The above descriptions are not intended as a catalogue, there being a number of important situations not described here. Nor is it intended as a typology, as there is clearly considerable overlap between the situations described. I have also said practically nothing about aetiology, not because it is less important – clearly factors in early childhood are of considerable importance, such as childhood trauma, including emotional and sexual abuse, emotional deprivation, mental illness in one or both parents – but because an accurate assessment of the inner situation is critical in rational management of these patients.

Case illustrations

Miss B was internally dominated by a cruel primitive superego which she felt watched her every move. She experienced any attempt at self-control as in the service of this superego, and so could not distinguish between it and ordinary ego functions that sought to protect her from danger; in other words, the superego masqueraded as the ego. This resulted in a wholesale projection of her sane awareness of the danger she was in, into her analyst. Thus left free of any concern for herself, Miss B took increasingly dangerous risks – such as driving whilst under the influence of sedatives – apparently with complete equanimity, whilst her analyst became increasingly horrified as the momentum of her self-destructiveness gathered pace. She said that she experienced the ending of sessions 'like a guillotine', and this was a very apt description as, having projected important ego functions into her analyst, she left the session in a 'headless' state. The situation deteriorated to such an extent that it became necessary to admit her to hospital.

On the ward, she behaved in a very provocative way towards the nurses. She would go off the ward without telling them where she was going, leaving them with an overwhelming anxiety that she was about to carry out a very self-destructive attack. She might say, for example, in an apparently calm state, that she was 'going to the shops', as if this was a quite ordinary and banal event, whilst at the same time conveying that she would be near the pharmacy where, by implication, she *might* buy some paracetamol. At other times she would telephone the ward from outside but not speak when a nurse answered and then hang up. The nurses found this unbearably tantalising. This resulted in an escalation of the need of the staff to control her and she was restricted from leaving the ward. The situation then further deteriorated and the nurses became worried that she might carry out a serious attack upon herself, at any moment. The final result was that she was restricted to a small room where she was continuously observed. She then became acutely anxious and declared in a terrified voice, 'I can't stand this place. I'm being imprisoned.'

The patient has 'actualised' (Sandler 1976) her inner situation. What started out as an inner conflict between aspects of herself, an intrapsychic situation, has now been transported into a conflict between herself and the nursing staff, namely an interpersonal situation. The superego watching her all the time is, of course, inescapable, but temporary escape is achieved through projecting it elsewhere in this way. It is not her own superego but instead the nurses on the ward who are felt to be imprisoning her.

It is also important to note that the patient's provocative manner did engender a good deal of hostility towards her which was never really owned by the staff. Although the maintenance of the patient under continuous observation served, manifestly, a wish to protect the patient from suicide, at a deeper level, it also, I think, satisfied a hatred which had been recruited in the staff and which was associated with some excitement.

In the schizoid world, internal good objects are felt to be under considerable threat from the subject's own murderous impulses. Some patients feel that the internal good object just cannot survive inside them and so must be projected elsewhere, in order to survive. This procedure can be life-saving as it is through such processes that the patient recruits others to look after him. However, through a subtle shift in the balance of forces, the patient can, as a result of these projective processes, become totally identified with his own cruelty, whilst the wish to live, and to secure help, becomes the target for mockery and contempt. In this perverse world, strength comes only from hatred, and the wish to preserve life and obtain help is regarded as evidence of weakness. Rosenfeld (1971) gave a very detailed analysis of this process which he termed 'destructive narcissism', where life-seeking parts of the personality are imprisoned and tormented by a cruel inner organisation which he termed the 'internal Mafia'. Such patients are inexorably drawn into a perverse world where life and sanity, regarded as evidence of weakness, are treated with contempt. Segal (1993), in discussing similar processes, gives a striking example from a literary source.

At the end of Jack London's novel *Martin Eden*, Martin, the eponymous hero, commits suicide by drowning. As he sinks he automatically tries to swim.

It was the automatic instinct to live. He ceased swimming, but the moment he felt water rising above his mouth his hands struck out sharply with a lifting movement. 'This is the will to live', he thought and the thought was accompanied by a sneer.

Segal goes on:

London brings out vividly the hatred and contempt Martin feels for the part of him that wants to live. As he drowns he has a tearing pain in his chest. 'The hurt was not death' was the thought that oscillated through his reeling consciousness. It was life – the pangs of life – the awful suffocating feeling. It was the last blow life could deal him.

Such situations can result in a particularly deadly scenario. The patient recruits more and more people to become responsible for his own life. But the more individuals allow themselves to feel so responsible, the more the patient dissociates himself from the wish to live, now located in others. Further, as the patient becomes increasingly taken over by the cruel inner organisation, the sanity and concern now located in external others become the object of scorn and derision.

Ms C was referred to be considered for admission by a psychiatric team who had become very worried at the possibility of her suicide. From what I could gather, threats of suicide had become one of the principal modes of communication. When I went to meet her in the waiting-room she had the air of someone who is very seriously disturbed. She was sitting in the waiting-room, with her head bowed low, and apparently did not see or hear me arrive. I had to attract her attention. What ensued was a very disturbing experience. For much of the time she disowned any knowledge about herself, claiming she had come 'because they sent me'. When I commented on how difficult she found the interview, she replied with a defiant air, 'Well anyone would in this situation, wouldn't they?'

Throughout the interview I felt acutely aware of the dangerous suicidality, whilst she remained almost entirely cut off from it and apparently superior. However, when I pointed out that she was doing everything she could to stop me helping her, and went on to say that she might succeed, she looked at me, smiled, and said, 'You've pulled the rug out from under my feet.' She added that getting treatment was 'her only lifeline'. Although this was, in a certain sense, true, what I want to convey here is the way in which, right from the beginning of the consultation, it was I who was to carry responsibility for her condition. The waiting-room situation where I had to try in a rather awkward way to attract her attention was emblematic of what was to transpire. When she said to me that getting help was her lifeline, this was not a moment of contact and reassurance. It filled me with anxiety. I felt that if I did not accept her for treatment then and there, it would be I who was pulling away the lifeline, I who would be responsible for her suicide. Having projected her wish to live into me and made me responsible for it, I, as the representative of that wish, was being taunted with the terror of her suicide. I carried not only the responsibility for her life, but also the threat of an omnipotent persecuting guilt. The smile was a smile of perverse triumph at my impossible position. It did turn out that this was an enactment of an internal situation in which she herself felt continuously threatened and mocked. Any reference that she made to mental pain was quickly followed by a contemptuous attack on that part of herself that experienced this vulnerability, labelled as 'whingeing and whining'.

These situations are not uncommon. Many patients use admission to psychiatric wards to provide them with an immediate context for these projective procedures. Although, in the last instance, no one can be absolutely prevented from committing suicide, it is easy for staff to become identified with an omnipotence which dictates that it is entirely their responsibility. They come to believe themselves to be the *only* ones capable of *really understanding* the patient. The determination to save the patient acquires a religiosity, the staff believing themselves to be specially selected for this mission. Hostility that is denied and split-off to this extent can quite suddenly return, and with a vengeance. Yesterday's poor suffering patient, who only needs help and understanding and constant support, easily becomes tomorrow's hopeless case who should be immediately discharged, given high doses of medication or even ECT. These measures may even bring an apparent improvement, not based on any real development but brought about through the gratification of the patient's need for punishment, relieving him, temporarily, of the persecuting omnipotent guilt.

It was Tom Main (1957) who originally studied these processes in detail, showing how the splits in the patient's mind are relived, in the ward, as divisions among the staff. The 'saintly' group, described above, who endlessly suffer on behalf of the patient, and who believe the patient to be *only* a victim of his damaging early relationships, have their counterpart in another group of staff who see the patient *only* as manipulative and 'attention seeking', which must be 'confronted'. Where these staff disturbances remain unacknowledged, the situation can quickly escalate, with catastrophic results.

A further marked feature of these cases where perverse elements are so predominant is the presence of negative therapeutic reactions. Here, just at the moment where the patient has made some real progress, there is a sudden deterioration, with real risk of suicide. It is as if the progress, with its acknowledgement of the extent of disturbance and vulnerability, provokes a furious counter-attack by the internal organisation which regards this contact with sanity as a betrayal. It is important to distinguish this sort of negative therapeutic reaction from that where the pull towards suicide is primarily a result of unbearable guilt and despair, which has different management implications.

> Ms D appeared at first as rather similar to Ms C, in that she too filled the staff with unbearable anxiety as to her suicidal capacity. Although at first perverse psychopathology seemed to predominate, this gave way to a more clearly melancholic picture. Ms D had made innumerable mutilating attacks on her skin by slashing it. Her skin seemed to represent her sexual body, which she regarded as disgusting. She felt full of 'bad disgusting thoughts', particularly of abusing children. She felt that she could rid herself of this identification with her abusing parent only through quite literally cutting it out of her body. She had managed, however, to spare her face and hands, and this appeared to represent a limited capacity to hold on to something good in herself. However, once on the ward, Ms D tended to project into the staff all awareness of these good aspects of herself, while sinking further and further into a melancholic state. The fact that in this case the staff felt able to maintain a belief in her, despite being constantly provoked, turned out to be of great therapeutic importance. The primary motive for this projection outside herself of her wish to live seemed to be more for 'safe-keeping', perverse mockery being much less evident. After some improvement, Ms D too, like Ms C, showed a marked negative therapeutic reaction and became more acutely ill. Although there were some perverse elements, the predominant difficulties arose from the unbearable psychic pain consequent on the awareness of damage done to her good objects, which to some extent really was irreparable.

Some important lessons are learnt from the management of such a case. There is a need to be constantly aware of both sides of the patient. Improvement brought an acute fear that the staff would become over-excited and so lose sight of the danger. Blindness of this type can, in some cases, precipitate further dangerous acting out, as the patient needs to have her dangerousness re-registered in the minds of those responsible for her, this being a source of profound reassurance. Even when the patient was, eventually, discharged, it was very important both to acknowledge the improvement, which was real, and at the same itme to accept the ever-present risk of further mutilating attacks or even suicidal attempts. These patients, I think, need to have a sense of the resilience of their object, namely an object that can bear to know of their murderousness whilst not being overwhelmed by it, nor driven to attempt to take complete control. There needs to be a capacity to recognise the possibility of suicide, without turning it into an omnipotent responsibility, thus facilitating management aimed at helping the patient, rather than evading guilt. Such functions support the patient's sanity. There needs here to be a recognition that toleration of the possibility of suicide is not the same thing as colluding with it. Institutions where these difficult patients are managed can easily themselves become vehicles for the enactment of these omnipotent processes.

At the Cassel Hospital, a regular weekly meeting of all the staff aims to discuss difficulties in the work, regardless of source. In the first meeting after a suicide had taken place, the staff were understandably stunned, especially as the patient was not thought to be in such immediate danger. During the meeting, one of the staff reminded those present that the staff at the previous week's meeting had spent much of the time discussing the nurses' re-grading. This referred to the implementation of new NHS policy, which required all qualified nurses to be re-graded. This meant that nurses who were at the same level in the hierarchy would, within a few days, find that some were now on a higher grade and thus receiving more money. This had been a considerable source of stress for the nurses and was interfering with their work. The meeting (at the time) was largely felt to have been useful. However, with the knowledge now at hand, it was asserted that this discussion had 'really' been a defensive distraction from anxiety concerning the patient who had killed herself. Soon there emerged the implication that if we had talked about the patient we would have saved her life. The meeting ended in an atmosphere of guilt and recrimination.

The following week, as I walked down the corridor to the meeting, I suddenly found myself wanting to use the meeting to talk about any patient under my care who was suicidal. I then remembered that it is often the patient whom one is not particularly worried about who actually commits suicide. So the category 'suicidal' widened its reference until it included all the patients under my care. I then felt impelled to discuss all of them in the meeting. Others wanted to discuss their patients. It became evident that the wish to discuss patients was no longer in any realistic relation to a wish to improve their care, but was now at the service of a wish to escape blame from an omnipotent organisation which, in the event of a suicide, would hold staff completely responsible and ensure they were punished.

Concluding comments

In this chapter I have, first, drawn attention to the different internal phenomenologies that underlie attacks upon the self. I have tried to show how an understanding of the patient's inner world can be an essential part of management. Inner situations can be externalised in various ways, result-ing in quite irrational management based more on countertransference enactments than sober consideration of the issues. A particularly dangerous situation is where the patient succeeds, through projective processes, in externalising his inner world to such an extent that external objects become indistinguishable from archaic inner figures, making reality-testing impossible.

Attention to the relationships staff form with patients and with each other is thus critical in management. We all enter the field of mental health for complex reasons, but probably common to us all is a wish to repair our own damaged inner objects. In order to be able to work effectively, we need to be able to tolerate the patient's attacks on these reparative wishes, our most vulnerable point. We need to be able to stand failure so that the patient can improve for himself, rather than experience the need for progress as a demand from those caring for him.

More than anything else, staff morale is the vital therapeutic ingredient, a morale that needs to be robust and not dependent on any individual patient getting better. I have described a common central structure in suicidal patients, a primitive psychotic superego which demands omnipotence, not knowledge. It is easy for such disturbed modes of thinking to find a home, not only in the staff but in the institution itself, especially when this is backed up by an external world that demands the impossible. To insist that mental health personnel accept a level of responsibility that is quite unrealistic seems increasingly to be a part of mental health policy. Such policies, based less on thought and more on the wish to project unmanageable anxiety into those faced with an already very difficult task, set the scene for a deterioration in the real care of these patients. Management plans come to serve as a defence of the self against any possible blame, rather than acceptance of the complexities of the task. An attitude of enquiry is transformed into one of protection of the self from the Inquisition.

Notes

1 This chapter was originally published in *Psychoanalytic Psychotherapy*, 2000, 15: 21–37. It is reproduced here with permission of the author and the editor of *Psychoanalytic Psychotherapy* and Taylor and Francis Publishers.

2 Illness and breakdown are viewed as developments that arise out of a particular personality structure when exposed to stress arising from internal and external sources.

3 Of course every suicide attempt needs to be taken very seriously. I remember well a patient who went to the Casualty Department having taken three paracetamol tablets which, she pointed out, was more than the recommended dose. The unwitting Casualty Officer told her she needn't worry as she would need to take many more to do herself any serious harm. She returned the following day, having taken fifty tablets. Similarly it also pays to be wary of the patient's reassuring statement 'it was all a silly mistake'.

4 From a phenomenological point of view it is important to differentiate between the anxiety and psychic pain that derives from the feeling of being persecuted by an object that has been attacked, and the pain that has a more depressive quality, arising out of awareness of the damage done to the object and which mobilises reparative wishes. There is a further category, however, that appears to combine both qualities. I am referring to a particular sort of tormenting psychic pain which arises from the feeling of being internally persecuted by the recriminations of damaged objects – as if, so to speak, they are saying, 'We are all suffering, look what you have done to us.' This latter situation may lead to suicidal acts or other types of violence, motivated by the need to be rid of this type of pain which is often so unbearable.

5 The word phantasy is spelled here using 'ph', following the convention that this spelling be used when it is unconscious phenomena that are being emphasised, distinguishing them from the more conscious events described as 'fantasies'.

6 Mason (1983) gives a very helpful and detailed account of this claustrophobic situation, brought about by what he calls 'the suffocating superego'.

References

Alvarez, A. (1974) *The Savage God*, Harmondsworth: Penguin Books.

Campbell, D. (1999) 'The role of the father in a pre-suicide state', in R. Perelberg (ed.) *Psychoanalytic Understanding of Violence and Suicide*, London: Routledge.

Freud, S. (1917) 'Mourning and melancholia', in J. Strachey (ed.) *The Standard Edition of the Works of Sigmund Freud, XIV* (pp. 237–258), London: Hogarth.

Klein, M. (1935) 'A contribution to the psychogenesis of manic-depressive psychosis', *International Journal of Psycho-Analysis* 16: 145–74; and also in *Writings of Melanie Klein*, Vol. 1, London: Hogarth, 1975.

Klein, M. (1940) 'Mourning and its relation to manic depressive states', *International Journal of Psycho-Analysis* 21: 125–153; and also in *Writings of Melanie Klein*, Vol. 1, London: Hogarth, 1975.

Klein, M. (1952) 'Notes on some schizoid mechanisms', in M. Klein, P. Heimann, S. Isaacs and J. Riviere (eds) *Developments in Psycho-Analysis*, London: Hogarth.

Laufer, M. (ed.) (1995) *The Suicidal Adolescent*, London: Karnac.

Main, T. (1957). 'The ailment', *British Journal of Medical Psychology* 30: 129–145; and also in T. Main (ed.) *The Ailment and Other Psychoanalytic Essays*, London: Free Association Books, 1989.

Mason, A. (1983) 'The suffocating superego: psychotic break and claustrophobia', in J. Grotstein (ed.) *Do I Dare Disturb the Universe?*, London: Karnac/Maresfield Library.

Rosenfeld, H. (1971) 'A clinical approach to the psychoanalytical theory of the life and death instincts: an investigation into the aggressive aspects of narcissism', *International Journal of Psycho-Analysis* 52: 169–178.

Sandler, J. (1976) 'Countertransference and role responsiveness', *International Review of Psycho-Analysis* 3: 43–47.

Segal, H. (1993) 'On the clinical usefulness of the concept of the death instinct', *International Journal of Psycho-Analysis* 74: 55–61; and also in J. Steiner (ed.) *Hanna Segal Papers 1972–1995: Psychoanalysis, Literature and War*, London: Routledge, 1997.

Stekel, W. ([1910] 1967) 'Symposium on suicide', in P. Friedman (ed.) *On Suicide*, New York: International Universities Press.

Chapter 5

A psychoanalytical approach to suicide in adolescents

Robin Anderson

Suicides are extremely distressing at any age but there is something particularly tragic about adolescent suicide. Adolescence is a time of the achievement of much greater competence and independence. Adolescents have arrived at a point in their lives when they can make their own mistakes and learn from them. Even when adolescents break down, interventions can begin which can help young people to try to make better decisions about themselves and see where they have gone wrong. One of the more encouraging aspects of working with adolescents is that we can often feel that it is not too late and that they can have a chance to put things right. There is a sense of a whole life ahead without too many irreversible decisions, in contrast to older patients who can often only make the best of the situation they are in. When this sense of hope in the future is cruelly cut short by suicide it has a powerful effect on anyone involved with them. For parents and siblings it is devastating, even fatal, and can certainly produce effects which may never be recovered from, as can also to a lesser extent happen to the friends and peer group. For professionals too the effect can be very distressing as well as persecuting, particularly if inquiries become suffused with the blame and destructiveness of the suicidal state.

Adolescence is a time of great turbulence and, apart from possibly infancy, is the time of the greatest biological, psychological and social change that occurs at any time during life. Any features of the personality development which predisposes a young person to suicide can be activated by this turbulent period. In this chapter I will explore adolescent suicide and attempted suicide from the point of view of what is going on in the minds of these young people at this time of their lives and how this may result in breakdown and seriously suicidal states. I will illustrate these ideas by describing some cases where suicide and self-harm were part of the clinical presentation.

Adolescent suicide in context

It is important to set the private tragedies in context. Suicide in young people has been identified as a serious public health problem worldwide

(WHO 1999). Rates of adolescent suicide have been increasing in many parts of the world. Every year, out of 10,000 adolescents 1,000 will make some kind of suicide attempt, 100 will come to medical attention, and one will die. In the UK and Republic of Ireland suicide is now the most common cause of death after car accidents in young people. Suicides by men outnumber those by women by 2:1, but in adolescence the ratio is 3:1. The paradox here is that girls make far more attempts than boys whilst boys' attempts are more likely to be fatal. Someone who attempts suicide has a much greater risk of eventually killing themselves (around sixty times greater) (Hawton *et al.* 2003). On the other hand, it is an uncommon event.

What do these larger studies say about the state of those who commit or attempt suicide? A diagnosis of depression is certainly present in a large number of cases – around 40 per cent in a US study of 894 cases of completed suicide in young people (Fleischmann *et al.* 2005) – which means that the risk of suicide must be seriously considered in such cases and also in the presence of a major psychiatric illness like schizophrenia. However, there is no doubt that impulsive behaviour related to acute distress caused by an issue such as the break-up of a relationship or academic failure in those who are vulnerable can lead to suicidal behaviour which can sometimes prove fatal (ibid.). If these states are modified by drugs or alcohol, this is even more likely. Often when we try to assess suicidal risk we do not know much about this individual and have to make decisions based on limited knowledge.

Many of the suicide methods chosen by young men in these acutely disturbed states seem to be more inherently dangerous and, although we are considering the deep aspects of unconscious processes here, we cannot ignore some of the more circumstantial aspects. For example, the most at-risk group of adolescents in the United States are the sons of policemen and women. Why should this be? It may be, of course, that being the son of a police officer in the United States is a highly pathogenic situation. However, it is more likely that in the United States – where suicide by shooting is the most common method chosen by young men – if a weapon is going to be readily to hand for those young men (in a way that it is not for most young men in the UK – contrary to popular opinion over here), then they may, in the emotional state they find themselves in, go and use it.

If someone is determined to kill themselves, in the long run, there is little that can be done to stop them. The point is that probably only a minority of suicides have that degree of determination. The American finding suggests that if someone is in this dangerous state of mind – and often this is a relatively transient state – then they are in more danger if the means to kill themselves is readily at hand. Similarly, making it more difficult to obtain large quantities of drugs such as paracetamol and aspirin has made actual suicide by these methods less common. There does, though, often seem to be an attempt to calibrate the degree of danger, for example, by controlling the extent of the overdose.

A young woman whom I assessed had attempted to hang herself from a light flex which was not strong enough to take her weight and so she survived. She probably knew at least unconsciously that this would be likely to be the case. The danger here is that young people may be unaware of the dangers of what they are doing and so put themselves at great risk even when they may not wish to die. For example, I was consulted about a depressed student who had got drunk and gone onto the roof of her student residence in a drunken and suicidal state. This showed an aggressive and desperate contempt for her safety but I doubted that she intended to fall. In fact she did not, but this had as much to do with good luck as any care on her part. This is a kind of Russian roulette which has an element of a desperate and dangerous game of playing with one's life, and this is of course a game that can be lost. Boys, with their more violent methods, have less scope for modifying the danger – if you use a gun you either pull the trigger or you don't.

In Britain the higher risk groups include those with serious depression or psychosis (schizophrenia), a history of sexual abuse, depressed young Asian women, young men in custody, and those with a history of being bullied. Suicide is more common among white males. Suicide is also contagious. When Michael Hutchence, the pop star, hung himself, there were many copycat attempted suicides around the world, including some fatalities. Along with another child and adolescent psychiatrist, I came across a situation in a very prestigious London school where a 'suicide club' was formed and young people had to make suicide attempts to get into this club. There were extra points for seeing a consultant psychiatrist! The activities included overdoses and cutting. This was a particularly manic and perverse situation but there is no doubt that those who are drawn to this activity seek out others who share similar impulses either covertly (almost unconsciously) or quite explicitly. This behaviour is another sign of its disturbing nature and the wish to cloak guilt and disgust behind a kind of group acquiescence.

Psychodynamic aspects of suicide

I now want to move on to think about some of the internal factors which I think are important in adolescent suicide. Although suicide attempts occur in younger children, they are very rare, whilst in adolescents both actual suicide and suicide attempts are much more common. So the inevitable conclusion is that there is something about the state of being an adolescent which makes suicide and suicidal behaviour more likely. So what is it about the mental life of an adolescent which might make suicidal behaviour understandable? Suicidal acts are attacks on the body. Is that significant or is it simply the means of getting at the mind? The answer is that it is both, because in certain states of mind there is no clear distinction between mind and body, symbolic and concrete. In order to understand this it is important to consider some of the changes triggered during adolescence.

Adolescents are thrust into a state of rapid change. Puberty results in hormone-induced physical changes to sexual organs, and changes in physical size and strength. These changes are accompanied by powerful feelings, not only as a direct result of circulating hormones, but also as a consequence of the alterations in psychic balance which come from changes in how young people feel about themselves – for example, from the knowledge of being stronger and being able to conceive or father a baby.

There is also a need to become someone who defines themselves in quite a different way – no longer somebody's son or daughter, brother or sister, but a person's potential wife or husband, and on the way to developing the capability for intimacy and sexuality in relationships; and somebody who will have a job, or who will be aware of the significance of not having one. These biological, psychological and social factors interact strongly with infantile feelings, so that the young person's phantasies about themselves and their body are given a powerful new context.

All these changes to the young person's identity require a giving up of old relationships, primarily the giving up of dependence on the parents. Perhaps the most difficult aspect of this is the facing of the disillusionment that the parents can no longer provide a protective screen of caring for and thinking for their children in the way that they once did. This is a loss which exposes the young person to the cold draught of reality as they face the world as it is, damaged and uncertain without the defence that it is their parents' problem and not theirs. In more healthy adolescents these changes as well as being disturbing bring a sense of hope and reassurance.

The movement towards adulthood therefore requires the ability to deal with separateness and loss and creates a process which is not unlike mourning. However, the capacity to deal with loss is never straightforward and the distinction between mourning and melancholia described so wonderfully by Freud (1917) is never clear-cut. All of us grapple with failed mourning to some extent, but for those who arrive at adolescence with serious impairments in their ability to face loss this period can feel like an unbridgeable abyss.

It is during this period that all the major developmental processes that have preceded it are further played out in the new situation of the adolescent being at the beginning of young adulthood. It is not easy to grow into greater independence and it does not happen smoothly. The deepest infantile desires do not go away, and many old mechanisms are revived, and need to be. In healthy splitting, dependency moves away from parents and yet is expressed even more intensely towards friends – those two-hour telephone conversations – or towards pop/fashion and sports idols or radical politics.

There is often a marked discrepancy between physical and emotional maturity. At certain times the young person may be grappling with the issues of young children or even infants yet they have the equipment of the young adult. The very concreteness of these changes means that the experience of the young person may be that the phantasies that were still not quite realised in childhood can now really be made to happen – oedipal sexual desires or destructive wishes. Thus, before puberty most children can manage to live fairly happily with the contradiction between their physical bodies and, say, their phantasies of being the opposite gender. After puberty it is much more difficult to manage this because of the indisputable facts of the enlarged genitalia in boys or the presence of breasts and periods in girls. Enhanced sexual feelings also confront the young person with their sexual nature which adds powerfully to the experiences of whatever the sexual phantasies served or were directed at. Similarly the massive increase in muscle growth adds to the strength and power of young people, especially boys, which means that they are actually more dangerous. This makes infantile aggressive phantasies that much more disturbing because they are more realizable.

A 14-year-old boy was referred to me by his school because of his violent behaviour. He had grown eight inches in a year and was now over six feet tall. He had always had quite a temper but before puberty neither he nor his family were terribly worried about this and his family easily helped him to calm down. But now the adults were afraid of him, and he in turn felt more anxious. He came to be seen as a danger, which to some extent he was. If you want to kill your father and you are 2 years old, then you will have quite a job and your father can easily stop you, but if you are a six-foot adolescent who is still caught up in infantile issues, then you really might be able to. The sense of this possibility becomes like a nightmare both to the child and those adults involved who are caught up in the shared phantasy as well as the reality.

Suicidal behaviour is often associated with commonly presenting symptoms such as a preoccupation with body image and denial of appetite, deliberate self-harm, especially cutting, drug abuse, and other forms of self-destructive behaviour. These disturbances have an outlandish violent quality which confronts us with a way of relating to and seeing the world which is concrete and dominated by borderline psychotic thinking. It is in this area of mental functioning that we can see the roots of the savage and self-destructive behaviour of suicidal acts.

Wilfred Bion (1957) categorised these phenomena as coming from what he called the psychotic part of the personality. Based on his work with borderline and actual psychotic patients he concluded that the personality divides developmentally quite early into the more healthy part, which he called the 'non-psychotic' or 'neurotic' part, and the 'psychotic' part. The neurotic part develops in a way that is familiar in Melanie Klein's usual classification. The personality does go through developmental phases of paranoid schizoid to depressive positions but the tendency is towards integration. However, when there is anxiety there is a tendency to regress to the paranoid schizoid position, and when anxiety diminishes then the move is back towards integrated depressive functioning. The point is that the splitting is fairly straightforward, projective identification is used more for the purpose of communication and the personality develops a preference for introjection and integration. So in adolescent development we see for example the 'healthy' splitting that I referred to of the adolescent who rejects the parents as fairly useless, compared to their friends, as a way of dealing with the need to move on from them towards adulthood. Once that is less necessary then the parents will once more be valued but in a newer and more mature relationship. On the whole there is more love than hate governing this non-psychotic part of the self.

Bion (1957) understood this development to result from the interaction between the baby and the mother. He saw that the baby needs and indeed seeks out the mind of the mother from the moment of birth. In early life the distressed baby's primitive unbearable feelings which Bion described as beta elements could only be processed by a maternal object. The baby projects these beta elements into the mother. The mother receives these experiences, and unlike the baby can do something with them apart from projecting them which is the only option available to the baby. They cause her discomfort and pain but she has the means of dealing with them, processing them and then responding to the baby with understanding which is appropriately communicated to the baby. The capacity for this so-called alpha process gradually develops in the baby who eventually can manage much more of this her/himself and can manage to reach towards the depressive position in the way I have described.

The situation in the psychotic part of the personality is very different. The psychotic part develops when the degree of violent explosiveness is not contained for the baby. This might be either because of the mother's inability to do so or because the baby gets into states which are so violent that she or he cannot any more bear to relate to the mother and cannot use what is available. Constitutional or environmental factors contribute in varying amounts, though the environmental ones are often very significant. In these primitive states of failed containment what develops is the opposite of what is seen in the neurotic part of the personality. Projective identification is carried out with such violence against a perceived non-available object that the baby has experiences of fragmented and damaged objects and this is what is internalised. It is a world dominated by hatred and revenge rather than love and forgiveness. Objects are felt to hate the baby and to push unwanted feelings into him/her. Sometimes this is in the context of actually intrusive and projecting objects (as in sexual abuse for example).

This part of the personality shows a strong predominance of destructive drives so that the impulse to love is transformed into sadism. There is a hatred of internal and external realities, extending to all that makes for awareness of them. The dominant anxiety is of the integrity of the self/

body and there is often a dread of imminent annihilation. The object world of this part of the mind is full of damaged and twisted objects conceived and internalised in hatred and violence. The psychotic part of the personality is dominated by a preference for projection and evacuation. Disintegration is preferred and the personality is governed by an intolerance of frustration. There is much more violence and hatred present and the splitting that does take place is frequently fragmentary; the objects which dominate the self are bizarre and named as such by Bion (1957). Bion felt that this division of the personality was present in all of us. In healthy individuals it is simply that the neurotic part is much stronger and is more in control of the mind, but when there has been a skewing of the personality for constitutional or environmental reasons then the psychotic part of the personality becomes able to dominate and sometimes even totally obscure the non-psychotic part, though Bion felt that it never obliterates it entirely.

During adolescence these more disturbed areas make their presence known even in normal adolescents and contribute to the more frightening aspects of the working through of the separation and readjustment of the identity at this time. The acquisition of an adult body, which so profoundly challenges the adolescent's identity, leads a return into the personality of parts of the self and objects which were split off and projected either into the adolescent's own body or often into the parent's body and sexuality. This leads to great increases in anxiety.

The containing and processing of these disturbed states require a more healthy part of the self identified with a good object and supported enough by good parental objects that can process these disturbed parts of the self and integrate them with more healthy parts. However, when the personality has not managed to be governed by a better functioning self, then these split-off aspects can re-emerge with a vengeance – literally. For example, a young male patient told me that when he began to notice pubic hair on himself at puberty he was disgusted and horrified. For him, the presence of a sexual body confronted him with very disturbing phantasies of his parents, especially his father, arising out of his very disturbed oedipal relation to his parents, which had remained split-off and projected into his father's sexuality. Puberty was experienced as an enforced intrusion, a bodily invasion of his father's body into his – a very concrete version of the more benign phantasy of becoming like his father. In his world there could be no such peaceful order: he was either a non-sexual little boy or he had his parents' hated sexuality forced into him in the form of his father's sexual body.

A somewhat similar and catastrophic reaction occurred with a pretty 13-year-old girl. She had been described as a bit of a tomboy, but happy and outgoing. Her periods had recently started when she attended sexual development lectures at school in which a woman was shown giving birth rather graphically. During this same session she had also been told about breast cancer. Shortly after this she had become acutely school-phobic and had become so disabled that she had to have her parents with her at all times, and when this settled a bit she still needed to know exactly where they were. She virtually stopped all social activities and her psychosexual development ground to a halt.

In her analysis it emerged that her own increased sexual libido made her terrified that there would be a terrible disaster if she had a sexual life even in her mind. For example, she had to stop herself from thinking about an attractive boy. When she was a little better, her parents went away and her grandfather came round and showed her and her sister some old home videos of when she and her sister were babies and young children. She had little memory of these but the main emotional reaction was to be rather disgusted at seeing these films. It seemed likely that she was reacting to the idea of her parents as a couple away enjoying themselves, with a phantasy that they were having intercourse and making babies, which disgusted her. She seemed to believe that any sexual activity on her part was terribly confused with her mother's sexual activity, which reminded her of the birth of her sister when she was 5. She had been more of a tomboy until puberty made that impossible, and, like the boy shocked by his pubic hair, became very confused with her sexual parents whom she had to stop, otherwise there would be near fatal consequences.

In these darker parts of the mind the dramas of the oedipal situation and the consequences of envy and jealousy are felt to be fatal. Persecutory guilt dominates and is felt as a violent murderous assault on the self or even the body, and the responses are dominated by wishes to be rid of, to surgically remove, to amputate.

A young man whom I was seeing for intensive psychotherapy – to whom I shall return later – was chronically and severely suicidal for many years. He had made many very serious attempts to kill himself. He told me that he had a phantasy that he would jump out of a window and his scarred and battered body would fall to the ground leaving him in a purified state to fly away. He believed that he could solve terrible internal conflicts by literally ridding himself of his ill and damaged self, and unconsciously he believed he would then live in peace.

Another example of the logic of this part of the mind was revealed in the assessment of a boy of 14 in an acute psychotic state. This boy came to see me in an extremely disturbed state. His breakdown had begun with a row with a friend. This other boy had complained to the boy's father and the patient feared that his friend's father would kill his own father and then frame him so that he would be held responsible, though of course he knew was entirely innocent. This belief gradually increased in strength and became a delusion. I thought the delusion was derived from his hostility to his own father which he attempted to deal with by disowning it and locating it in the other man – the friend's father. But instead of being able to face this hostility and deal with his guilt about it, gradually withdrawing these projections, he was quite unable to do so.

His anxieties escalated and, instead of just one danger, he started to believe he was now surrounded by hundreds of Afghan rebels who he was convinced were trying to kill him and actually were poisoning him and breaking his legs. He was very upset that 'they' were also attacking his father and mother, and in addition killing hundreds of people whom he was sure would turn up as bodies in his home. It was as though this 'bad father' (with the defence that this was not his, but his friend's father) had now become fragmented, disseminated into a wider and wider world so that each fragment, as it were, became another bad father – the Afghan rebels. Moreover, his perception of this badness and danger had become quite bizarre. While in the room with me, he believed that a siren, from a passing police car outside my window, was evidence that the enemy were after him. This was probably a split-off transference reaction towards me, who he probably thought, as well as trying to help him, was also part of this persecutory blaming. Noises in my room became evidence of listening devices. Running through all this was the thought that others were dying because the killers were unable to reach him, but his death would put an end to all this suffering, even though it was undeserved. He imagined that he might have to sacrifice his own life to save the world or possibly even his parents to save them from torture.

This case illustrates how the primitive anxieties about death and destructiveness, and the primitive feelings of possessiveness, love, and jealousy, if not worked through early in life, can remain dormant. But when there is a late upheaval, say, precipitated by some crisis or perhaps the changes of adolescence, these primitive feelings break through and dominate the personality, leading to violent eruptions, which in certain people can lead to self-directed violence. In this particular boy I thought that there was a real risk of suicide.

Of course, not all developmental failures will lead to a psychotic breakdown as happened in this last case. This boy was clearly suffering from schizophrenia or a schizoaffective disorder which urgently needed to be treated. Nevertheless his symptoms still conveyed a clear meaning and the power of his impulses may well have been the precipitating cause of the breakdown even if there was a biological aspect to his vulnerability to breakdown in this way.

Yet another case that illustrates some of the dynamics I have been considering is that of a 19-year-old seen in three-times-weekly psychotherapy. She had a history of self-harm and serious suicide attempts which had required lengthy in-patient treatment. She had been a very neglected child. Her mother had a borderline personality disorder and had been alternately violent to her and over-dependent on her. Her father was an alcoholic.

After some time in treatment she was no longer so suicidal and did not self-harm any more.

On one occasion this patient had cancelled a session due to toothache. In the following session she told her therapist that the dentist she had consulted had told her that there was nothing wrong with her tooth. In the session she was then able to think with her therapist that she might find the source of the pain in her mind.

She had been travelling home from her sister's house in the car with her parents and had seen a broken billboard, one of the ones that have rotating slats and show alternating pictures. It had got stuck and both images were mixed up with each other. After seeing this it seemed to her as if her mind started to break, and she blamed it on the broken billboard, although she felt this made no sense.

She said that when she got home to her parents' house, she went outside to have a cigarette. She suddenly felt 'like crap' and had the urge to burn herself in the way she had done many times in the past but not recently. She was embarrassed telling her therapist about this.

Later in the session she returned to the weekend and what had happened. She said she feared that she was actually going to break down. She spoke with real intensity about how much she hated her mother. Whilst at her sister's she had felt the hatred so intensely that she could not bear to hear her mother breathing. They were sitting at the table eating dinner and she couldn't bear the sound of her eating and breathing. Then she realised with horror that she and her mother were eating in time with each other, that their mouths were opening and closing at the same time, and she had to stop eating. She had to stop because this meant that her mouth and her mother's mouth were the same. She could not stand that thought and had to break the connection with her mother.

The following morning she woke up to find her 'mother in her face'. She explained how she had gone to bed in her old room with her cat asleep next to her. When she awoke she found her mother lying across her, playing with the cat so her face was 'in the patient's face'.

This captured well the patient's horror at feeling that her body and her mother's body were literally confused with each other. She felt not only that her mother was intrusive but that she actually had her mother's infantile hunger and greed pushed into her. This was linked in the transference to the patient having to own her previously denied dependency on her therapist and her tendency to retreat back to her parents at weekends to avoid the experience of separations from her therapist (she had her own flat and knew that her parents were not a good influence on her). In this way she was confronted with her own oral needs which had for years been split off and projected with considerable hatred into her mother.

The young woman clearly had a disturbed mother who treated her as if she was a kind of mother, but in this part of her mind, this inappropriate behaviour was entirely concrete and felt mad to her (and probably represented her infantile experience too). The wish to burn herself might be seen as her modified wish to destroy her mother and the dependent part of herself projected into her mother, and so had a suicidal intent since she would have to destroy herself to achieve this. However, I think it also served to give her a very vivid sense of her own skin boundary which she felt had been lost in her mad and very concrete identification with her mother.

Conclusion

In this chapter, I have been trying to convey that suicide and attempted suicide acts in adolescence are, as Egle Laufer (personal communication) asserted many years ago, acts which have a psychotic component to them. The adolescent is confronted with the need to be able to process massive biological, psychological and social changes which bring about what one might think of as a kind of capsize of the personality, rather like the way massive icebergs turn upside down when the warmer seas melt the lower part.

The adolescent has to move from everything being orientated upwards towards the parents and the adult world, to becoming an adult who is capable of being a parent. This means that all the more disturbed parts of the personality have to be helped into the new situation. In those vulnerable adolescents the violent and murderous version of human relations which exists in all of us breaks out from its place of residence in the mind and can be played out in reality, with all the pain and distress that those who work with these patients are all too familiar with.

References

Bion, W. (1957) 'Differentiation of the psychotic from the non-psychotic personalities', *International Journal of Psycho-Analysis* 38: 266–275.

Fleischmann, A. (1999) *Figures and Facts about Suicide*, Geneva: World Health Organization

Fleischmann, A., Bertolote, J.M., Belfer, M. and Beautrais, A. (2005) 'Completed suicide and psychiatric diagnosis in young people: a critical examination of the evidence', *American Journal of Orthopsychiatry* 75: 676–683.

Freud, S. (1917) 'Mourning and melancholia', in J. Strachey (ed.) *The Standard Edition of the Complete Works of Sigmund Freud, Vol. 14* (pp. 243–258), London: Hogarth.

Hawton, K., Zahl, D. and Weatherall, R. (2003) 'Suicide following deliberate self-harm: long term follow-up of patients who presented to a general hospital', *British Journal of Psychiatry* 182: 537–542.

WHO (1999) *The World Health Report 1999 – Making a Difference*. http://www.who.int/whr/1999/en/index.html

Chapter 6

Treatment priorities after adolescent suicide attempts

François Ladame

Introduction

In this chapter I will discuss the model of treatment I have developed with my colleagues in Geneva. This has been developed from psychoanalytic thinking about the meaning of a suicide attempt in adolescence, particularly the idea that a suicidal crisis is a trauma that ruptures previous experiences of containment. Accordingly our treatment model starts from the view that in-patient assessment and treatment are a necessary starting point for suicidal adolescents. I will discuss the model of treatment and I will explain this with reference to the psychoanalytic framework as it has developed in French-speaking countries.

The need for containment

With experience, and from a psychoanalytic perspective, my colleagues and I in Geneva have come to understand the suicidal crisis as a *psychic trauma* in which a collapse occurs in the usual way of functioning of the psychic apparatus. This means that the usual boundaries existing between internal and external worlds are no longer present. Similarly, the boundaries between intrapsychic structures are no longer functioning. As a consequence, mental representations are also no longer able to freely circulate, since such circulation relies on the binding capacity of the psychic apparatus. Our therapeutic approach aims to reconstitute the capacity of the mind to symbolize, giving verbal expression to these mental representations.

Therefore I make a plea for intensive psychic care in specialized in-patient units once physical threats to life have been either excluded or removed in the emergency room. Such intensive crisis treatment aims at fighting with adequate means against the natural inclination of suicidal adolescents to repress or deny the psychical conscious and unconscious meaning of what happened a few hours or days ago. Often there is collusion by their parents in this process.

During this acute care, priority should be given to 'containing' the patient to enable her/him to be in touch with the internal reality that compelled her/him to the enactment. Internal reality has a powerful compelling effect, so that the suicidal adolescent feels that she/he could not help but do it. Containment means providing both a structured environment and an approach that enables the internal reality to be faced and kept in mind. Second, the treatment aims to avoid repression and/or denial of that internal reality. Third, once the adolescent has acknowledged the loss of control underlying the suicidal enactment, including the shame involved, the aim is to help her/him to understand why ongoing treatment is needed after discharge from the in-patient unit.

It is important, in order to secure the suicidal adolescent's compliance with our recommendation for out-patient treatment, that the treatment and the reasons for it make sense to them. According to our experience in Geneva, once the continuity of psychic functioning has been re-established, through the process of containment, patients are able to develop the insight that they may be trapped again in similar situations where they are left without any choice but the suicidal solution. This insight is very helpful in enhancing their motivation to engage in out-patient psychotherapy.

The objective of psychoanalytic psychotherapy is to allow the adolescent to be in control of aspects of her/his internal reality which previously seemed to be out of her/his control. More than this, it aims to treat the vulnerabilities that lie beneath the suicidal act and which could be responsible, in the future, for the risk of repetition. The process of psychotherapeutic treatment aims to enable the young person to feel safe from internal persecution and therefore to rely less on splitting and denial. He/she should feel protected from the risk of alienation when internal persecutors control his/her mind – in other words feel protected from psychical death (psychosis) as well as from physical death (committing suicide).

The traumatic dimension

In order to discuss these ideas I would like to illustrate the *traumatic dimension* of the suicidal crisis with a brief vignette: the story of a young woman called Gina.

> When she was close to her fourteenth birthday, Gina, whose mother had recently died, decided to kill herself. Gina's past was tragic: her father was violent and alcoholic and had called her a whore since she began menstruating a year or two earlier. Before dying Gina wanted to know what love meant, at least once. She went to bed with the first boy who came along and then took an overdose of medication. She was revived, and she discovered some time later that she was pregnant, and decided to keep the baby.
>
> A few years later, when she was nearly 18, she met a man, fell in love and settled down. The young man adopted the child. Gina's grandmother reacted

to this by saying: '*I am so happy, at least this will shut your father up because he has been telling everyone he is your child's father!*'

Years went by. Gina was living with the same man she still loved. She was 22 when she had another breakdown and made a second suicide attempt. Upon awaking from her coma she discovered that the man she so loved had abused her. Thereupon she went and bought a gun, and killed her lover, the only man she had ever loved. Since then Gina has been a prisoner somewhere in a French jail.

Gina's story raises many questions pertaining both to inner reality and suicide prevention and treatment. Moreover, as the story was published years ago in a French book on 'Women and jails' (Ginsberg 1992: 224–226) it does not raise complex issues of confidentiality, as do cases from clinical practice. It also illustrates one of the main points regarding the traumatic dimension, which is to remind us that, although suicide means 'murder of oneself', there always remains something unpredictable regarding the direction of the violence necessary to commit such a 'murder': it can be directed either inside against the self or outside against another.

Gina's story can be understood through the application of Aulagnier's (1984) concepts of 'telescoping' and 'unveiling'. For Aulagnier these concepts are central in accounting for the movement from a potentiality for psychosis towards a psychotic breakdown. She writes:

> I define unveiling or the phenomena of telescoping as an experience, or event which confronts the self with a representation of oneself in an unexpected manner that imposes itself on the ego with absolute certainty. Suddenly an event, the gaze of another, whose view is valued, sends back to the ego an unveiled image which, paraphrasing Freud, has 'the horror of an image of oneself that has been discarded'.
>
> (Aulagnier 1984: 12–13)[1]

Though Aulagnier herself did not make this connection, I think that the concepts of unveiling and telescoping also help to conceptualize psychic trauma. Particularly, I consider the traumatic state to be a 'psychotic moment' in which both the Preconscious and reality testing do not function. I shall return to this discussion later in the chapter.

Gina killed her companion, but later, while in jail, recognized that at the time of the enactment she was convinced she was killing her father. The loved object of her past childhood which she had to relinquish after puberty was totally confused with her new love object. Past and present were so tightly condensed that they acted like a red bullet putting her in a state of '*awakened nightmare*' (see Ladame 1991). I highlight the word nightmare because many young patients, when interviewed about their pre-suicidal itinerary, use that word to describe their recent life and convey to us the feeling that they were indeed living in a state of 'awakened nightmare'. In my view, there are many analogies between nightmare and psychic trauma which may help us to understand what happens at the time of a suicidal act. The most essential is that the Preconscious is disabled in the nightmare state. Hence the Preconscious is not able to tame the crude instincts of the Unconscious through the mechanisms of binding and displacement.

In Gina's case the problem is not to know whether the real father of Gina's child was the boy with whom she went to bed before her first suicide attempt when she was 14 or her father. The trauma which overwhelmed her as a young woman of 22 was linked to the statement made by her grand-mother when she was 18. At that time she was in the adolescent develop-mental process of remodelling her childhood identifications to become an adult woman. Her grandmother's words (*'I am so happy, at least this will shut your father up because he has been telling everyone he is your child's father!'*) resonated like an oracular statement that unconsciously pinned her down in the unacceptable identity of an incestuous girl. Its traumatic effect was put into abeyance for some time and it did not immediately trigger a catastrophe. But its murderous potential exploded as Gina was compelled to face the horror of her own unrecognized reality, the horror that she had become, at least unconsciously, what she could not but refuse to be, an incestuous and parricidal subject. What I referred to above as an 'awakened nightmare' is precisely that: something that the subject has ignored until that point in time about his/her own reality traumatically explodes, creating a confusion between the categories of reality (internal versus external) and time (past versus present).

The management of suicidal crisis

Gina's story, which I have used here to illustrate the explosive complexities of many patients' clinical histories, helps us to understand the treatment priorities in Geneva.

A specific model for the management of suicidal crisis has developed in the French-speaking parts of Europe. This model involves admission of suicidal adolescents to a specialized in-patient unit where the therapeutic approach is psychoanalytically inspired. The first unit of this kind was the Centre Abadie in Bordeaux, France. The intensive initial hospitalization is designed to offer motivation for longer-term psychotherapy and aid compliance with such an approach.

Initial reports by Pommereau and Penouil (1995) suggested that the unit in Bordeaux has had a positive impact on outcome of suicidal behaviour in young people. In a retrospective study of 357 subjects – 85 per cent of the population admitted – traced one year after admission to the specialized unit in 1994, 20 per cent had attempted suicide again, and 0.8 per cent had died by suicide. This compared with rates of 29 per cent for repeated attempted suicide and 1.3 per cent for death by suicide at one-year follow-up found in a similar study in 1989–90, prior to the opening of the unit. Whether these results were statistically significant was not reported; however, the results were encouraging.

The Geneva in-patient unit for suicidal adolescents and young adults (aged 16 to 21) opened in November 1996 and has admitted an average of 140 patients annually. The unit offers an intermediate healthcare structure between emergency treatment and long-term treatment, which we believe to be essential. Young people are admitted on a full-time voluntary basis to the eight beds of the unit, which is located in an apartment building in the immediate vicinity of the hospital complex. Psychiatric nursing staff are present and available on a twenty-four-hour basis.

The therapeutic approach is inspired by psychoanalytic principles and includes daily psychotherapy sessions on weekdays with a psychiatrist or psychologist accompanied by a psychiatric nurse, along with group sessions twice weekly. Individual sessions focus on the 'here and now' of the suicidal crisis and its traumatic impact on thought processes, whilst group sessions deal with the difficulties of sharing experiences and emotions. The adolescent's family are seen by the social worker within forty-eight hours of admission and further family sessions are offered as indicated or required. Admission is for a maximum of one month, and the average length of stay is fifteen days. The principal objectives for the therapeutic work with adolescents are to overcome initial resistance to treatment and improve long-term compliance with therapeutic interventions, thus offering adolescents an improved quality of life and reduced risk of recurrent suicide attempts.

The approach is based on a number of principles. Admission to the crisis unit acknowledges the psychic breakdown enacted through the suicide attempt. It offers a 'controlled' break with the outer world, giving the adolescent a temporary haven from the concrete burden of everyday life. Thus we routinely propose a complete break with the outside for forty-eight hours, with no visits or phone calls.

We promote psychic functioning which has been temporarily 'frozen' through the rupturing effect of the suicidal episode and the disabling of the functioning of the Preconscious. This implies paying great attention to the issue of containment in order to allow re-functioning of the psyche at the level of symbolization, thus allowing words to have the meaning of words, and thus to act as symbols, instead of, concretely, being experienced as things without symbolic content or as 'symbolic equation' (Segal 1986).

As I have mentioned above, we put particular focus on the here and now, the suicidal crisis in the present, in order to prevent the young person's denial of all painful affects and fantasies that led to the suicidal act and were 'washed out' through the enactment. Psychotherapists should avoid falling into the trap of (re)constructing a remote past of early childhood, which can be used defensively to escape the present. However painful it may be to the patient, they have to focus on the panic-like anxiety and moment of loss of control, on the fear of madness that traumatically overwhelmed them, and left them with no other solution but to enact a suicide bid. Such a technique is appropriate only with the guarantee that the patient is contained by the structure and environment of the ward as well as by the caring environment. Once inner containment becomes strong enough and the process of binding, unbinding and rebinding begins to work again, it is possible for the young person to move towards reflecting on meaning instead of acting.

We also aim to help the patient and her/his family to understand why she/he needs long-term treatment after leaving the unit. Put simply, this is based upon the knowledge that unless real change occurs in the underlying mental and dynamic structures, what happened once might well happen again. It is therefore important to build in adequate and reliable protective strategies against the risk of repetition. Through the daily sessions with the adolescent in the in-patient unit, we encourage the patient to ask for and see a therapist outside the unit. And we assist her/him in the process of finding someone who is available either in private practice or in public service. Our experience is that 90 per cent of young people admitted to the unit do request follow-up therapy. Once the patient has established mean-ingful contact with a psychotherapist outside the unit, he/she may leave more or less safely.

Underpinning our insistence on the importance of long-term treatment is our belief that this is the only way to impact on ongoing developmental difficulties and the narcissistic fragility that made the suicidal crisis and the enactment possible. The long-term psychotherapeutic treatment is the essential second step of the therapeutic process. Its principal aim and focus is to enable the adolescent to achieve the process of subjectivation (becoming-a-subject).

Subjectivation is an important concept in French psychoanalytic thinking about adolescence (Cahn 1998). Cahn's view of subjectivation is that the individual adolescent is involved in an internal struggle and a social process leading to having a sense of self in the world (individual identity) and holding a sense of truth(s). If the adolescent is unable to engage with and accomplish the process of subjectivation, there is unfulfilment and the adolescent may be 'lured into a closed ideology or delusion, alienating or imprisoning her/him and distorting her/his inner world' (Cahn 1998: 159). This can lead to a feeling of not knowing oneself and therefore being out of control of internal reality. Subjectivation is a three-step process of getting to know oneself and inner truths, through ownership of the body (that is, the developing adult sexual body), ownership of one's own thinking, and ownership of one's own drives and desires. Once this process is established, the risk of alienation is over; the adolescent or young adult is now able to control what was previously out of his/her control, and to feel safe from internal persecution without relying on splitting and denial. It also means that she/he is protected against psychical death (psychosis) and physical death (committing suicide).

Advantages and disadvantages of the model

The model I have described has powerful advantages in addressing the traumatic suicidal crisis. In the initial phase of treatment the priority is given to containment of the patient. Following the successful reintroduction of containment through attending to the psychic trauma, the second phase is to offer long-term psychoanalytic psychotherapy on an out-patient basis with the aim of achieving the process of subjectivation. There are some disadvantages in practice, which I will now discuss.

As admission to the unit is strictly on a voluntary basis, the main limitation concerns those who refuse to enter the unit. Unfortunately these are very often the same young people who refuse any kind of help, even as out-patients, challenging our therapeutic strategies and proposals. Therefore the issue of engaging such young people is not restricted to psychoanalytic approaches for it concerns public health policy as a whole and, as such, is beyond the scope of this chapter.

Another limitation is the gender gap. We have a sex ratio of 8:2 (female patients to male patients), whereas the sex ratio of suicidal adolescents and young adults in the community is somewhere between 6:4 and 5:5. Again, the issue is not restricted to psychoanalysis, and not even to psychiatry. We have the same evidence in somatic medicine. As young males are more at risk than young females, in terms of both their future psychical and physical health, we have to deal again with a very worrying public health issue regarding preventive strategies for suicidal male adolescents.

Finally we are also concerned by those patients who, once discharged, don't comply with our therapeutic recommendations. Those patients who do not comply with our recommendations do nevertheless wrap themselves in the caring network configured by the unit. They nearly all enter the telephone number of the ward in their mobile phone book, and they know they may call round-the-clock if they need to. The nurse they developed the closest relationship with will answer their call. In this way, the unit, including its staff, as a human environment represents a safety belt and a means of maintaining contact. This function is very useful as a preventive strategy and enables further opportunities for therapeutic work to take place.

Conclusion

In this chapter I have discussed the model of work with suicidal adolescents that has developed in Geneva and in other French-speaking centres. The model offers initial in-patient containment of the suicidal crisis followed by long-term psychotherapeutic work. The model has been developed in accordance with our psychoanalytically informed thinking which sees the suicidal crisis and enactment as a psychic trauma, through which the capacities for distinguishing external and internal, past and present, are diminished. The model also recognizes the importance of working in the here and now to address the psychic conflicts that led to the suicidal enactment but which are quickly lost through the traumatic effects of the enactment and the reliance on splitting and denial. When, through containment, the psychic processes are restored, long-term psychotherapy is essential to prevent repetition and to achieve subjectivation. This model has some powerful merits and advantages in treating suicidal adolescents and preventing repetition.

Note

1 The passage is worth quoting in full. Aulagnier continues, 'The discarded image of oneself would have been one of the identifications that one would have rejected. Often in psychosis, one can rediscover the catastrophic experiences which initiated the decompensation phase. The phenomenon of "unveiling", which can also be encountered outside of psychosis, is one of those most important experiences that signal the passage from one mode of relating to another: experiences that confront the ego with evidence of what it wished to become and what it is, the gap that separates who you are from what you imagined you wanted to be' (Aulagnier 1984: 12–13).

References

Aulagnier, P. (1984) 'Telle une zone "sinistrée"', *Adolescence* 2: 9–21.
Cahn, R. (1998) 'The process of becoming-a-subject in adolescence', in M. Perret-Catipovic and F. Ladame (eds) *Adolescence and Psychoanalysis: The Story and the History* (pp. 149–159), London: Karnac Books.
Ginsberg, G. (1992) *Des prisons et des femmes*, Paris: Ramsay.
Ladame, F. (1991) 'Adolescence and the repetition compulsion', *International Journal of Psychoanalysis* 72: 253–273.
Pommereau, X. and Penouil, F. (1995) 'Détermination du devenir et des taux de récidive des jeunes suicidants, douze mois après leur hospitalisation à l'UMPAJA du centre Abadie (Bordeaux), du 16 novembre 1993 au 15 novembre 1994', *Rapport final de l'Association pour l'Étude et la Prévention du Suicide en Aquitaine*, Paris: Direction Générale de la Santé, Bureau SP2.
Segal, H. (1986) 'Notes on symbol formation', in H. Segal (ed.) *The Work of Hanna Segal: A Kleinian Approach to Clinical Practice. Delusion and Artistic Creativity and Other Psychoanalytic Essays* (pp. 49–65), London: Free Association Books/ Maresfield Library.

Chapter 7

Mental pain, pain-producing constructs, the suicidal body, and suicide

Israel Orbach

Introduction

This chapter will address two questions: what makes some people wish to commit suicide, and what makes it possible to carry out a self-destructive act against one's self. The answer to these questions will be sought within the realms of the *suicidal mind* and the *suicidal body*. The suicidal mind will be explored using Shneidman's (1993a) concept of mental pain. I proffer that the suicidal wish is an end-result of unbearable mental pain stemming mostly from pain-producing inner constructs. These pain-producing inner constructs are triggered by sensors and sensitivities to circumstances that arouse mental pain such as loss, narcissistic hurt, guilt, and failure. The inner constructs also include beliefs and attitudes towards life and death, concerning the conditions under which life is worth living, as well as self-destructive tendencies. When the inner constructs are set in motion, they can produce unbearable mental pain, as a result of which a person may wish to kill her or himself. Yet in order to be able to carry out a self-destructive act against one's self, special bodily states and processes come into play. The suicidal body is characterized by dissociation, numbness, anhedonia, indifference to physical pain, and a heightening of thresholds of senses. Such bodily states can facilitate suicidal behavior, as they make it easier to aggressively attack the body.

As both mind and body take an active part in the suicidal act, therapy with suicidal persons should take into consideration both the suicidal person's mind and body. Some of the ideas presented in this chapter have been discussed separately elsewhere (e.g. Orbach 2003, 2006, 2007), but here these ideas are presented in a more integrative way.

The suicidal mind: theories of mental pain

Freud: mental pain as longing

Freud (1917, 1926) was one of the first to write about the concept of mental pain. He attributes this experience to a child's longing for reunification with the his/her mother. Internal pain, according to Freud, can take place only after the child has experienced the pleasure and satisfaction of the mother's presence and from the union with her. The mother's intermittent appearance and disappearance arouse the pain of longing for her. Subsequently, mental pain in adulthood is actually a manifestation of the archaic longing for one's mother. Freud also drew a distinction between mental pain and similar experiences. He posed the following questions: 'when does separation from an object produce anxiety, when does it produce mourning, and when does it produce, it may be, only pain' (1926: 169). Freud suggests that anxiety arises in response to the fantasy of losing an object, depression comes about when the object has been lost, and pain is the experience of longing for the mother (see also Joffe and Sandler 1965).

Joffe and Sandler (1965) discuss Freud's attempt to define pain and suggest that Freud barely touched upon this concept, and did not develop it sufficiently. They suggest that there are different qualities and degrees of mental pain and that this experience should be further scrutinized. In recent years the concept of mental pain has become an important focus of attention, especially as it pertains to suicidal behavior.

Shneidman: 'Psychache' – as the frustration of the most important needs

Several years ago, Ed Shneidman wrote in his book *Suicide as Psychache*: 'Nearing the end of my career in suicidology, I think I can now say what has been on my mind in as few as five words: *Suicide is caused by psychache*' (1993a: 51). Psychache, in Shneidman's terms, is mental pain of the mind. Suicide occurs when mental pain is deemed by the person to be unbearable. This means that suicide has to do with thresholds of psychological pain endurance (Shneidman 1993b). A 17-year-old-adolescent, who planned to commit suicide, left a message on the internet, echoing Shneidman's assertion: 'I am going to kill myself because it hurts so much. What do I do to make the pain go away? Now I just want to make it all go away.'

Shneidman (1993a) argues that as long as modern suicide research ignores the most fundamental aspect that centrally relates to suicide, that is, the intolerable mental pain, empirical endeavors are doomed to miss the mark. According to Shneidman, depression itself does not cause suicide – the clinical symptoms of depression are debilitating, but not deadly. Moreover, correlating suicide with DSM categories is irrelevant to understanding the inner experience of the suicidal person. The immediate cause of suicide is unbearable pain. Shneidman actually views suicide as the last defensive action against mental pain.

According to Shneidman, mental pain – 'Psychache' – is a mixture of hurt, anguish, sorrow, aching, misery in the mind, shame, guilt, humiliation, loneliness, loss, sadness, dread, and the like. The various negative emotions and experiences turn into a generalized experience of unbearable mental pain – a kind of emotional perturbation (Shneidman 1980). Shneidman (1996) suggests that mental pain is energized by a frustration of the most important needs – needs that the individual lives by, and would die for. These needs, in fact, define the individual's day-to-day intrapsychic and interpersonal functions and makeup, so that the frustration of these needs constitutes an existential threat which the individual simply cannot tolerate.

Maltsberger: mental pain as a shocking sense of disintegration

Maltsberger (2004) views mental pain as an instigator of suicide from a psychoanalytic perspective. In Maltsberger's terms, mental pain or anguish is, in essence, the experience of self-disintegration. The sequence of disintegration begins with a traumatic event (e.g. loss) which causes a weakening of the ego and its defenses. At this point, the integrative forces of the ego subside, and the good self representations and good object representations are overshadowed. Further in the disintegration sequence, the suffering person experiences a flood of inward and outward aggression, self-criticism, and self-hate. External and internal objects are experienced as hostile and frightening. An individual in the throes of this disintegration process experiences it as something ego-dystonic and uncontrollable, a flood of insanity, as it were. When attempts to gain control over this sense of insanity fail, the suffering person redirects his/her desperate attempts towards the body. Attacking the body is an attempt to save the mind. I met a 24-year-old woman, who wanted to join the Israeli Association for Suicide Prevention as a volunteer. She told me that one day, within a few hours, she tried to commit suicide by such various methods as drowning herself, cutting her body, taking pills, and finally by pouring gasoline on her body and setting herself on fire. As a result, her face, neck, and hand were severely burned and distorted. When I asked her what happened the morning she tried to kill herself, she replied: 'I was standing on the beach, and, suddenly, I felt that I was losing my mind.'

Bolger: mental pain as a sense of brokenness

Bolger's (1999) conceptualization of mental pain has been extrapolated from her analysis of narratives of former patients describing their experiences of mental pain. The narratives produced by the participants suggest that the cause of mental pain is a rupture in the relationships with significant others. Bolger asserts that mental pain is essentially characterized by a sense of brokenness. Bolger figuratively describes brokenness as 'woundedness', experiencing the self as a feeling of being damaged, disconnection (broken bonds, loneliness, aloneness), loss of self (meaninglessness, loss of identity), loss of control (helplessness and hopelessness, inability to symbolize the experience), and sense of alarm (anxiety, fear, shame, panic). The experience of brokenness can also take on bodily manifestations, such as physical pain, heaviness, and sense of emptiness. Following Bolger's analysis, it is possible to define mental pain as the sense of being broken and shattered, accompanied by loss of control and caused by a rupture in relationships with significant others.

Styron: mental pain as a turmoil of uncontrollable inner hostile forces

One of the most moving descriptions of the experience of mental pain is provided by Styron (1992), who himself suffered from a severe episode of depression, which he documented autobiographically. Utilizing this documented personal experience, I performed a content analysis of his descriptions, picking out all of the sentences with direct or indirect relevance to mental pain, and then categorizing these sentences into several key categories (Orbach 2003). The following is a sample of that analysis:

A. *Description of the pain intensity*: (e.g. 'I experienced a curious inner convulsion that I can describe only as despair beyond despair' [p. 6]); B. *Perturbation*: (e.g. '. . . upheaval convulsing my system' [p. 26]); C. *Emotional freezing*: (e.g. 'I felt a kind of numbness, an enervation . . . an odd fragility . . . lacking normal coordination' [p. 43]); D. *Estrangement*: (e.g. '. . . the sense of being accompanied by a second self – a strange observer who, not sharing the dementia of his double, is able to watch with dispassionate curiosity as his companion struggles against the oncoming disaster . . .' [p. 64].); E. *Surfeit of the pain*: (e.g. '. . . a trance of supreme discomfort . . . in which cognition was replaced by that positive and active anguish' [pp. 17–18]); F. *Submission to a torturing evil force*: (e.g. '. . . panic and dislocation, and a sense that my thought processes were being engulfed by a toxic and unnamable tide that obliterated any enjoyable response to the living world' [p. 16]); G. *Destruction of the mind* (e.g. '. . . the mind continues in its insidious meltdown' [p. 26]); H. *Loss of self*: (e.g. '. . . I felt loss at every hand . . . the loss of self-esteem . . . and my own sense of self had all but disappeared, along with any self-reliance' [p. 56]); I. *Changes in perception*: (e.g. '. . . a sight and sound that would have exhilarated me . . . caused me to stop with fear, and I stood stranded there, helpless, shivering . . .' [p. 46]); J. *Physical pain*: (e.g. '. . . the gray drizzle of horror induced by depression takes on the quality of physical pain' [p. 50]; '. . . the pain is most closely connected to drowning or suffocation . . .' [p. 17]).

The content analysis indicates that what is particularly salient in Styron's description of his emotional pain is an overflowing sense of being controlled and destroyed by a hostile and estranged inner force that fully occupies his consciousness with agony.

Orbach and Mikulincer: pain as a sense of irrevocable negative changes in the self and its functions

My colleagues and I have conducted an analysis of mental pain narratives, described by various groups of suicidal and non-suicidal people (Orbach *et al.* 2003). The analysis yielded a mental pain scale, consisting of forty-five items grouped into nine factors as follows: (1) Irreversibility (e.g. 'I have lost something that I will never find again'); (2) Loss of control (e.g. 'I have no control over what is happening to me'); (3) Flooding (e.g. 'My feelings change all the time'); (4) Narcissistic wound (e.g. 'I am abandoned and lonely'); (5) Estrangement (e.g. 'I am a stranger to myself'); (6) Freezing (e.g. 'I can do nothing at all'); (7) Confusion (e.g. 'I have difficulties in thinking'); (8) Support (e.g. 'I want to be left alone'); (9) Emptiness (e.g. 'I have no desires').

According to this operationalization, mental pain can be defined as an irrevocable sense of hurt, and as a perception of negative changes in the self and in its functions, accompanied by negative feelings and cognitions (see also Janoff-Bulman 1992).

Intolerance for mental pain

One of the most important ideas in Shneidman's (1993a) theory of mental pain and suicide is that the most detrimental factor in suicide is not the intensity of the pain, but its intolerability. Many people can endure intense pain, and cope with it successfully. However, when the threshold for enduring mental pain is low, suicide risk appears. I have identified three experiential features of intolerability of pain as they emerge from patients' narratives of mental pain: the sense of the overflow or surfeit of the pain (e.g. I feel flooded by the pain); the inability to contain the pain (e.g. I cannot take any more) and the inability to cope with the pain (e.g. I don't know what to do to make the pain go away).

The inability to tolerate sudden pain is demonstrated in a young female patient's recollections of her mother's death. She remembers that at the age of 16, while talking to her mother on the phone, she heard a sudden noise of a car crashing, and the phone went dead. That afternoon she learned from her father that her mother had been killed in a car accident. She recounts: 'I started running around the yard, screaming "my mother is dead, my mother is dead!" Then I stopped.' This occurred several times in her life, when the memory of the tragic event became conscious.

This vignette demonstrates the intolerability of pain, which is experienced on such a concrete level that one tries to physically cast it off. This is, in fact, what actually happens in suicide – an attempt to get rid of the pain in the most physical manner.

Pain-producing inner constructs

Most of the theories and empirical data suggest that loss of any nature is the source of mental pain (e.g. Freud 1917). I would like to indicate the pain-producing inner constructs as another source of mental pain. Similar to Bowlby's (1973) working models, these constructs consist of a cluster of cognitions, emotions, sensitivities, and action tendencies.

The following aspects can be identified in these constructs. (1) Negative representations of the self and of others. (2) An acute sensitivity for specific pain-arousing situations and triggers, such as loss, narcissistic hurt, guilt, and failure. (3) Definitions of the conditions under which life is worth or not worth living. (4) Destructive action tendencies reflecting habitual patterns of self-abuse that erode one's sense of well-being. When the inner constructs are set into action, they can produce unbearable pain.

The pain-producing inner constructs stem from a lifelong internalization of negative experiences. Once the constructs have been internalized, the individual constructs his or her perceptions in a way that produces negative experiences and a negative orientation towards reality. The suicidal person reacts to these perceptions of life circumstances and of the self with habitual and ineffective coping mechanisms which in themselves create mental pain. In time, these experiences turn into self-destructive forms of action. The suicidal individual becomes entrapped in his own pain-producing constructs, eventually seeking total self-destruction to escape the intolerable pain.

The transactional relationship with the environment also contains an element of provocative engagement in pain-producing situations. Suicidal people tend to trap themselves in irresolvable dilemmas and choose to be involved in problematic situations. Some persistently set unattainable goals for themselves which invariably lead to failure. Cognitively, suicidal people tend to balance conflicting arguments in such a way that neither a solution nor a catharsis may be achieved. As inner pressure mounts, and conflicts about life and death intensify, suicidal individuals tend to provocatively escalate problematic situations, destroy relationships with beloved ones, and fail themselves on purpose. They carry the problematic situations to their extreme form, through active self-entrapment that proves to them once and for all that life is not worth living. In this process, suicidal individuals tend to increase the pain-producing constructs, by provoking situations in which new losses, rejections, and self-hate are created.

Sharon, a pretty and intelligent 28-year-old woman, sought therapy after she had attempted suicide for the third time. During her last attempt, her life was saved by an unexpected visit from her ex-boyfriend. The last suicide attempt was prompted by two recent events: she had broken up with her boyfriend – a break-up which she initiated; and she had been fired from work as a result of a dispute with her superior on the issue of her being non-compliant. When her superior tried to discuss the problem with her, she simply turned her back to him and walked away. She recounts: 'This is what I always do when somebody hurts me. I do not talk to him or her anymore. I wait for an apology. I can immediately recognize uncaring people. I am just like my mother, and I hate it.' She went to another superior and complained to him that her previous supervisor was indifferent to her, expecting him to help her out. As he was not responsive to her wishes, she reacted with rage, after which she was fired. Later that day she spoke with her father and had a dispute with him. She then went home, walked straight to the bathroom, reached for a bottle of pills, and started to swallow them frantically.

In a later session, Sharon recapitulated her sensitivities in interpersonal relationships. When, she experiences an interpersonal or personal difficulty, she expects that someone other than herself will take responsibility for her and solve the problem. When someone does take the responsibility, she feels loved and cared for. When no one steps forward to offer themselves on her behalf, she interprets this to mean that no one cares for her or loves her. In the absence of a desired response, she will always react with a temper tantrum, and then will turn to suicide. She reflected on these narcissistic tendencies and said, 'I think that I am spoiled and childish, but I cannot help it.'

The characteristics of the pain-producing constructs can be clearly seen in Sharon's description. First, Sharon's self-representations are negative – i.e. 'childish' and 'spoiled' – and so are the representations of others, whom she views as uncaring, indifferent, and disappointing. Sharon claims to have a detecting sensor, which is able to identify indifferent and disappointing persons. Thus, she is constantly monitoring her environment in search for such people. She looks for love, care, and affection in their most primal forms: life is satisfying and worth living only when others attend to her need to be taken care of, and extend themselves to take responsibility for her. A lack of any immediate responsiveness to her needs triggers mental pain in the form of narcissistic hurt – that is, feelings of being unloved, ignored, and rejected. Sharon exhibits self-destructive tendencies of uncontrolled rage, temper tantrums, and provocative interactions, and this behavior further triggers pain in the form of self-hate and disappointment, which, in turn, arouses suicidal urges and actions.

The suicidal body

An intolerability of mental pain, and pain-producing inner constructs, may indeed help to explain why some people wish to kill themselves, yet it is still unclear what makes it possible for these people to carry out aggressive attacks against their own bodies. Even as a decision to end one's life is consolidated, the idea of maiming one's own body is still carefully weighed. In order to understand this, one needs to consider the concept of facilitators of suicide.

A facilitator is not a 'cause' of suicidal behavior; rather, it is a process or condition which facilitates the actualization of potential suicidal states (see also Orbach 1997). One of the most potent facilitators of suicidal behavior is bodily dissociation. The body of the suicidal person is epitomized by bodily dissociation. Characteristics of bodily dissociation, such as unusually high thresholds for physical sensation, pervasive and negative attitudes towards the body, or active neglect of bodily care and protection, may yield a potential estrangement between the body and the self. This, in turn, facilitates the attack on the body. In the absence of a natural body-protecting shield, suicidal behavior may be carried out with greater ease than when self-preservation attitudes towards the body exist.

A case in point is Helen, a 19-year-old who made some serious suicide attempts. She told me that, while in basic training in the army, she missed her parents very much. When she was not given the leave of absence she desired in order to see her parents, she slammed her arm against a wall and broke it. Her injury enabled her to get sick leave and to see her parents. She did not mind the physical pain. In fact, according to her report, Helen could hardly feel any pain at all.

Attitudes and behaviors pertaining to body preservation or destruction are rooted in early bodily care. The body, as a source of satisfaction and pleasure, enhances the tendency for life preservation, and the attraction to life, and serves as a shield against self-destruction. Bodily sensations, such as responsiveness to pain, and sensitivity to internal bodily processes, produce warning signs aimed at alerting systems against bodily harm, due to internal and external dangers. These bodily processes regarding self-preservation attitudes are related to early positive bodily care experiences.

Van der Velde (1985) argues that bodily self-love, physical self-care, and body protection are acquired in early infancy. According to Van der Velde, the child associates the internal experiences of pain, hunger, thirst, and touch comfort with the external behavior and attitudes of the parents, such as body postures and cues of the caretaker (i.e. feeding, diapering, and caressing) which produce changes in sensations. The child identifies with the expressed parental love for his or her body, and learns to love it and protect it. The vital significance of early physical contact has been demonstrated by the Kangaroo Mother Intervention Technique (KMI), wherein twenty-four-hour skin-to-skin contact substitutes for the incubator treatment of low birthweight babies. The physical-contact facet of this method has shown that tactile interaction can even prove life-saving. When compared to the incubator, the KMI method has proved equally effective in terms of survival, and, in cases of serious illness, the KMI has often provided superior results (Sloan *et al.* 1994).

Hatred towards the body, rejection of the body, physical dissociation, physical anhedonia, insensitivity to bodily cues, and other distorted bodily experiences, may facilitate self-destruction. Studying a sample of institutionalized babies, Spitz (1965) demonstrated that their psychological maladjustment, developmental arrest, physical deterioration, self-harm, and high mortality were related not to medical neglect but rather to the absence of consistent maternal care. Field (1997) found in a sample of hospitalized children and adolescents with psychiatric problems, such as depression, conduct disorder, and suicidal behavior, that they had a history of touch neglect, or touch abuse, during early childhood.

My colleagues and I (Orbach *et al.* 2006) have also empirically tested the theory of the triangular link between early care, body experiences, and suicidal behavior through two hypotheses: (1) Suicidal youngsters manifest different feelings and attitudes towards their bodies and experience their bodies in a different way compared to non-suicidal youngsters. (2) Suicidal youngsters have more negative memories of early care than their non-suicidal counterparts.

Both objective measures and self-report measures were utilized in the collection of data on bodily experiences. A tactile stimulator provided recordings of tactile sensitivity, a measure for tolerance of tactile pressure and physical pain. The self-report of bodily experiences included accounts of physical anhedonia, bodily dissociation, anxiety about the body, and responses to various types of touch (tactile defensiveness). Data on the body-related attitudes of the subjects were collected through self-report on body image, body care, body protection, and similar items. Lastly, perceived early care, in the form of parental bonding, recollection of positive and negative touch, and history of maltreatment, was measured in the subjects. Also included were measures of depression, anxiety, severity of pathology, and suicidal tendencies. The study was comprised of three groups of adolescent subjects – suicidal in-patients, non-suicidal in-patients, and a control non-clinical group.

The results confirmed the two hypotheses stated above. The suicidal participants tolerated higher levels of tactile pressure and exhibited more negative body experiences and attitudes towards the body. Moreover, the suicidal group reported more negative experiences of early care, and these were found to be correlated with the negative bodily experiences and negative attitudes towards the body (see also Orbach *et al.* 1996a; Orbach *et al.* 1997).

Integrative summary

In this chapter, I have tried to present a phenomenological-experiential perspective of suicide. The main questions addressed were: why do people wish to commit suicide, and what makes it possible to carry out an ultimate aggressive act against the self and against the body?

I have attempted to answer these questions by referring to the suicidal mind (mental pain, pain-producing constructs) and the suicidal body. Following Shneidman (1993a) and others, it is suggested that the immediate cause for the suicidal wishes, from a phenomenological perspective, is unbearable mental pain. Although the different accounts of mental pain brought forth reveal various experiential aspects of mental pain, there are many similarities between these accounts. Shneidman's (1993a) theoretical account describes mental pain as stemming from a deep frustration of one's most important needs in life, resulting in an inner perturbation characterized by a mixture of negative feelings. Eventually, this composition becomes a generalized negative experience, which turns into a new, unique experience that, as a whole, is different from each of the negative feelings.

Maltsberger (2004) views mental pain as an experience of disintegration, including loss of control, madness, aggression, and self-hate. The personal account of mental pain by Styron (1992) points out the dreadful experience of being attacked by estranged and hostile forces from within. Bolger's narrative model places the sense of brokenness at the heart of mental pain, and describes brokenness as damage, disconnection, meaninglessness, loss of self, loss of control, fear, and panic. The empirical model suggested by my colleagues and me (e.g. Orbach *et al.* 2003) characterizes mental pain by the negative changes that occur within the self, accompanied by negative emotions and cognitions.

Clinical accounts of mental pain, as expressed by suicidal patients, seem to resonate with many of the conceptual aspects described by the various mental pain models presented in this chapter. Several common features emerge from the different accounts and models of mental pain. First, the pain is experienced as an irreversible state, stemming from irreversible negative changes in the self. Second, this said shift in the self brings about an emotional flooding to the point of loss of control over one's self. Third, these changes in the self are experienced as acting internally within the self as estranged destructive and hostile forces.

It has been stressed that the experience, not of the pain itself, but of the pain as intolerable, is the crucial factor in the suicidal wish. Intolerability of pain is enhanced by the intensity of the pain, the overflow of the pain, and by inability to contain and cope with the pain.

As was pointed out in this chapter, there are two primary sources of mental pain. One source is life stressors, which are individual in so far as individuals differ in their sensitivity to different life stressors as well as in which stressors trigger the pain. Yet, even allowing for individual differences, loss has been suggested to be the most common life stressor. The other primary source of mental pain is, in fact, internally produced and generated pain. Internally produced pain is actually manufactured by pre-modeled templates formed by early traumatic experiences and early conflicts. When pain is triggered internally, self-destructive tendencies are also set in motion, leading to even more pain. Unbearable mental pain can explain how the wish to kill one's self emerges, but it is not sufficient to explain how the potential for suicide becomes an actual act of self-destruction.

In order to move from the unbearable pain to self-destruction, further facilitating processes are needed. One of these facilitating processes is the creation of the suicidal body. Some clinical theoreticians (e.g. Bell, Chapter 4 this volume; Laufer 1995; Maltsberger 1993) claim that suicide cannot occur without a split between body and mind. The processes that enable this split to occur include bodily dissociation, physical numbness, physical anhedonia, insensitivity to physical pain and to tactile stimulation, and a general indifference or negative attitude towards the body. Detachment from the body via these psycho-physiological processes serves as a facilitator for the physically self-destructive act. The suicidal body is a necessary condition for suicide to take place.

Based on an integration of the theoretical, clinical, and empirical findings, we can carefully move forward to identify a unique personality configuration of at least some suicidal individuals. This configuration is a combination of high thresholds of physical pain, and a low threshold of mental pain. If this hypothesis is confirmed, it may well contribute to the further understanding of suicidal behavior and its treatment in suicidal individuals.[1]

Note

1 Viewing suicide and suicidal behavior from this perspective implies that the treatment of suicidal behavior should include a focus on both mental pain and the suicidal body. The pain can be alleviated by therapeutic strategies such as the therapist taking an empathic attitude towards the patient's suicidal wish, exploring the patient's death fantasy, learning about the fluctuations in the pain and their relation to mental and actual events, helping the patient to take responsibility for his/her own self-destructive tendencies and learning how these contribute to pain, and preparation for coping with the pain in the future (see Orbach 2001 for an extensive review). The therapeutic focus on the suicidal body can help revive the body by means of recently developed techniques such as body mindfulness (see Williams and Swales 2004).

References

Bolger, E.A. (1999) 'Grounded theory analysis of emotional pain', *Psychotherapy Research* 9: 342–362.

Bowlby, J. (1973) *Attachment and Loss: Volume 2, Separation: Anxiety and Anger*, New York: Penguin Books.

Field, T.M. (1997) 'Touch therapies for adolescents with suicidal ideation', Paper presented at a symposium, 'Early Attachment in Infancy and Self Behavior in Adulthood', Bar-Ilan University, Israel, December.

Freud, S. (1917) 'Mourning and melancholia', in J. Strachey (ed.) *The Standard Edition of the Works of Sigmund Freud, XIV* (pp. 237–258), London: Hogarth.

Freud, S. (1926) 'Inhibition, symptoms and anxiety', in J. Strachey (ed.) *The Standard Edition of the Works of Sigmund Freud, XX* (pp. 75–175), London: Hogarth.

Janoff-Bulman, R. (1992) *Shattered Assumptions: Toward a New Psychology of Trauma*, Toronto: Maxwell Macmillan Canada.

Joffe, W.G. and Sandler, J. (1965) 'Pain, depression, and individuation', in J. Sandler (ed.) *From Safety to Superego* (pp. 154–179), New York: Guilford.

Laufer, M. (ed.) (1995) *The Suicidal Adolescent*, London: Karnac.

Maltsberger, J.T. (1993) 'Confusion of the body, the self and others in suicidal states', in A. Leenaars (ed.) *Suicidology: Essays in Honor of Edwin Shneidman* (pp. 148–171), Northvale, NJ: Jason Aronson.

Maltsberger, J.T. (2004) 'The descent into suicide', *International Journal of Psychoanalysis* 85, 3: 653–668.

Maltsberger, J.T. (2006) 'Out-patient treatment', in R.I. Simon and R. Hales (eds) *The American Psychiatric Publishing Textbook of Suicide Assessment and Management* (pp. 367–379), Washington, DC: American Psychiatric Publishing.

Orbach, I. (1996) 'The role of the body experience in self-destruction: early attachment and suicidal tendencies', *Clinical Child Psychology and Psychiatry* 1: 607–619.

Orbach, I. (1997) 'A taxonomy of factors related to suicidal behavior', *Clinical Psychology: Theory and Research* 4: 208–224.

Orbach, I. (2001) 'Therapeutic empathy with the suicidal wish: principles of therapy with suicidal individuals', *American Journal of Psychotherapy* 55, 2: 166–184.

Orbach, I. (2003) 'Mental pain and suicide', *Israel Journal of Psychiatry and Related Sciences* 40, 3: 191–201.

Orbach, I. (2006) 'The body-mind of the suicidal person', in T.E. Ellis (ed.) *Cognition and Suicide: Theory, Research, and Therapy* (pp. 193–214), Washington, DC: American Psychological Association.

Orbach, I. (2007) 'Self-destructive processes in suicide', *Israel Journal of Psychiatry and Related Areas* 44: 266–279.

Orbach, I., Palgi, Y., Stein, D., Har-Even, D., Lotem-Peleg, M. and Asherov, J. (1996a) 'Pain tolerance in suicidal psychiatric and normal objects', *Death Studies* 20: 227–240.

Orbach, I., Stein, D., Palgi, Y., Asherov, J., Har-Even, D. and Elizur, A. (1996b). 'Tolerance for physical pain in accident and suicide attempt patients: self-preservation vs. self destruction', *Journal of Psychiatric Research* 30: 307–320.

Orbach, I., Mikulincer, M., King, R., Cohen, D. and Stein, D. (1997) 'Thresholds and tolerance for physical pain in suicidal and non-suicidal adolescents', *Journal of Consulting and Clinical Psychology* 65, 4: 646–652.

Orbach, I., Mikulincer, M., Sirota, P. and Gilboa-Schechtman, E. (2003) 'Mental pain: a multidimensional operationalization and definition', *Suicide and Life Threatening Behavior* 33, 3: 219–230.

Orbach, I., Gilboa-Schechtman, E., Sheffer, A., Meged, S., Har-Even, D. and Stein, D. (2006) 'Negative bodily self in suicide attempters', *Suicide and Life Threatening Behavior* 36, 2: 136–153.

Shneidman, E.S. (1980) *Voices of Death*, New York: Basic Books.

Shneidman, E.S. (1993a) *Suicide as Psychache: A Clinical Approach to Self-Destructive Behavior*, Northvale, NJ: Jason Aronson.

Shneidman, E.S. (1993b) 'Suicide as psychache', *Journal of Nervous and Mental Disease* 181: 147–149.

Shneidman, E.S. (1996) *The Suicidal Mind*, New York: Oxford University Press.

Sloan, N.L., Leon-Camacho, W.L., Rojas, P.E. and Stern, C. (1994) 'Kangaroo mother method: randomized controlled trial of an alternative method of care for stabilized low birth weight infants', *Lancet* 344: 782–785.

Spitz, R.A. (1965) *The First Year of Life*, New York: International Universities Press.

Styron, W. (1992) *Darkness Visible: A Memoir of Madness*, New York: Vintage Books.

Van der Velde, C.D. (1985) 'Body image of one's self and of others: developmental and clinical significance', *American Journal of Psychiatry* 142: 527–537.

Williams, J.M. and Swales, M. (2004) 'The use of mindfulness-based approaches for suicidal patients', *Archives of Suicide Research* 8: 315–329.

Part 2

Practice

Chapter 8

Hostility and suicide: the experience of aggression from within and without

Mark J. Goldblatt

Many authors have noted the association between suicide and aggression. Since Freud's (1917) formulation of suicide as anger turned back upon the self, many authors have taken up the aspect of suicide as internalized anger. Later authors have also taken up the role of suicide as an experience of hostility from significant others. In this chapter I review some of the literature about aggression and hostility. I suggest that suicide takes place in the context of unbearable hostility towards the self, which is experienced both interpersonally and intrapsychically. Therapeutic interventions should therefore focus on helping the patient to recognize internal aggression and violent rages that end up being aimed at the self. At the same time, efforts should also concentrate on developing a non-hostile external sustaining environment. Psychotherapy that recognizes the patient's emotional experience enables growth of internal sustaining resources. However, that might not be enough. Suicide prevention might necessitate changing the external environment as well.

Theoretical perspectives on suicidality

In 'Mourning and melancholia', Freud (1917) described how the melancholic's ego splits and is able to direct against itself hostility that relates to an object. In a later paper, 'The psychogenesis of a case of homosexuality in a woman', Freud put it this way, 'Probably no one finds the mental energy to kill himself unless, in the first place, in doing so, he is at the same time killing an object with whom he has identified himself and, in the second place, is turning against himself a death wish which had been directed against someone else' (Freud 1920: 162). Since then the cliché of suicide as anger turned upon the self has been over-used and its practical clinical usefulness has become limited.

Menninger (1933) developed this idea further in his description of the suicidal triad. The wish to kill, which he locates in the system ego, is an expression of hostile aggression, and is re-directed on the self, away from the hated-loved person.

Hendrick (1940) argued that in some patients suicide is used as a mechanism to escape aggression. In contrast to Menninger whose 'wish to be killed' represented a way to deal with guilt arising from the superego, Hendrick argued that suicide in some cases might be a way to deal with the aggression that is experienced from within.

In his 1969 paper on adolescent suicide, Sabbath described the pathology of the parent–child relationship that contributes to adolescent suicide. Suicides that take place in the context of a family usually reveal an ambivalence on the part of the family members towards the adolescent. The identified adolescent patient is loved and hated at the same time. Often this occurs in the context of the patient's chronic suicidality, which is experienced by family members as an emotional drain. At other times the rage at the patient appears to have been present from birth, or even before conception. Usually the ambivalence is covert, although in some cases it may be quite explicit. Sabbath proposed the concept of the 'expendable child' (1969: 285), which presumed a parental wish, which may be conscious or unconscious, spoken or unspoken, that the child interprets as their desire to be rid of him, for him to die. The child experiences this as a loss or abandonment, and feels expendable.

Sabbath saw this phenomenon as contributing to adolescent suicidal behavior although it is probably just as common in other age groups. This concept has also been extended to the 'expendable patient' where psychiatric hospitals may replicate the parent–child relationship. In these cases the ambivalent doctor–patient relationship (or nursing staff–patient relationship) may contribute directly or indirectly to the patient's suicide attempts.

Rochlin (1965) develops this further. He suggested that abandonment of the child by his parents evokes intolerable aggressive feelings toward the parents. In an effort to spare the object, the self becomes the target of the destructive wishes through suicidal wishes and actions. Through projection, the source of hostility is referred back on the self, sparing the object at the expense of the adolescent's life.

In considering aggression and suicide, Richman and Rosenbaum (1970) were struck by the amount of hostility that was directed towards the suicidal person. The families they studied avoided crises relating to change by blaming the identified family member, which subsequently precipitated a suicide attempt. They advocated confronting this aggression in the patient and the family in the treatment and prevention of further suicidal regression.

Suicide can sometimes be an expression of revenge by young people conscious of their own intolerable hostility towards their parents. In his paper on the 'Psychodynamics of suicide', Hendin (1991) suggests that in young people suicide is usually an escape from an intolerable affective state, and that the nature and intensity of these states are significant in assessing suicidal patients. Rage is one of these affective states, and he suggests that people who feel torn by rage and violence can view suicide as a way of controlling this sense of disintegration. Work by Weissman and colleagues (1973) reported that the open expression of hostility and rage distinguishes depressed patients who are suicidal from those who are not.

Novick (1984/1996) reminds us to be sensitive to the role of hostility and death wishes of the mothers of suicidal adolescents. He notes that the conviction by the adolescent that her mother wanted her dead was not just a projection, but 'had a substantial basis in reality' (1984/1996: 545).

Asch (1980) describes the suicidal patient who recruits others (often the therapist) into rationalizing the suicide and making it possible. Through unconscious fantasies of oral submission that attempt to restore an object loss, the suicidal patient enlists the aid of a significant object in causing his death. Asch suggests that in psychotherapy the suicidal patient evokes a negative countertransference and then uses his experience of such a response to justify his suicidal act.

Maltsberger (1988) has also underscored the importance of recognizing lethal affects in suicidal evaluation. He notes that murderous rage can often not be tolerated, and such patients turn on themselves as a way of protecting others from their own murderous hostility.

Clinical implications

Patients who become suicidal in the context of family aggression are most likely to develop an expectation of similar hostility from others, especially the therapist. In the transference, one would expect the patient to keep the therapist at a distance, and treat him with caution and suspicion, or more likely with fear and distrust.

I want to consider two different aspects of this clinical situation, namely hostility in the transference and non-transference hostile experiences of the patient (usually at the hands of family, friends or colleagues).

Hostility in the transference

Working in the transference may enable the patient to explore his anger and fears, especially through an exploration of how they may reappear in relation to the therapist. However, with some patients, re-experiencing fear and hatred for the therapist in the transference may contribute to a negative therapeutic reaction, and the possible abandonment of the treatment.

If the patient is to overcome the fear and distrust of the therapist, this will depend on two major factors. First, the patient's ability to form a therapeutic alliance to try to work with the therapist is typically connected with constitutional factors that allow for contact even under circumstances of traumatic withdrawal. Often this is predicated on the patient's having experienced an early, loving nurturing object who was able to convey a sense of worth despite the aggression that was the predominant experience. Sometimes a caring grandmother, sister or aunt may fill this position. Other times it might be an interested teacher, coach or clergyman.

The second significant factor in developing a trusting relationship is the therapist's ability to provide a safe nurturing environment in which the therapy can take place. Generally this occurs through the structure that is provided by the frame of the therapy and the boundaries that are created. The therapist's ability to define the frame allows the patient to feel secure, even though the frame limits the time of the session and the nature of the therapeutic contact.

However, suicidal patients sometimes require additional measures to overcome the obstacles in the way of the working alliance. When the therapist is able to convey in words and actions that he really is a safe, caring, new object, then the treatment is more likely to proceed successfully. Often this is accomplished through interventions such as clarification and interpretation. But more often these patients need additional supportive measures. Sometimes *actions* on the part of the therapist are the necessary therapeutic steps.

Actions involving the therapist and patient have received increasing attention in the psychoanalytic literature, where enactment has become a widely used term. Although it originally implied something pathological, enactment has come to describe a normal range of interpersonal occurrences (Frank 1999). Goldberg has narrowed the definition to those interactions 'that may be conceptualized as transference and countertransference issues' (2002: 882).

Special therapeutic accommodations arise frequently and are necessary in the treatment of suicidal patients. Often such patients need to be seen at inconvenient times, or they may need in-between-session phone calls, or reduced fees. To deny these therapeutic accommodations would leave the patient feeling abandoned and assaulted. To interpret the unconscious hostility would also be experienced as attack. Yet to make therapeutic accommodations takes some sacrifice on the part of the therapist: demands made on the therapist's time and energy for which he is usually not compensated.

Defenses like reaction formation lead susceptible therapists into trying to provide more and more for the suicidal patient in the hope that they can stave off a suicide attempt. When the therapist is held hostage to the patient's threats of suicide (Hendin (1991) has referred to this as 'therapeutic bondage'), the treatment (and often the patient) is doomed (Sabbath 1969).

The therapist is caught in the dilemma of needing to be more accommodating to the suicidal patient while at the same time being aware of countertransference reactions that are enacted. Awareness of countertransference rage and hostility may provide important clues to the dangers involved in boundary crossings. Boundary violations that invariably hurt the patient are dangerous and naturally contraindicated.

Non-transference experiences of hostility

Experiences of hostility and rejection at the hands of family, friends or colleagues at work seem to appear with great frequency. Technically, dealing with these 're-traumatizations' can be very trying. Patients display their ambivalence in their inability to acknowledge what they have described. When the therapist repeats the patient's statements back to him (often word for word), these statements are then repudiated and denied, and the patient becomes angry at the therapist for grossly missing the point. It often takes a great deal of work before the patient is able to accept his ambivalence and recognize both sides of his dependency and hatred for the attacking object. Helping the patient to clarify his feelings, and his experience, will gradually lead to an increased recognition of these painful affects.

Case example

Stella was a 20-year-old, African-American university student who came for treatment for severe depression and profound suicidal distress. I treated her for three years in twice-weekly psychoanalytic psychotherapy before she moved away to begin graduate school and pursue her career as a lawyer. At that point she was no longer suicidal.

Stella would be a classic example of an 'expendable child'. Her parents abandoned her to the care of a sadistic aunt so that they could each pursue their own professional careers. Later on they showered love and gifts on their 'golden child', Stella's brother, who was four years her junior, while ignoring Stella's needs for money and attention.

Stella was referred to me in the throes of a suicidal crisis, which had arisen out of a severe depression, chronic self-hatred and self-attack. She had tried to kill herself as a teenager, but since then she had managed to control her self-loathing and suicidal thoughts through her devotion to her religious beliefs. This was only partially successful. Over the past year or so prior to entering treatment, her self-hatred and self-attack had escalated and she was now armed with a serious suicide plan which she had formulated one month prior to seeing me.

When I met her, Stella appeared as an attractive young woman who seemed physically awkward, casually dressed in jeans and a sweater. She had several visible body piercings, two on each ear lobe, and one on her tongue. She made almost no eye contact, looking off to the side throughout the sessions. She had a full range of affect, but revealed very little of her emotional experience, usually in a constricted manner, unless she was overwhelmed, in which case she cried freely. She met criteria for a Major Depression with depressed mood, irritability, anhedonia, fatigue, poor sleep, loss of appetite, and low energy. Her concentration was poor, and writing her school papers was difficult. She felt hopeless, helpless, worthless and guilt-ridden. She also met criteria for Borderline Personality Disorder. When she experienced internal agitation she obtained relief by cutting herself on her arms. She was then able to calm herself down. The cutting had initially been superficial, but was becoming deeper and deeper.

On the side of internal sustaining resources I noted that she was able to see some goodness in herself. She recognized herself as smart and compassionate. She had recently begun to work, which raised her self-esteem, and gave her a sense of value from helping others. She valued her love of children, her baby-sitting abilities, and her cooking skills. She had intense and conflicted feelings about sex. She wanted to be in a relationship, but thought that she was unattractive, and that young men would not like her. Stella had a few close friends with whom she spent her free time, and would call on them in times of crisis. She also was in regular contact with her parents, and even though she felt she could not really talk with them, she continued to hold on to the hope of a deeper relationship with them.

Stella said she did not like her previous attempts at therapy because it reminded her that she had a problem; that she was not really in control of how she felt, and that she was angry.

Past history

Stella is the oldest of three children born to an African-American family. She has two younger brothers – one four years younger, and the other eight years younger. Her father was a successful lawyer, with a much sought after expertise. Although he was well respected with several areas of expertise, he was jealous of Stella. He felt he was poorly educated, and that she was an intellectual. He was also quite competitive with her. When Stella proudly told him of her extraordinary academic achievements he complained about payments that he had to make for psychotherapy. When she won a prestigious award for her writing, the father did not read her paper, but felt insulted that he was not mentioned in it. The father favored her younger brother who played basketball. The family turned a blind eye to this brother's drug use.

Stella initially refused permission for me to speak with her parents. 'I can't make him pay for therapy. I feel I'm a big burden. He pays for my education. He's proud of me and I'm smart like him. I don't show them anything wrong. So they think I'm being a hypochondriac. If you talk to him, you'll tell him things he won't believe, and then he'll call me, and I'll have to tell him.'

Three months into the treatment, when Stella agreed to let me speak with her father, he told me that he cared about his daughter, and would like to help. He was concerned about her ability to cope, and found it difficult to know how she was doing because she remained high functioning despite her suffering. He did not want to invade her privacy, but asked me to call him if I needed to. He agreed to pay the full fee for weekly psychotherapy. He invariably paid two or three months late, and complained to Stella (but never to me) about the huge cost.

The mother too was a legal specialist. She was less emotionally available. Stella thought that her mother felt guilty for leaving her in the care of the aunt throughout her childhood. Stella remembered crying in front of her mother about the aunt calling her ugly and saying hurtful things. The mother started crying too, but continued to leave her with the aunt for another four years. 'If they knew how awful she was, why did they leave me with her?'

Stella felt competitive with her mother whom she resembles physically, but said that at 'my age' she was skinny and gorgeous. The mother had 'a huge temper' and was easily enraged, especially at her younger son who had learning difficulties and could not read well.

The most important and destructive influence on Stella appears to have been her father's sister. She spent the last few years of her life in a nursing home, and died during the course of Stella's therapy with me. Throughout her childhood Stella was sent off to her aunt's home, where she experienced chronic verbal sadistic attacks.

When Stella was $4\frac{1}{2}$, her first brother was born. Her parents were just out of Law School, and they asked father's sister and brother-in-law to come and live with them to help care for the children. Stella says they mostly raised her, as she spent most of her time with them. 'My aunt Mary is a bitch.' The aunt seems to have spent most of the time treating Stella poorly, and calling her fat and ugly and worthless. 'I hated her so much. Now she's old and dying. You're supposed to love your family, and I feel guilty.'

Uncle Charlie, Mary's husband, on the other hand was greatly loved by Stella. He seemed to have suffered similar abusive tirades from his wife. He always accepted her ranting in silence, and Stella wondered why he did not say something. He was seen as smart and sweet, and Stella felt cheated out of her relationship with him due to the abuse from aunt Mary.

Stella remembered feeling helpless very early in her life. Aunt Mary would tell her repeatedly that she was fat and worthless. She felt unlovable. She felt she could not complain to her parents about this treatment and did not reveal to her parents the extent of the abuse – partly because she felt her mother already felt guilty enough about abandoning her as a child, and partly because mother already hated Mary, and wanted her to die.

'I didn't have the greatest childhood. I was fat as a kid, and kids are cruel. I was constantly teased. I hated my childhood, a lot!' By seventh grade Stella was grossly overweight. She entered junior high school where they had stratified classes, and then began to appreciate her intellectual capacity. She gained a measure of self-esteem, lost 50 pounds, and began to find friends. She joined a youth group and became intensely religious. 'This was really great, because people had to like me.' Being part of this religious youth group also helped Stella deal with her conflicting impulses. 'Being a Christian is about negating yourself, so it's wrong to follow your desires.'

During her sixteenth year Stella began slashing her wrists, and taking sleeping pills. She then tried to kill herself. 'I wanted people to notice me. It was a cry for help . . . There was too much of a good thing all at once. I wanted to be the center of attention, and when I didn't get it, I got depressed and weird. I thought suicide would make people care more.' She finally told her friends and they encouraged her to talk with her youth group leader. At length he persuaded her that she had to tell her mother. 'It was awful. She didn't say anything. She just got up and left. We drove home in silence, and went to bed. Mother was so angry she didn't want to talk to me. She said she was so disappointed.'

Stella began treatment with an adolescent psychiatrist who diagnosed Bipolar Disorder. She hated this experience. It was a fifty-minute drive in silence, with either parent. Father constantly complained about having to write out a check. After a short time, Stella could not stand it any more, so she told everyone that she felt better, and could stop treatment.

Course of treatment

After the initial evaluation I proposed twice-weekly psychodynamic psychotherapy as well as appropriate medication for depression and agitation. Stella could not agree to either recommendation. She herself could not afford twice-weekly therapy, and her insurance would only cover twelve sessions in total for the year. She felt she could not ask her father to pay for treatment, as he would be angry at her, and she would have to let him know how desperate she was. She had not actually told her parents how suicidal she was. She was thinking of leaving university, but realized that things were not better at home.

Here was the first instance of a therapeutic accommodation or perhaps an enactment: I agreed to begin treatment without a full commitment to full fee coverage. Stella agreed to use her insurance coverage (substantially lower than my usual private pay fee), and we began to meet weekly, with the understanding that we would consider ways to begin a dialogue with father around payment for therapy. Stella agreed she would come in more frequently if her suicidality worsened. I thought that I needed to be flexible about frequency of meetings, payment for sessions, and contact with her parents, in order to establish a working alliance. If we were able to establish such an alliance, I thought we would then be able look at her emotional situation, alleviate her depression, and then attend to the relationship with her parents, and address long-term issues of the treatment.

We dealt with medication in a similar way. I felt strongly that Stella's depression and agitation would respond to medication. She felt that she had tried many medications previously, with mixed results. She did not want to undertake any further medication trials as she would invariably experience side effects and obtain little or no relief. Once again, I felt that I did not need to press this issue. When she felt more trusting of my judgment, or if her distress worsened, then she might be more open to medication relief.

My approach in the therapy was first to help her see that she suffered from a severe depression. Despite her great efforts this is a debilitating illness and she deserved credit for how hard she persevered. Relapses of depressive symptoms are incapacitating, but depression can respond to appropriate treatment. Second, due to the psychological trauma of her childhood she had developed coping mechanisms which helped her get through the past, but she now found herself re-experiencing similar destructive interactions in the present. Third, I was also exceedingly clear on boundaries and limits – for example, cancellation policy – and pointed out how she had intense reactions to boundary violations, which sometimes included her own partial re-enactment. I tried not to get into power struggles with her, such as over the frequency of sessions, or the use of medications.

During the early stages of the therapy I would limit my comments to the material she brought up, making clarifications about her affective response to the interactions she was describing. Certain behaviors (especially her self-destructive urges) were extremely bothersome to her. I did not suggest that she change them. In fact, I would recognize that trying to change them had been very difficult, despite her best intentions. I also made a point of acknowledging the hostility that she described from others, commenting on the aggression and sadism that had not been acknowledged. I actively participated in the therapy, trying to help her to describe her experience in words.

Stella seemed to improve almost from the first few sessions. By the fourth session she said, 'This therapy is going well. You made me feel a lot better. You legitimized the way I felt. That was good.' I responded by saying that, due to her past experiences, I felt I could not remain silent or passive to her material. I thought that silence on my part or even neutrality would come across to her as hostile, or condoning her own self-attack. She attacked herself and treated herself poorly, perhaps because that was all she had experienced others doing to her. She responded that she valued other people's opinions more than her own, and she would be happier if she had a boyfriend, because that would make her feel worth something. But, it was impossible for her to feel it from within.

This was another instance of therapeutic accommodation. I tried actively to convey without judgement my sense of what she was revealing. In other circumstances I might have allowed more silence for her associations to develop, but here I felt I had to step in earlier with comments that I hoped would convey my efforts to try to sort out her emotional experience.

We acknowledged that she 'falls apart when things go wrong'. When people she counted on were not reliable, she worried about them. She had a difficult time experiencing anger, fearing that it would result in her losing the people who might care about her.

We also noted that she took on a lot of activities – for example, school projects, work, and social activities. She then felt overwhelmed by the stress that came with these activities, but she could not slow down because then she would feel very sad, and she could not 'handle that'; therefore she felt intense anxiety/agitation, which made her 'freak out' and led to her cutting or overdosing. This made her think poorly about herself, and she blamed herself for acting badly. I interpreted to her that she appeared to be sensitive to feelings of loneliness, which was understandable given how isolated she felt as a child. When she felt she was losing the support of someone she needed, she became panicked, and did all these activities, like cutting, to deal with her panic. Then she blamed herself for acting in this way, and for causing the loss of her supports. She responded that she felt some pressure not to cut herself, but when she got into that state, the suicidal pressure became more and more intense.

After eight sessions we started to discuss how to continue the therapy when the insurance sessions would run out four weeks later. At that point Stella agreed to allow father into the process. She said that she had a glimpse of hope that therapy could help bring about big changes. She was already showing increased coping skills. She reported that even though things had been very stressful, she 'didn't go crazy like usual'. 'I've never been as seriously suicidal as February . . . I used to feel special about the depression. I realized in February I didn't want it. That's what's different this time, I don't like the depression anymore.'

By session 11, Stella began to take better care of herself. She realized that her times of 'freaking out' had to do with being really tired, and getting to sleep would change her perspective. She agreed to try an over-the-counter hypnotic for sleep, as she admitted that it was now taking her about an hour to fall asleep. 'This is the most normal I've felt since 16. It's a weird identity shift. Feeling like a new person, like the depression is something from the past.'

Soon after getting father's agreement to pay for weekly therapy, Stella had a relapse of depressive symptoms, associated with loneliness and the loss of relationships over the summer. She was terrified that she would regress back to her previous suicidal state. At this time (week 17) she agreed to a trial of an antidepressant along with an anti-anxiety drug for sleep.

Stella seemed to consider the fluctuations in her mood as something that had an independent course, un-reactive to things in her life. 'I used to feel chronically suicidal. I didn't think it would ever get better, but it did. Something worked. But, how long do you wait for it to get better? You can't make someone want to live. Nobody could make me want to live. It just went away.' I confronted her about how she saw it as fortuitous, despite the therapy we had engaged in, and the medication. She was able to reflect on the course of treatment and associated to illness and bodily pain, which she usually ignored.

I pointed out that she had taken in that attitude from her parents, and continued to treat herself in that same dismissive way. By expressing my interest and concern for her physical health I tried to reinforce the need to be aware of her physical and emotional needs, and to take them seriously.

At this point (week 25) she began to show some interest in me. She asked about my accent. She was fearful about changing our relationship. She felt that the therapy had worked well, because I legitimized her feelings. In her previous treatments the relationship with the therapist had not been explored, and she had never had a relationship with a therapist before. She was scared to have a relationship with me. 'I don't want to. If I start to like you, I don't won't to get too attached. If you moved, you would be hard to replace. If you run out of toilet paper, you get another roll, but therapists perform a function. If I decide to like you as a person, it opens you up to liking me as a person, and maybe you won't like me, and that would be awful. Right now, this has been a business transaction. Liking you goes beyond that.'

I responded: 'This is the issue you keep being faced with, and it's not surprising that it comes up over here. In fact, it's helpful, because we might be able to find a way to sort it all out. On the one hand, you want to feel close, and experience your feelings in a safe way. You find your emotional experience to be interesting, and exciting, and even compelling and essential, but at the same time you feel that you are vulnerable to getting hurt, and having a bad experience, which might lead to feeling worse, and lead you back down to the terrible place you were in several months/years ago.'

She replied: 'I didn't like you very much at first. You seemed very serious. It made me feel that my illness was legitimate. That felt good, but I also thought, I really am in trouble and I have to deal with it. He thinks it's serious, and I really have to deal with it. And there was the money. I didn't want to ask my dad. But I got over that. I was really anxious over the weekend. I called you and left a message. I realize I don't do well with ambiguity [about relationships with her friends]. I just wanted to talk to someone to calm me down. It helped to call your machine, and I took a Xanax and it calmed me down.'

I finished off the session by reiterating, 'The more things can be put into words, the clearer it becomes for you, and you can calm down.'

She replied: 'Yes. I really need things to be said.'

Although there were ups and downs in the treatment, within six months Stella showed improvement in all areas of her functioning, including feeling less depressed, not suicidal, and functioning better at school, home and socially.

Summary of treatment

Therapy aimed to clarify Stella's affective experience, and the aggression in her interactions. The therapy focused on treating her depression, and interpreting her feelings and behaviors in terms of her traumatic experience. By providing understanding and consistency I tried to help her realize the nature of her experience, and what caused her reactions. This was done actively, to combat her impression of silence in the therapist as indicating tacit agreement with her own self-hatred and criticism. I also asked questions that focused on bodily safety and appreciation. By showing my interest in this aspect of her well-being, I tried to convey my own value of bodily integrity, as a way to help her to begin to appreciate her own bodily self-worth. I also tried to point out pitfalls ahead, which she might not consciously want to deal with. These included her reaction to pending losses, her tolerance of others' hostility, and the need to understand the nature of our relationship, and the possibilities for our work to continue, or to terminate.

I have described the therapeutic accommodations or enactments that appear to have facilitated treatment through a suicidal crisis, and during a three-year-long psychotherapy. Extra therapy sessions were suggested when necessary, as were phone calls and emails. All were treated according to the patient's needs and ability to tolerate affective intensity. When the suicidal crisis was no longer an issue, the question of characterological change arose. I suggested increasing the intensity of the treatment to several times a week. At that point Stella considered how to afford this, as she felt she could not ask her father to pay. She therefore found a job with health insurance in order to afford treatment. Although the insurance was less than my usual fee, I agreed to accept it, with her self-payment of the remaining portion. At this point I felt that there was still a need for some therapeutic accommodation although the intensity of her needs was substantially decreased, and her own ego strengths were notably increased.

Conclusion

Destructive aggression directed at patients from important family members can coincide with intrapsychic deficits to produce hopelessness and a longing for death. Therapy for such patients works well when it is able help the patient recognize the hostile forces that he is subject to, and the internal conflicts that contribute to his self-attack.

When the therapist is able to counteract the destructive internal and external hostility the patient is able to regain his own sense of self-worth. Sometimes this involves countertransference actions that recognize the needs of the impaired patient. Boundaries are always crucial for such patients, but the needs of such patients are extra-ordinary, and with thoughtfulness, care may be provided that counteracts self-destructive habits.

References

Asch, S. (1980) 'Suicide, and the hidden executioner', *International Review of Psychoanalysis* 7: 51–60; reprinted in J.T. Maltsberger and M. Goldblatt (eds) *Essential Papers on Suicide* (pp. 524–548), New York: New York University Press, 1996.

Frank, K. (1999) *Psychoanalytic Participation: Action, Interaction and Integration*, Hillsdale, NJ: Analytic Press.

Freud, S. (1917) 'Mourning and melancholia', in J. Strachey (ed.) *The Standard Edition of the Works of Sigmund Freud, XIV* (pp. 237–258), London: Hogarth.

Freud, S. (1920) 'The psychogenesis of a case of homosexuality in a woman', in J. Strachey (ed.) *The Standard Edition of the Works of Sigmund Freud, XVIII* (pp. 147–172), London: Hogarth.

Goldberg, A. (2002) 'Enactment as understanding and misunderstanding', *Journal of the American Psychoanalytic Association* 50, 3: 869–883.

Hendin, H. (1991) 'Psychodynamics of suicide, with particular reference to the young', *American Journal of Psychiatry* 148: 1150–1158; reprinted in J.T. Maltsberger and M. Goldblatt (eds) *Essential Papers on Suicide* (pp. 612–632), New York: New York University Press, 1996.

Hendrick, I. (1940) 'Suicide as wish fulfilment', *Psychoanalytic Quarterly* 14: 30–42; reprinted in J.T. Maltsberger and M. Goldblatt (eds) *Essential Papers on Suicide* (pp. 104–117), New York: New York University Press, 1996.

Maltsberger, J.T. (1988) 'Suicide danger; clinical estimation and decision', *Suicide and Life Threatening Behavior* 18: 47–54.

Menninger, K.A. (1933) 'Psychoanalytic aspects of suicide', *International Journal of Psychoanalysis* 14: 376–390.

Novick, J. (1984/1996) 'Attempted suicide in adolescence: the suicide sequence', in H. Sudack, A.B. Ford and N.B. Rushforth (eds) *Suicide in the Young* (pp. 115–137), Boston: John Wright/PSG Inc., 1984; reprinted in J.T. Maltsberger and M. Goldblatt (eds) *Essential Papers on Suicide* (pp. 524–548), New York: New York University Press, 1996.

Richman, J. and Rosenbaum, M. (1970) 'A clinical study of the role of hostility and death wishes by the family and society in suicidal attempts', *Israel Annals of Psychiatry and Related Disciplines* 8: 213–231.

Rochlin, G. (1965) *Griefs and Discontents: The Forces of Change*, Boston: Little, Brown.

Sabbath, J.C. (1969) 'The suicidal adolescent: the expendable child', *Journal of the American Academy of Child Psychiatry* 8: 272–289.

Weissman, M., Fox, K. and Klerman, G.L. (1973) 'Hostility and depression associated with suicide attempts', *American Journal of Psychiatry* 130: 450–455.

Chapter 9

Attacks on life: suicidality and self-harm in young people

Jeanne Magagna

Introduction

Elisa loves her husband who no longer loves her. Her baby is crying for her; turning away Elisa walks slowly up the stairs. She is supposed to take the box filled with wooden clothes pegs, pull the pieces of washing out of the basket, one by one and hang them all along the line. And then? Another task to do. Why? With what aim in view? For no reason at all – there is no aim. And at the end of the day what will happen? Nothing. And tomorrow? The same as today. No, she just cannot do it.

She has one thought. Just wait, don't give up on yourself, just wait! But Elisa doesn't think, doesn't hear, doesn't see. She feels only this strange void all around her. She can't live without her love – even for a single day.

She moves forward, her arms outstretched, groping along in a dead world in which she can no longer find her place. Elisa raises her hands, grips the window frame, climbs up onto the narrow sill: she is so tall that she has to bend her head a little so as not to touch the beams. For a moment she leans her cheek against the plaster of the wall, her eyes closed, her face serene, smiling almost. Eyes still shut, she will lean out a little, and in a slow, impassioned gesture, let go the hands that hold her in life.

Elisa has lost not only the love of Gilles her husband, but more importantly, her love for him. As her love for him is the only justification for her existence, she is in effect already dead, gazing into the abyss. When Elisa no longer is anything, she no longer wants to be anything any more.

This passage from Bourdouxhe's (1992) novel, *La Femme de Gilles*, illustrates the theme of this chapter which is that attacks on the self, including annihilation, come when love dies. In every suicide, every attack on life, we must acknowledge the multi-faceted violence, the murdering of the body, of the psyche and of the designated internalized external object of the killing impulse.

Currently I work as a child and family psychotherapist in Great Ormond Street Hospital for Children and Ellern Mede Centre for Eating Disorders. In these treatment centres I witness the following:

- an 18-month-old child consistently turning his head away from mother as she attempts to give him a spoon of food, necessary for life
- a 15-year-old girl rarely opening her eyes and not eating, speaking or moving
- four anorectic young people aged from 12 to 18 years, all of whom have said 'I just want to die' not only in words but also in their not eating, overdosing, and self-harming actions

Throughout all these current experiences I have been trying to understand these young people who are expressing the wish to die, slowly dying by not eating, and sometimes actively attempting to cut or kill themselves. In this chapter I shall describe aspects of therapeutic work with these young people who, unable to have or to maintain a loving link with a good internal object, attach themselves to destructive forces within. I will begin by showing the enormous variation in the intensity and quality of their destructive impulses, the nature of their relationship to the internal object, and the conscious and unconscious intentions underlying their self-harm and/or attempted suicide. These ideas will be linked to important treatment issues which individual psychotherapists and in-patient multidisciplinary teams should consider when working with depressed young people. Throughout the chapter I shall intersperse vignettes describing therapeutic work with these self-harming, suicidal, non-eating children and young people.

Transference and countertransference issues

From a psychological point of view, attacks on life are very complex. In order to understand self-harming, suicidal young people, I must understand not only their feelings about themselves and their parents, but also their feelings about the professional staff involved in their treatment. I realize that *at the time* of any young person's threatened attack on life, I also need to understand my and other multidisciplinary staff's current feelings towards the young person. In addition I must understand both our attitudes *subsequent to* an attack on life and our attitudes which fluctuate as the young person's self-destructive ideation and activity persist.

Questions to ask regarding the transference–countertransference relationship

Dr Henri Rey (1994), former Maudsley Hospital Consultant Psychiatrist and Psychoanalyst, suggests that the following questions are important to ask at the time of any self-harm or thoughts of self-harm:

What part of the young person is involved?
In what emotional state?
Situated where in space and time?
Does what?
With what motivation?
To what part of the significant other?
In what state?
Situated where in space and time?
With what consequences for the significant other?
And with what consequences for the young person?

I will use Dr Rey's questions to help analyse the relationship of the patient to the therapist in the following psychotherapy session.

Susan's session

Eighteen-year-old Susan said she wanted to torture me. She felt I simply couldn't understand how hurt she was. Susan had arrived early for the session and had seen my previous patient leave the session and get into the car with her mother. Being raised in an emotionally and sexually abusing family, Susan had had to depend on herself. Seeing my previous patient get into a comfortable car with her mother stirred up all Susan's feelings of isolation, loneliness and envy. After she seated herself in the session Susan complained that I did not realize how lonely she was, how alone she had felt during all her life. She felt I could never comprehend that. She ascertained that she could tell that my middle-class background was different. She felt I probably had had caring parents. Then she was silent.

I replied that I was all she had. It felt so unfair, so painful, when she saw the girl with her mother. I was trying to help her have more in her life . . . she had found therapy and that was helping her to have a better life.

At the end of the session, Susan remained seated, refusing to leave the room. I talked about her needing to look after the little girl that wanted to stay always with me and now had to leave. Susan still didn't move from her chair. I then added that she seemed to be not allowing space for the next person who would come to see me. Susan remained immobile, so I also suggested that she would rather have the next person see Susan with me for then Susan could spoil her session the way hers had been spoilt. Susan got up and very uncharacteristically she threw her chair hard against the door which was still shut. This created a startling bang and was accompanied by the seat of the chair falling off. I was visibly startled.

Susan rushed out of the room shouting, 'I hate you and I am going to kill myself!' Susan had deliberately left her diary on the floor, giving the message that it wouldn't be needed any more.

Subsequently, one and a half hours later, Susan phoned me. She apologized for being so out of control and after a pause she said she was all right.

She was calling from a railway station. I asked what was the matter. What was happening? Susan said that she couldn't talk as she had to rush to get the train.

I wasn't at all clear where she was going for she lived near the consulting room; however, she had gone to visit a friend and safely returned for the next session.

Later, as I pondered over Susan's suicide threat, I asked:

What part of her is speaking?	An infant.
In what emotional state?	Feeling jealous of the girl who has a mother all the time, feeling abandoned at the end of sessions, feeling helpless in the face of this painful hurt and overwhelming rage.
Situated where in space and time?	She arrives to feel my lap soiled by others and departs feeling a hard, shut door and a cold outside place.
Does what?	Attacks, injures 'my lap' – the chair and my door, representing the boundaries to the session, particularly the ending of the session.
With what motivation?	To attack my uncaring heart and non-understanding mind so I can feel and understand what she feels. She also wishes 'to bang her feelings into me' so that I feel deeply hurt.
To what part of the object?	My lap, my heart, my mind, my boundaries.
In what state is the object?	My lap is soiled, my heart is felt to be hard, my mind is non-comprehending.
With what consequences for the significant other?	My heart is shocked and hurt and I feel extremely worried about Susan. I am aware in her phone call that she leaves me 'shut out'.
And with what consequences for the young person?	Susan initially feels pleasure and relief from the feelings which have overwhelmed her thoughtful self. Subsequently she becomes extremely worried that I will abandon her and that she will lose a loving contact with a 'good me' inside herself. Her phone call suggests Susan also feels sorry that she has been very worrying and hurtful to me.

It is crucial to ask these questions when a young person makes a threat to kill herself.[1] Such a threat represents an attack on the good internal object, an attack on the significant others in the young person's life, *as well as* a possible physical attack on life.

Six of the observable phenomena in attacks on life

In answering the questions Rey posed regarding the suicidal young person's relationships, I have noted six rather distinct relationship patterns:

1   The young person in an active, deliberate way *chooses death.*
2   The young person *uses the threat* of suicide.
3   The young person *retreats from* feeling persecuted in her life.
4   The young person *is threatened by destructive voices* demanding and threatening the self with death, but she still feels slightly separate, rather than completely identified with these voices or thoughts.
5   The young person *is overwhelmed by feelings and by destructive voices* and passively submits to the death impulse. Often there is some sense that the body may be destroyed, but the soul might be entering a better place than life. In other words, a denial of death is present.
6   The young person *tries to recover the self* through hurting or killing the body. She is depersonalized at this point so that the self-destructive phantasies are not fully acknowledged as hurting the self; rather, they represent an attempt to gather together the disintegrated personality and locate the sane mind.

Now I shall describe some of these types of attacks by young people.

Further exploration of the six types of relationships underlying suicide or self-harm

1 The young person in an active, deliberate way chooses death

John Bowlby (1969) states that a child's suicide attempt is a response to the loss of a good relationship to an external attachment figure. The suicide attempt may also represent a lack of a good internal attachment figure, based either on the lack of opportunity to have sufficiently good experiences with a satisfactory attachment figure, or loss of the good internalized parents due to the incapacity to bear frustration and subsequent destructive attacks on the primary attachment figures who are subsequently internalized. Any one of these experiences may prompt the adolescents to feel there is nothing left. They perceive the external environment to be unresponsive and/or abusive in some way. Furthermore, prior to the suicide or self-harm they do not experience a sufficiently good enough internal object. This lack of a good *internal object* makes it impossible for them to sustain the perceived lack of love and sense of rejection by the *external attachment figures*.

I have given examples of this experience of 'nothing being left' in the story of Elisa described at the beginning of the chapter. As in the suicide of Elisa, the young girls in the films *The Story of Adele H.* and *The Lacemaker* are abandoned by their lovers. Lacking the security of previously established good internal objects, they depend almost completely on their lovers. When abandoned, the girls, now left without any good internal objects, are filled with only a sense of hate which creates even more of a sense of bad abandoning objects. Thus they experience 'nothing being left' and they both become suicidally depressed. Perhaps their experience is similar to that of an 11-year-old who was abandoned by her parents. She says:

> The beauty of love has not found me.
> Its hands have not gripped me so tight.
> For the darkness of hate is upon me.

Hate, rather than love and sadness for what is lost, creates a sense of profound despair of 'having nothing'.

In the hospital where I work, Amelia, aged 15, is suffering from anorexia nervosa, which masks a psychotic depression. During the Easter holidays Amelia takes an overdose of tablets, saying that all she wants is to die. She actively chooses to kill herself.

What part of her chooses this death?	The uncaring adult part of Amelia.
In what emotional state?	The infantile self suffers a sense of abandonment by her key worker, the nurse, her therapist and her case manager.
Does what?	Amelia identifies with the abandoning figures felt to be cruel in leaving her.
With what motivation?	To attack the cruel figures leaving her.
With what consequences for the inner object?	The inner object is further attacked and becomes a cruel uncaring figure.
With what consequences for herself?	Amelia attacks her self physically and emotionally.
With what consequences for external rescuing others?	Amelia forces the 'designated rescuing others', the multidisciplinary in-patient team, to acknowledge the effects of their joint abandonment during the holiday. In the future, they will be more careful in planning spaced-out holidays and working through the patient's feelings about their absences.

2 The young person uses the threat of death to save the self and avoid breakdown of defensive omnipotent thinking

When parents in an enmeshed relationship with their anorectic daughter attempt to provide firm boundaries and rules for the child, the parents sometimes seem to move from being helplessly impotent to unleashing their inhibited aggression and becoming harsh and physically punitive.

Ten-year-old anorectic Alice does not obey her parents' exhortations to eat and to stay at home. When Alice throws a tantrum instead of obeying, her parents lock her in her room. Alice has built up a 'hard shell' of defiance, through which she attempts to protect her vulnerable self.

On these occasions when her parents become hard and punitive in their countertransference to their difficult child, Alice makes half-gestures towards suicide: she puts a plastic bag over her head, puts a rope around her neck, cuts her wrist with a knife. On one occasion when she is feeling very perse-cuted by me in a psychotherapy session, Alice makes a mock attempt to strangle herself with the tied-up arms of her jumper. She asks her mother to pull the jumper arms to make the noose even stronger. In these activities, I feel Alice expresses at least three violent experiences.

First, Alice becomes 'like ice' to herself. She feels her parents, her family, and individual psychotherapists are hard, non-understanding figures, cold and insulated from tender feelings. Feeling a lack of love, Alice turns to a cold, unfeeling 'ice in her heart'. She becomes violent to herself; however, she succeeds in projecting her distress into us through an attacking, shocking event to pierce our hard, uncaring armour.

Second, Alice attempts to split off her 'crazy' state of mind, and project it into me. In one session, she makes a drawing of a very distorted face filled with voices dictating messages against us. Meanwhile she speaks in an intellectualized way, trying to remain aloof from her emotional experience. When Alice doesn't get her own way she icily says, 'I get so upset I just feel I'll have an epileptic fit, go mad, or suicide.' It seems I am to contain the horror and terror of this crazy state which Alice, through her emotional aloofness and drawing, attempts to split off and project into me.

Third, through her suicidal gestures and suicidal threats, Alice shows that she feels her omnipotent self, which she depends on for emotional safety, is being attacked and killed by external authoritarian controls. When there is an attack on this omnipotent self upon which she depends for security in lieu of the parents, the *omnipotent self* rears its cruel head, dictating to her, 'You don't need life, death is the answer. Everything will be nice then.'

In all three of these violent experiences, I, as the therapist, experience Alice's terror of death – death of her sane self, death of her *omnipotent self* protecting her, and death linked with her primitive infantile anxieties of dying. These infantile terrors of dying have never been sufficiently con-tained in Alice. Since infancy her terror of catastrophic death has been dealt with through *omnipotent* phantasies instead of being dealt with through depending on the parental capacities for mentalization (Allen and Fonagy 2006) and containment of her primitive anxieties.

I am suggesting that treatment interventions, including psychotherapy, in-patient treatment and feeding, which do not sufficiently contain the child's anxiety about losing the *omnipotent protective armour* to hold the self together might lead to destructive acting out. Herbert Rosenfeld (1987) has described various functions of the omnipotent self to which the infant may cling in moments of psychological adversity. Originally the *omnipotent self* might have offered the infant protection in relation to abusive relationships and pathological attachment relationships including emotionally uncontaining relationships. However, when overused, the *omnipotent self* becomes a *destructive omnipotent self* which binds the healthy personality to it. By binding the healthy personality to it, the *omnipotent self* thus attacks the strength, goodness and vitality present in the relationship with the therapist. It doesn't allow access to the understanding of the therapist. It also attacks the young person's thoughtful self trying to get in touch with intense feelings. Ultimately, the *omnipotent self attacks the link with life through self-harm and/or suicide.*

3 The young person retreats from persecutory figures

In a film of food-refusing children made by Professor David Skuse, one 18-month-old child is rejecting the gaze and refusing the food given by her mother. In the film, each food-refusing child has felt abandoned or mis-understood by the mother. Food refusal also implies that the child has never achieved a harmonious attunement (Stern 1985) while trying to find love, nurturing, pleasure and a mentalizing mind in the mother. Mental-izing (Allen and Fonagy 2006) is the part of mother required for healthy development of the baby. Mother's ability to mentalize for herself and the baby allows the baby to develop his/her own innate capacity for mental-ization. By *mentalizing* I am referring to a process by which the person concerned holds emotions alive internally and through thinking gives meaning to the desires, needs, feelings, beliefs and reasons underlying interpersonal interactions.

A baby needs mentalizing more than simple basic comforts to stay psychologically healthy. *Mother* is perceived to be bad if she is depriving baby of a satisfactory, properly attuned mentalizing relationship. As a result, anger towards mother is projected onto her and her spoon. Mother and spoon are filled with baby's projections of aggression, resulting in baby's experience of spoon and mother being perceived as bad and perse-cutory. Subsequently the baby refuses mother's rhythm of caregiving and also refuses to open her mouth for mother's food. I am not saying that the mother is bad, but rather suggesting that the mother and baby are not in a harmonious relationship. Alongside a misattuned relationship with the mother, the child simultaneously begins to develop a style of using *omnipotent control*, a kind of pseudo-autonomy (Bick 1968) in relationships. Omnipotent control is used in lieu of mentalization of feelings. Gradually the use of omnipotent control captures parts of the healthy self. Subsequently it becomes destructive and the base of obsessional control so prevalent in eating-disordered young people.

4   *The young person is threatened by destructive voices demanding and threatening the self with death, but she still feels slightly separate, rather than completely identified with these voices*

Some young people have a destructive omnipotent self in the form of hallucinatory voices attacking healthy, intimate attachments to important figures in a young person's life. Caterina, a 14-year-old anorectic girl, begins telling me about the voices which haunt her. There are three voices; they are women's voices. They feel like the three cruel witch figures in *Macbeth*. They tell her what to do and threaten her if she doesn't obey or does the wrong thing. For example, the witchlike voices forbid her to eat anything, at times. They criticize her if she does not follow her minute-by-minute programme for the day. When she leaves the therapy room, they criticize her for speaking to me. They are very forceful, cruel and demanding voices. She feels suicidal because she can't bear the loudness of the voices.

Although her situation is extremely severe, a young person who is depressed, self-harming and/or suicidal may have less assertive destructive thoughts to which she turns when in a crisis or disappointed and hurt in the process of trying to establish a meaningful, helpful relationship with someone important to her. The therapist's work is to help the young person find a way of becoming cognizant of the moments when these destructive, omnipotent thoughts occur. This is the first step in taking responsibility for them. Eventually the young person can then struggle, with the help of the psychotherapist, to fend off their luring appeals. If these destructive omnipotent thoughts are not held in mind and struggled with, they ultimately result in depression, some form of self-harm and/or suicidal thinking.

Caterina notes that the voices tell her not to eat. They drag her into depression and make her cry. They are luring her back into the in-patient paediatric ward, suggesting that being an in-patient is the solution to all her difficulties. They tell her it would be wonderful to starve, to go back to the in-patient ward, to have biscuits and tea, to watch a children's programme called *Playschool* and to talk in a baby voice. They don't want her to be like the adolescent girls in their tight jumpers and jeans.

The statements of a young person's hallucinatory voices are gradually transformed and become less virulent during the course of therapy. These phases of therapy with Caterina are presented in detail to show a rather dramatic version of fairly typical phases of psychological development, with the destructive voice attacking hope, in severely depressed young people. These are the five fairly distinct dialogues with destructive voices with which I help Caterina struggle during the course of her therapy:

A. As I am talking with her, Caterina hears the cruel voices dictating orders to her, threatening her with complete starvation if she disobeys them. They shout at her until she cries because of their loudness. She feels herself to be a helpless victim of their cruelty. They threaten her with death. They are so loud she wants to kill herself to get rid of them.

B. While in my presence Caterina says she feels imprisoned by the voices, but begins to feel slightly antagonistic towards them. She has the courage to tell me that she really doesn't like them much although she can't let them go. She cannot yet talk back to them.

C. Caterina begins to disobey the voices and talk to the students at school. She is beginning to have some hope that she can have a life with friends; however, the voices threaten her when she disobeys their messages, creating despair, and they put her on a concentration camp schedule, early to rise, starving, following the old rigid routine of minute-by-minute procedures for living her life.

D. The voices seem to get somewhat kinder and more infrequent/ less intrusive/less pervasive. They seem to have less power to grab Caterina's attention, because her psychotherapeutic work is becoming a base of security for her. The problem is that when she is disappointed with me she can easily turn to these destructive voices as an ally against me.

E. The voices disappear much of the time. They appear intermittently but only at times when Caterina is alone. However, Caterina becomes panicked when she experiences herself as alone and lonely without them. At times, before her own internal objects are more benevolent and functioning as a source of internal security, she substitutes the therapist's 'good voice' to keep her company.

Caterina's experience demonstrates how terrifying it is for a young person to let go of the death wish represented by the destructive voices prompting suicidal despair. For example, if the young person's attachment is to this destructive part, as was the case with Caterina, the patient fears that losing *the destructive part* will result in *falling to pieces*. Getting better can feel like being flung out of a secure prison. The prison is experienced as secure even though this imprisoned mental state involves massive confusion and clinging to death as a solution. Caterina says that when she is alone without the punitive voices she feels in such *an empty space*.

5 The young person is overwhelmed by feelings accompanied by destructive voices which lead to submitting to the death wish

Emaciated, eyes closed to every object or person, Tanika lay on the hospital bed. She refused food and drink and seemed not to notice urine trickling out of her. With her striking dark hair and smooth Modigliani oval face, she looked like a porcelain doll. She looked as though the cord which held her in life had been broken. There seemed to be no emotional point to her existence. She was motionless through the day and night. After some time she began to respond by greeting any nurse's touch or word like a mosquito creating a stinging irritation.

Tanika suffered a depressive stupor. As she was Japanese and her parents spoke very poor English, we were not even certain whether or not she spoke English. It was not clear during the times her eyes were open whether or not she responded to the meaning of English words. To the observer, Tanika felt almost dead. It is difficult to know what happens to a dying girl who barely opens her eyes let alone speaks. It seems to me that even the wish to die has wilted and become, instead of a wish, a drowning in death or sleep. In the psychiatric textbooks, psychotherapy would not be recommended for her – she does not speak, she doesn't show any motivation for psychotherapy, she may not even speak English. Although the psychotherapy sessions I offered to her were briefly successful and she began to 'awaken' and look at me, Tanika subsequently retreated into her former comatose state. I didn't know from her history how anorectic she might be, but now she was in a depressive stupor, or pervasive refusal syndrome as described by Lask *et al.* (1991).

This 15-year-old Japanese girl had felt abruptly torn away from all that she knew: her culture, her friends and her grandmother. She had nothing to which she could anchor herself in this new world in London. She had developed through holding onto external relationships without ever really internalizing the capacity to think about the feelings which she had. She used massive denial to cope with intense feeling.

With Tanika I used the method I often use with children who do not intend to speak to me or may not feel ready to speak to me about their experiences. I took the family dolls to each session and slowly began telling a story about the Tanika-doll losing familiar friends, her grandmother, her country, her language, her brother. I did this in very short stories, inter-spersed throughout our daily 15–30-minute psychotherapy sessions. I always told the story of the doll family so that Tanika would be free to reach towards any feelings if and when she felt ready. I waited until I saw a flicker in Tanika's eye or movement of her fingers and then I would talk more about the point to which her movement referred. For example, a tear dropped, on one occasion once and on another she showed a hint of interest before she fell asleep. Then Tanika 'awakened' as she became interested in the next story, but often she said nothing.

Later, as she was recovering, Tanika told me about some former thoughts. The air was spinning round the earth. All the houses had fallen over. She said she felt like breaking through a glass window, throwing herself out of the window. At this moment, when she was so ill, I felt she was being submerged by the death impulse, enclosed in a dead object. Yet part of her had been trying to come to life with me. From the start of her depression, even though Tanika didn't speak, she required my thoughtful presence to move psychologically and physically towards life.

With Sean, another psychotically depressed boy, the situation was slightly different. He slept. He was very drowsy, both because of medication and because he retreated defensively into sleep. I again used the family dolls. Holding the dolls in my hands, I asked Sean if he could wake the Sean doll up. He became surprisingly awake as he took the 'mother doll' and very cruelly awakened the 'Sean doll'.

I talked about the 'Sean doll' feeling there was a cruel mother making the child do just what she wanted. I added that this mother doll didn't care about what her child wanted. The boy doll just wanted to sleep and sleep and forget about everything. Once he felt understood, Sean awakened fully with a smile.

In psychotic depression the *self is submerged by the death wish*. If I could, I would begin treating the psychotically depressed young person the day she was hospitalized. I do not agree with the prevalent English psychiatric notion that psychological understanding of a young person needs to wait until the young person is a fairly healthy weight or is talking. In my experience, if we wait to provide a containing psychotherapy, we prolong the illness by depriving the young person of the understanding she needs to hold onto or rediscover the wish to live. If we keep demanding speech from a young person we drive her into a state of persecution. *First we must give our understanding*.

In order to come to life, to emerge from being smothered by death, both these young people, Tanika and Sean, required a mentalizing adult, an adult who could bring emotional nourishment to their wilting and wasting self. It seemed essential that someone should attempt to provide understanding of their wish to die, to drop off into sleep or death. They could not live without an emotional rope gently tugging them to emotional life. After the first time she heard the story of her life with the doll family, Tanika was willing to be fed. She would not feed herself initially, but she would swallow food put into her mouth.

6 The young person tries to recover the self through hurting or killing the body

There have been observed to be remarkable similarities between the psychic state in trauma and the mental state of some suicidal patients (Shneidman *et al.* 1976). Indeed, some suicide attempts and repeated self-mutilations may represent a means of interrupting the traumatic state (Simpson 1976) and trying to find the sane self.

Both holocaust victims and suicidal patients describe a 'break in the lifeline' and a 'loss of personality' (Venzkaff 1964). When psychic numbing sets in, the person becomes aware of a feeling of 'deadness and depersonalization'. The internalized external figures are felt to be numb and uncaring to the self, and the self is in identification with these hard, uncaring internalized figures. The self is then left psychologically surrendering to destructive craziness and a sense of psychological emptiness. It is this sense of being left with destroyed internal objects and the resulting state of emptiness which feels so lethal.

In this situation one often sees an overwhelming danger of loss of self. There is a blocking of, and dissociation from, one's experience. Self-observation, cognition and symbolic thought are reduced to a minimum. There is a sudden wish to make *a violent exit* from this state of helplessness and depersonalization through actively taking one's own life. Or there may be *a wish to obtain relief* from this depersonalized state through cutting the self, or injuring the self in some other way. It is as though destroying the self or hurting the self provide solutions to the tension of being depersonalized. The razor can represent comfort and reassurance, a perverted form of self-care. However, repeated cutting ultimately only compounds and deepens the link with the *tyrannical destructive omnipotent self* enslaving the young person (Gardner 2001).

Cutting may also help the young person feel 'real': Amelia, 15, said, 'I had to cut myself – I didn't know who I was before. I had to see the blood.' She needed to have a sense of *a live object that could experience pain and a live self*. In her book, *Nobody, Nowhere*, Donna Williams (1992) wrote of experiences and feelings similar to Amelia's:

> At home I would spend hours in front of the mirror staring at my own eyes, whispering my name over and over, sometimes trying to call myself back. At other times becoming frightened at losing my ability to feel myself. I was losing my ability to feel, my own world may have been a void, but losing my grip on it left me unmercifully in some sort of limbo without any feeling or comfort whatever. I began to hurt myself to feel something.
>
> (1992: 54)

Depersonalization followed by self-harm or suicide attempts can become addictive processes to a *tyrannical omnipotent self* which substitutes itself for thinking about conflictual, painful, terrifying emotional experiences in relation to important caregivers.

The suicidal child's or young person's motives in relation to potential rescuers

Alongside the wish to die is generally an unfulfilled wish to be rescued

The young person, through a suicide attempt, tries to restore the mother who has abandoned her. Who is the designated rescuer? Obviously it is the person (or people) to whom the young person is most attached. The *designated rescuer* is also the one upon whom the young person may originally have projected a great deal of aggression. The therapist – who is, in the transference, a representative of the original object – can be the specific *designated rescuer* as old or new traumas are experienced.

The designated rescuer is also the person whom the suicidal person unconsciously holds responsible for her own impending death

Imagine a young person who takes an overdose and then reproaches her mother, the object of her hostility, because she experiences her mother as being uncaring. The young person still hopes, paradoxically, that the mother will change from being the uncaring mother of her perception and rescue her. Through the mother rescuing her, the young person hopes that she will experience herself as being actually loved and lovable. Also, by rescuing, the mother shows that she actually cares about the child; she is not the 'bad' mother the girl tried to 'kill off'.

The request to the rescuer includes the need for the designated rescuer to be receptive to the threat of suicide

As Rey (1994) stated, it is important to assess the motivation of a suicidal person in relation to the *designated rescuer*. Although the young person attempting suicide has a perception of uncaring internalized external figures, usually the young person hopes that the *external designated rescuers* will transform themselves and be able to reach out to the victim, be empathic to the victim and be strong enough to recognize and acknowledge destructive impulses both in the suicidal young person and in the *designated rescuer*.

A dangerous designated rescuer

A *dangerous designated rescuer* is a person who implies consent or unconsciously colludes with the suicide. An actual attack on the body during the pre-suicidal state can be precipitated by an actual experience of rejection or a feeling of having been abandoned or dismissed. The suicidal patient experiences rejection in a particularly potent way when the rejection is experienced in relation to someone who is valued. When the rescuer refuses to respond as unconsciously or consciously desired by the pre-suicidal person in need, the suicide occurs.

Those people working with depressed and suicidal individuals are vulnerable to being provoked or subtly led into attitudes and reactions which are experienced by the individual as rejection or collusion with the suicidal phantasy. In other words, prior to the suicide, the pre-suicidal person could have externalized the bad, uncaring, punitive internalized object relationship, thus prompting uncaring in the countertransference relationship with the *designated rescuers*. Of course in some situations the *designated rescuers* may simply be uncaring. Therapists should beware of professional defences against feeling deeply – this may lead to becoming perceived as a *dangerous rescuer*. On the other hand, feelings need to be tempered by thought and self-scrutiny, so that therapists don't 'act out' in the countertransference.

Dreams as a means of assessment of the suicidal risk

In *The Dream in Clinical Practice*, Litman (1980), who worked on analysing in depth the dreams of suicidal young people, suggests that a young person rarely commits suicide as an impulsive, unpremeditated act. However, some clinicians believe that suicide acts are frequently impulsive. Usually, the idea of suicide is first considered as a potential avenue of escape from intolerable mental pain. Initially, the idea of suicide is alien and frightening. Other solutions to the mental pain are sought and attempted, but when these alternatives fail, the idea of suicide often becomes more attractive. Suicide can be rehearsed in both phantasy and reality.

In clinical practice, understanding the young person's dreams and drawings can provide clues to potential suicides before the young person is able to speak about suicidal feelings and act upon them. For this reason, I always look at young people's drawings and dreams during the initial assessment as well as throughout the course of therapy. There are some basic themes in drawings and dreams (Litman 1980) which can alert the therapist to potential suicidal activity. They include the following:

Themes of death and dead persons:
Example: 'I am burning to death in a house on fire.'

Themes of destruction of the self and other persons:
Example: 'I had a horrible dream. I am being fired at by soldiers. I die. Then they die. What is the best way of dying? Fast firing guns is better than dying slowly.'

Images of being trapped and struggling unsuccessfully:
Example: 'I am running on the beach being chased by a lion looking like a man with claws. I can't escape.'

Peaceful dreams of taking leave of the world and significant others:
Example: 'The woman is being crushed by a roller-coaster then walks
to a beautiful house in the country and has tea and a long conversation
with a friend.'

It is important to note that these dreams all involve death and can be used
to warn the clinician that the young person is at risk of killing herself to end
all feelings. Self-mutilation is different in that the self-mutilator seeks to feel
better (Favazza 1998: 262). Of course, it is essential for the therapist to look
at death as a metaphor expressing death of internalized figures and death of
part of the personality. In listening to dream reports, fine-tuned clinical
judgement relying on use of the countertransference is needed. The young
person's conscious motivations and intents linked with suicidal ideation in
the dream will help the clinician to differentiate between the young person's
aggression which can be symbolized and the young person's aggression that
will be acted out.

Conclusion

The question commonly asked is, 'Can we prevent suicide?' In many
situations we can certainly note that a young person is at risk of self-harm
or suicide by careful use of our countertransference and the child's transference to us when we are working in assessment or in in-patient or out-
patient psychotherapy. The denial of the reality of death, however, can
permeate professional and family systems. For this reason it is important to
see young people who have attempted suicide within twenty-four hours after
the act (Campbell and Hale 1991). Because denial of death can so easily
occur, it is also crucial to discuss clinical work with self-harming and
suicidal young people with one's colleagues (Laufer 1995). Parents, general
practitioners, teachers and other professionals should always be aware of
risk when the young person has an excess of hate, anger, or depression;
there is also risk when, during times of serious conflict, she does not seem to
'hold the hope' either of turning to a secure attachment figure or of
changing her inner situation.

The careful assessment of dreams and suicidal thoughts and the use of Dr
Rey's (1994) penetrating questions will assist in predicting risk and taking
appropriate safety measures to support the young person. There is, however,
the reality that the destructive inner object beckons a suicidal young person
during times of disappointment and particularly during separations from a
trusted significant other, including the psychotherapist, the treatment team
and the parents.

It is important to note that currently in the United Kingdom most adults
who commit suicide do so in the first seven days subsequent to discharge
from in-patient treatment. For these reasons it is particularly important to

plan absences of others significant to the young person (parents/therapists) with sufficient warning and to work through the emotional complications presented by scheduled separations from therapeutic treatment and, especially, by termination of in-patient treatment and psychotherapy.

During therapeutic work with a suicidal young person who feels trapped in despair, it is essential to patiently receive and bear the brunt of the young person's painful emotions. At the same time it is necessary to provide some realistic hope and an adequate, consistent and reliable therapeutic structure. The individual psychotherapist's task is to assist in the development of the young person's capacity for mentalization, rather than self-harm and suicide, as a way of coping with intense emotions of rage, hatred, disappointment, and psychic pain. Anne Sexton (1981), a poet who eventually took her own life, said, 'I have got to have something to hold onto.' 'The family therapist needs to be the catalyst for building meaningful connections between the young person and her parents, peers, teachers, key members of her social network and involved helping professionals from larger systems' (Selekman 2002).

Finally, I would like to cite Donna Williams (1992) who says in her book *Nobody Nowhere*:

> As much as one might want to, one cannot save another's spirit. One can only inspire the other's spirit to fight to save itself. Perhaps love can inspire but sometimes people must love you enough to declare war.
>
> (1992: 54)

Note

1 I have used the female pronoun in the chapter simply for ease of writing. At present 75 per cent of the young people I see with eating disorders and pervasive refusal are girls.

Bibliography

I have drawn on the following texts in my practice and when writing this chapter.

Allen, J. and Fonagy, P. (eds) (2006) *Handbook of Mentalization-Based Treatment*, Chichester: John Wiley and Sons.

Beck, A.T., Resnik, H.L.P., Lettieri, D. (eds) (1974) *The Prediction of Suicide*, Bowie, MD: Charles Press Publishers.

Bick, E. (1968) 'The experience of the skin in early object relations', *International Journal of Psychoanalysis* 49: 484–486.

Bourdouxhe, M. (1992) *La Femme de Gilles* (trans. Faith Evans), Champaign, IL: Lime Tree Publications.

Bowlby, J. (1969) *Attachment and Loss, Vol. 1*, New York: Basic Books.

Campbell, D. and Hale, R. (1991) 'Suicidal acts', in J. Holmes, (ed.) *Textbook of Psychotherapy in Psychiatric Practice*, London: Longman, 1991.

Dare, C., Szmukler, G. and Treasure, J. (1995) *Handbook of Eating Disorders: Theory, Treatment, and Research*, New York: Wiley.

Farmer, S. and Hirsch, S. (1979) *The Suicide Syndrome*, Cambridge: Cambridge University Press.

Favazza, A.R. (1998) *Bodies under Siege: Self-mutilation and Body Modification in Culture and Psychiatry*, Baltimore, MD: Johns Hopkins University Press.

Gardner, F. (2001) *Self Harm*, Hove and New York: Brunner/Routledge.

Green, A.H. (1978) 'Psychopathology of abused children', *Journal of the American Academy of Child Psychiatry* 17: 92–100.

Haim, A. (1970) *Adolescent Suicide*, London: Tavistock Publications.

Hale, R. and Campbell, D. (1991) 'Suicidal acts', in J. Holmes (ed.) *Textbook of Psychotherapy in Psychiatric Practice* (pp. 287-306), Edinburgh: Churchill Livingstone.

Krystal, H. (1978) 'Trauma and affects', *Psychoanalytic Study of the Child* 33: 81–116.

Lask, B., Britten, C., Kroll, L., Magagna, J. and Tranter, M. (1991) 'Pervasive refusal', *Archives of Diseases in Childhood* 66: 966–990.

Laufer, M. (1984) *The Suicidal Adolescent*, London: Karnac Books.

Leff, J. and Vaughan, C. (1983) *Expressed Emotion in Families*, New York: Guilford Press.

Litman, R.E. (1980) 'The dream in the suicidal situation', in J.M. Natterson (ed.) *The Dream in Clinical Practice*, New York: Jason Aronson.

Magagna, J. and Segal, B. (1990) 'L'attachment et les procès psychotiques chez une adolescent anorexique', in Groupe de recherché et d'application des concepts psychoanalytiques à la psychose (eds) *Psychoses et Création, L'Ecole Anglais*, Paris: Diffusion Navarin/Seuil.

Malan, D.H. (1997) *Anorexia, Murder and Suicide*, Oxford: Reed Educational and Professional Publishing Ltd.

Palazzoli, M.S. (1974) *Self-Starvation: From Individual to Family Therapy in the Treatment of Anorexia Nervosa*, New York: Jason Aronson.

Racker, H. (1968) *Transference and Countertransference*, London: Hogarth.

Rey, H. (1994) 'Anorexia nervosa', in J. Magagna (ed.) *Universals of Psychoanalysis*, London: Free Association Books.

Rosenfeld, H. (1987) *Impasse and Interpretation*, London: Routledge.

Segroi, S. (1982) *Handbook of Clinical Interventions in Child Sexual Abuse*, Lexington, ME: Lexington Books.

Selekman, M. (2002) *Working with Self-Harming Adolescents*, New York: W.W. Norton.

Sexton, A. (1981) *Complete Poems*, Boston: Houghton Mifflin.

Shneidman, E.S., Farberow, N.L. and Litman, R.E. (eds) (1976) *The Psychology of Suicide*, New York: Science House.

Simpson, M.A. (1976) 'Self-mutilation', *British Journal of Hospital Medicine* 16: 430–438.

Tucker, C. (1983) 'Proximate effects of sexual abuse in childhood', *American Journal of Psychiatry* 139: 1252–1256.

Turp, M. (2003) *Hidden Self-Harm*, London and Philadelphia: Jessica Kingsley.

Venzkaff, U. (1964) 'Mental disorders resulting from racial persecution outside concentration camps', *International Journal of Social Psychiatry* 10: 177–183.

Williams, D. (1992) *Nobody Nowhere*, Toronto: Doubleday.

Wolpert, L. (1999) *Malignant Sadness*, London: Faber and Faber.

Films

The Story of Adele H. (1975) Director: Francois Truffaut. Based on a novel, *The Story of Adele H.*, by Victor Hugo.

The Lacemaker (1977) Director: Claude Goretta.

Chapter 10

Suicidality and women: obsession and the use of the body

Benigna Gerisch

Suicide, sex and gender

In this chapter, I will focus on the links between femininity, obsession and suicidality, and to explore these connections I will present an illustrative case example from which I shall develop some theoretical considerations. However, in order to put these discussions in context I will begin by taking a brief look at the connection between suicide and gender from an historical research perspective.

There is probably no other symptom comparable with suicide that, if looked at closely, reveals the reflexive interplay of nature and culture, sex and gender, both inwardly and outwardly. This interplay refracts and condenses impressively through the social preconditions enabling, or, rather, not preventing, such an act, alongside the individual's inner world also formed by the outer reality (Kappert and Gerisch 2004).

This I want to explain in my following remarks. On the one hand the extent of the problem of suicide has always been linked with striking, even spectacular, empirical differences between the genders: the frequency of male suicide is over twice that of women, whereas *the frequency of female suicide attempts is twice that of men*. On the other hand, if one takes a look at scientific research into suicidality, which began its established life as suicidology when Durkheim published his sociological study *Le Suicide* (1897), the terminology used to describe the interplay between sex and gender, nature and culture seemed to become compressed in a special way. In several papers (Gerisch 1998, 2003a) I have illustrated, through the detailed and critical study of the epidemiological, medical-psychiatric and psychoanalytical explanatory models from the turn of the last century until the present, that suicidology research to date has barely progressed from the reproduction of gender role stereotypes expressed in the myth 'She died for love and he for glory' (Canetto 1992). Our understanding has thus not yet extended beyond the reflection of biological prejudice. The extent of female suicide problems has always been located where women differ most clearly from men: in the body (Gerisch 2000).

According to Canetto (1992), the scientific 'vicious circle' lies in the fact that the view of the scientist, and in addition that of traditional suicide theories, is to a large extent influenced by male and female gender role stereotypes. These summon up normative, conformist male and female suicide behaviour and also shape the preconceptions and research methods of the suicidologists. Canetto postulates that it is not only the individual suicide behaviour that is dependent on sex and culture; rather, it is the scientist who is shaped by culturally conditioned assumptions, bringing about the difference between the sexes, with the result 'that what the researchers "found" depended upon in which direction they looked and what they were prepared to recognize' (Canetto 1992: 13).

Reverting to a naturalistic argument seems oddly like coping with an insult scientifically, as the comparatively high suicide rate of married women – still true today – contradicts Durkheim's central theory that social integration of the individual and the protective function of marriage reduce suicide. There are only a limited number of papers dealing explicitly with female suicidal behaviour (Canetto 1992; Rachor 1995; Suter 1976), and that number is reduced even further if one tries to find psychoanalytical studies of female suicidal behaviour. Psychoanalytic clinicians writing about adolescence are an exception. Some of them have formulated very differentiated theories concerning suicidal behaviour among the young, incorporating some consideration of gender-specific differences – for instance, the extremely important work by Laufer and Laufer (1984, Laufer 1995), Berger (1989, 1999), Campbell (Chapter 2, this volume), Perelberg (1997, 1999) and Bell (Chapter 4, this volume).

Recourse to traditional research provides the following information which is not infrequently used in tautological arguments: women make more suicide attempts – especially with soft methods, because they are different from men, that is, they have a different biological-hormonal makeup. And, because their actions do not have death as a goal, and they cannot cope with object loss in any other way, these are hysterical-manipulative acts to put pressure on the object who is typically experienced as in some way abandoning.

'She died for love and he for glory'

Even in antiquity, a central theme in Greek tragedy was that of women killing themselves because of disappointed love (Neumer-Pfau 1987; Higonnet 1985). Our clinical experience, however, shows that conflicts with relevant reference persons, as well as separation or loss of significant love relationships, were given as the main reason for seeking help by both men and women equally. Freud (1917) wrote that suicidality and (object) loss seem to be inseparable constants which, and this must be emphasized, have a gender-specific correspondence meaning. Among men, reactions of anger and revenge are likely, comparable to *loss of property*, as described by Rousseau-Dujardin (1987). Their aim is to ward off the feelings of insult and loss. Attempts to assert their 'phallic right' can manifest as murderous impulses and threats. In contrast, and far more frequently than men, women react to separation with masochistic-depressive modes of self-devaluation and the classical form of aggression directed against the self. Re-actualization of a chronically damaged narcissistic self occurs. The suicidal act aims not only to kill the introjected object, but also to alter and secure it (Kind 1992).

There are other central differences between the genders. The greatest of these is found in how the body itself is experienced. In my argument, I presume that for women and men there is a different, also gender-typical, cathexis and instrumentation of the body. The central question resulting from this is: what does the body represent, and how and in what way does it become the place where intrapsychic conflicts are enacted? In brief, these differences may be formulated as follows. Men outwardly tend to externalize and manipulate objects. They are more likely to attempt to repair felt narcissistic damage by engaging in extreme and highly challenging sporting activities, and by turning away from animate objects in favour of inanimate ones, for instance, alcohol and lifestyle drugs up to and including forms of perversion.

In my clinical experience, it is more frequently women who, whether suicidal or not, react with a specific alloplastic conflict-solving strategy projected at the body. In this way, women attempt to control the objects within the body or on the surface of the body, the skin. Also, with a noticeably higher frequency, women feel their bodies, which they experience as inadequate and lacking, to be the cause of insults, rejection and loss of objects. The tormenting feeling of inadequacy, which is blamed on and bound to the body, can intensify to such an extent that it appears as delusional dysmorphobia, especially during adolescence. Coping attempts include a wide variety of cosmetic and operative re-shaping measures, psychosomatic responses, and self-destructive behaviour of any type, including *addictive* types of relationships.

Casuistry: 'I can see no further than you'[1]

I would now like to present a few excerpts from the psychoanalytical treatment of Ms A, a case that I have already discussed elsewhere (Gerisch 2005), in order to illustrate these ideas.

Ms A initially made contact by email. At that time she was in the USA on a research programme. She had become involved some months earlier with an older, married colleague who, out of the blue, had ended the affair. This was all reported briefly in her email, which she ended by asking whether I could help her. I advised her to come to the Centre for Therapy and Studies of Suicidal Behaviour where I work, and a week later she did so. I was immediately fascinated by her: she was tall, slim and very curvaceous, with a wild mass of black curls and green eyes.

'I cannot live without that man; it was the greatest and most passionate relationship I ever experienced. I was everything with him: intellectual, emotional and sexual. Through him I finally knew who I really was. It was like coming home from a long journey. I want him back, no matter how', she burst forth. She described how the relationship had been marked by waves of sadomasochistic attempts and rejections right from the start, which had 'almost driven her mad'. He had blazed a trail towards her and into her, and then withdrawn, only to again renew his involvement with her. The interim periods were filled with unbearable waiting: for a sign, his telephone calls, his appearances. Her mobile phone was her life-support machine: if it sounded, it aroused hopes that it was him, providing assurance that she was still alive; if there was no call, she immediately fell into something 'raw, black' which could not be filled with anything else. The longer she had to wait, the more desperate, empty and paralysed she became, interrupted by rare bouts of sobbing, but in the grip of a deathly-living state.

Her sexuality had been marked by intense passion, such as she had never experienced before, and he too had been obsessed with her and her body. Only in these embraces was she totally sure of his love and of herself. It was unimaginable that anything could have separated them. Outer reality and the horrendous periods of waiting disappeared on this island of joy. It was only in this 'never-never-land' with him that she felt he saw her truly, authentically and totally.

But then, overnight, X suddenly left her, although they had just planned a research trip to the west coast together. In fact, he had not really separated from her, he had just suddenly disappeared. He simply no longer reacted: not to her calls, her text messages or emails. She fell into an unbearable frenzy and, initially believing there had been an accident, death or some other catastrophe, she had checked all the hospitals and emergency wards until she gradually realized that he was indeed alive, but not for her.

In this state of hopeless impotence and unbearable vulnerability she had made her first suicide attempt with tablets. She wanted to end this tortuous condition that she found herself in because of the lack of 'overall body reaction', but even more than that, to force his return by risking her life. She could no longer eat, nor sleep; work was only possible with the greatest effort, and she no longer wanted to, nor *could* she, go on living. Finally, after further weeks of senseless waiting in agonizing despair, she took sleeping pills in an attempt to commit suicide for the second time, without a flicker of hate, anger or indignation. Six months later we arranged a four-times-a-week analysis.

Biographical aspects

There were no early or later actual traumatic object losses in Ms A's bio-graphy. She was the youngest in a 'normal', complete family with a mother, father and two siblings. Experiences of deficits were hidden, barely visible and written in her body. We can imagine a mother who did not necessarily wish to have another child, who was quite unable to cope at the time of her daughter's birth and was herself tortured by experiences of loss. She seemed to have little inner space for this infant, who, also in competition with the father, had clinging attacks, whose cries insulted her narcissistically, and for whom breast-feeding was torture until she finally gave up in exhaustion. Therefore, an early, always present, sad and traumatic shadow clouded her body-to-body existence with her mother, which was marked by the paradox of forced physical proximity together with inaccessibility. For her mother she was an infant, who was secretly accused of ruining her female attractions and of hindering her career prospects. In addition, we imagine a mother who was envied for everything she was able to give her children – milk, security, a comfortable home – while she herself felt totally unsatisfied and unloved.

Ms A was disappointed and frustrated by her later attempts as the 'bright, intelligent sunshine of the family' to turn to her father, a man who was totally absorbed in his work, unemotional, professionally successful and frequently absent. He occasionally stroked her hair absent-mindedly, but more often the children were the recipients of achievement expectations voiced in a demanding-threatening manner, which they tried desperately to fulfil.

Addiction and sexualization

In her intrapsychic matrix, shaped by the shadow of physical proximity and absence, Ms A remained fixated on an inaccessible, highly idealized love-object who became the saviour in person but who, however, soon recoiled, shocked at her absoluteness, her insatiable oral greed, her unconditional and passionate intensity. I was also impressed by how spontaneously she unfolded her eroticism and sexualization, both of her entire body-ego as well as of significant object relationships – dynamics that also became apparent in the relationship with me. It seemed that as soon as she felt more connected, reference to the (inaccessible) love-object caused her to regress immediately to her earliest fantasies of fusion that had always been frus-trated. She now re-experienced this as an unbearable deprivation. She sought to ward off these feelings with an auto-erotic stimulation of the body, resulting from a reactive precocious body-ego and premature sexual-ization, with the aim of being able to feel alive and integrated (Khan 1979; Grubrich-Simitis 1984).

Physicality, eroticism and sexualization also became metaphors for the essential binding and securing of an object. A perpetual state of being in love provided the existential confirmation and reinforcement of the self. And the constant need for a state of being in-love, and the 'dumbfounded body', guaranteed the existential confirmation and reinforcement of the self. Without doubt, Ms A needed this fearful lust which she repeatedly reproduced because it was irrevocably linked with the 'absent' tortuous presence of the primary object, while her joyous moments of intense physicality were for her analogous with a 'second birth' experience.

Her desire for the attentive object could only be satisfied by concrete sexual union. She gave a vivid description of her absolute need for passionate physical embraces which encompassed all of the senses and corresponded with an experience of time that I would describe, along with De Lillo (2003), as 'body-time'. Only in these moments of experienced body-time did she feel alive, authentic, anchored within herself and the world.

Gutwinski-Jeggle also emphasizes the deformation of time–space continuum in these conditions when she writes that addiction and sexualization are attempts to

> recover the symbiotic condition of concrete continuity and thereby apparent timelessness, attempts which are subconsciously laden with death, the exact thing that we consciously wish to escape from because death is the most extreme and powerful moment that transports us from discontinuity to continuity.
>
> (2003: 17)

At the beginning of the analysis, Ms A was only able to keep going thanks to her unbroken work mania. When spaces of unfilled time occurred, occasionally at the weekend for instance, she tried to cope with the unbearable loneliness through half-hearted attempts at relationships from which she duly emerged disappointed and frustrated because she never found what she had lost with X. '*I wanted another man so that he could chase him from me but at the same time I could not bear another person touching me.*' Therefore, she often had no choice but to turn from the animate to an inanimate object to calm herself. She smoked, drank a lot of alcohol and spoke to women friends on the telephone for hours, staring at her mobile phone all the while. But these attempts proved fruitless: her lover was, in fact had to be, constantly present – in her thoughts, feelings, in her dreams, when awaking, falling asleep, always.

She clung to this imaginary presence and in this way was able, albeit tortuously, to experience herself fulfilled and not separated. Her shock if she 'forgot' him for a second, which occasionally happened, was such that she feared she had begun to abandon him, to be unfaithful; she felt it was a form of treachery, but even stronger was her loss of self which led to renewed and increased real or imagined attachment. Sometimes, in a state of inebriation, like a *drunk dialler*, she left long and desperate cascading messages on her lover's answerphone. The constantly available addictive drugs (especially alcohol and cigarettes), which projected no desires or needs of their own, nor insults or disappointments, for a while satisfied her insatiable hunger for togetherness and endless continuity (Voigtel 2001). But even they in time seemed to her to be a disturbing third element. Or, the effect of alcohol enveloped her in a wave of insulating comfort which carried her back to her generously spun cocoon of love.

Ms A made manic and persistent use of modern technology (especially mobile phone and email) which in contrast to conventional addictive substances has an in-built and obvious object-communication function. Furthermore, this indicated a particular form of fantasies of fusion which encouraged a specific manipulation of time, thus fuelling the fantasies. Her desperate use of the cold object almost brought it to life; she was constantly tapping text messages into her mobile as if it were a body substitute, in the insatiable hope of being rescued by an answer. However, most attempts at imagining that the object was always available in this way proved deceptive, and when no answer was forthcoming she immediately sank back into the state she had just tried to escape from.

Mourning, melancholy, body, gender and suicidality

Ms A's use of the body in her suicidal acting out fits with the clinical observation I have made above, namely, that for women suicidality is a conflict-solving strategy projected at the body. This raises the obvious question as to whether there are aspects of female development that make it incomparably difficult for women to be able to separate and mourn, which can contribute to self-destructive behaviour when their hate, anger and disappointment are directed towards themselves, particularly towards their bodies.

One significant difference between male and female development is that female psychosexual development is more strongly marked by radical morphological changes to the subjective body image and specific physical experiences that are intimately connected with the mother. In short, we can say that the process of separation and individuation for girls is aggravated by gender specifics. This has led me to generate two hypotheses.

My first hypothesis argues that a central and highly conflictive dilemma runs through female development like a fragile, potential point of fixation and is continued in the ubiquitous separation and detachment aggression experienced in a highly ambivalent way by girls. It is directed at an object that is both the primary love-object, as well as the identificatory object in terms of the essential development of female identity. The specifically close primary bond that a girl has with her mother – the phenomenon of flowing into each other and the curious permeability of both bodies – is a gender-bound and, effectively, insoluble 'adhesive' identification. The tendency to physical 'symbolic equation' (Segal 1957) – in the sense of the mother–self–body – fosters a same-gender mother–daughter dyad in general. This is particularly so when a third person (typically the father) is unavailable or unusable as a pre-oedipal and oedipal triangulation object (Gerisch 2003b).

Continuous constriction, or even removal, of the threatened inter-subjective and intermediary space hampers the developmental need to transform experiences of separation and of being separate. It also impinges on the capacity to transform archaic aggression and destructiveness and so allow symbolization to replace enactment through the body (Fonagy and Target 1996, 1999).

My second hypothesis argues that the shared gender between mother and daughter increases the risk that the body with its perceptive functions, particularly in the pre-verbal developmental phase, acts as the central structure-providing apparatus of unconscious and inter-subjective processes in the mother–daughter dyad. If the ability to symbolize and represent experience has been insufficiently developed, dissociative phenomena can occur at times of crisis, especially when the woman is faced with loss. The body can then repeatedly become the place of enactment for complex residues of mostly unconscious primary, bodily sensory information. I have in mind here conflicting, as well as traumatic, shards of experience that have become engraved in the female body during the difficult separation and individuation processes.

Suicidality and the body

Before concluding, I would like to return to Ms A and her use of the body in suicidal experiences. My interest here has nothing to do with doubting the lethal intention of her suicidal behaviour, but rather emphasizing the body-related complexity of her suicidal acting out.

Ms A's love-object, condensed as 'I cannot live without you', in the sense of a spoken performance, indicates the same failed detachment and separation drama that led to this specific projective and concrete use of the body. Her body becomes a stage on which a reactualized highly charged and dramatic play for two or more characters is performed. The less X reacted, the more he distanced himself, the more she experienced her unquestionably beautiful body as something monstrous. She now discovered all of the shortcomings in her body that must have driven X away. The body that once was passionately and sensually enflamed through his desire was changed in her fantasy to a misshapen abnormality which she could not even bear to approach in masturbation, because this 'fat monster' did not deserve it.

Then, also because of the forced realization of X's absence, she was regularly overwhelmed by spasms of desperate weeping. Ms A's constantly excited body was harassed by attacks that predominated in her suicidal fantasies, a body that ought to be eradicated because it constantly desired X's presence, and because nothing was able to calm or soothe it. This both excited and excitable body was a representation of the unbearable presence and absence of the lost lover, who was inseparably fused with a highly ambivalently burdened maternal introjection. The meaning of this is also that the (imagined) death is not the most extreme resolution. Rather, to the extent that the desiring-insatiable body is an unsettling threat to psychic harmony, experienced as a loss of the self, there is this attempt to eradicate the imagined fantasy, the upset body – in the sense of representing that part of the self that is dependent, needy and clinging – and so counteract the feared disintegration.

'In the two opposite situations', Freud (1917: 252) wrote, 'of extreme love and of suicide, the ego is overwhelmed by the object, although in quite different ways.' Based on the thought of being overwhelmed by an object it is not surprising that the part-for-all solution also surfaced here, and that Ms A's suicidal fantasies sometimes seemed like medieval exorcist rituals: she wanted to cast out X from within her at all cost, to free herself from the demon that was far more than just a shadow on her ego, that prevented her continued existence. The more unbearable this condition became, the more brutal and bloody were her suicidal fantasies. They were, however, not connected with an idea of final death, but rather of release: 'death is only terrible for the body, the soul thinks not of it', wrote the poet Marina Zwetajewa (1989: 164f) shortly before her suicide.

In summary, I am suggesting that both core complex (Glasser 1979) anxieties generated by the wish to fuse with the object, and oscillation between the paranoid-schizoid and depressive positions (Klein 1957), are enhanced in female development in a particular and gender-specific manner. This can result in a concrete need to physically cling to a love-object. This view broadens the scope for understanding the following key question: *why does the inability to separate and the resulting use of the body as an object and symbol seem to be a specific female way of solving and coping with conflict?* (Hirsch 1989, 2003).

Having posed these questions, it is now important to follow up these ideas through undertaking further differentiated interdisciplinary examination of these aspects under the working title, 'Body–pathology–gender – interdisciplinary research into gender-typical body practices'.

Note

1 Quotation from the film *Damage*, directed by Louis Malle (1992), with Jeremy Irons and Juliette Binoche.

References

Berger, M. (1989) 'Zur Bedeutung des "Anna-selbdritt" – Motivs für die Beziehung der Frau zum eigenen Körper und zu ihrem Kind', in M. Hirsch (ed.) *Der eigene Körper als Objekt* (pp. 241–277), Berlin: Springer.

Berger, M. (1999) 'Zur Suizidalität in der Adoleszenz', in G. Fiedler and R. Lindner (eds) *So hab ich doch was in mir, das Gefahr bringt* (pp. 29–65), Perspektiven suizidalen Erlebens, Bd. 1, Göttingen: Vandenhoeck & Ruprecht.

Canetto, S.S. (1992) 'She died for love and he for glory: gender myths of suicidal behavior', *Omega* 26: 1–17.

De Lillo, D. (2003) *Körperzeit*, München: Goldmann.

Durkheim, E. (1897) *Der Selbstmord*, Frankfurt: Suhrkamp.

Fonagy, P. and Target, M. (1996) 'Den gewalttätigen Patienten verstehen: Der Einsatz des Körpers und die Rolle des Vaters', in M. Berger and J. Wiesse (eds) *Geschlecht und Gewalt* (pp. 55–90), Göttingen: Vandenhoeck & Ruprecht.

Fonagy, P. and Target, M. (1999) 'Towards understanding violence: the use of the body and the role of the father', in R.J. Perelberg (ed.) *Psychoanalytic Understanding of Violence and Suicide* (pp. 53–72), London: The New Library of Psychoanalysis.

Freud, S. (1917) 'Mourning and melancholia', in J. Strachey (ed.) *The Standard Edition of the Works of Sigmund Freud, XIV* (pp. 237–258), London: Hogarth.

Gerisch, B. (1998) *Suizidalität bei Frauen. Mythos und Realität – Eine kritische Analyse*, Tübingen: Edition Diskord.

Gerisch, B. (2000) '"Auf den Leib geschrieben": Der weibliche Körper als Projektionsfläche männlicher Phantasien zum Suizidverhalten von Frauen', in P. Götze and M. Richter (eds) *'Aber mein Inneres überläßt mir selbst.' Verstehen von suizidalem Erleben und Verhalten. Hamburger Beiträge zur Psychotherapie der Suizidalität* (pp. 78–115), Bd. 2. Göttingen: Vandenhoeck & Ruprecht.

Gerisch, B. (2003a) *Die suizidale Frau. Psychoanalytische Hypothesen zur Genese*, Göttingen: Vandenhoech & Ruprecht.

Gerisch, B. (2003b) 'Suizidalität als Ausdruck einer Symbolisierungsstörung', in H. Lahme-Gronostaj (ed.) *Symbolisierung und ihre Störungen. Tagungsband der Herbsttagung der Deutschen Psychoanalytischen Vereinigung* (pp. 313–326), Bad Homburg: Geber & Reusch.

Gerisch, B. (2005) '"Nicht dich habe ich verloren, sondern die Welt" Liedenschaft und Obsession bei suizidalen Frauen', *Psyche – Zeitschrift für Psychoanalyse und ihre Anwendungen* 59: 918–943.

Glasser, M. (1979) 'Some aspects of the role of aggression in the perversions', in I. Rosen (ed.) *The Pathology and Treatment of Sexual Deviations*, Oxford: Oxford University Press.

Grubrich-Simitis, I. (1984) 'Vom Konkretismus zur Metaphorik', *Psyche* 38: 1–28.

Gutwinski-Jeggle, J. (1992) '"Trauma und Zeiterleben". Theoretische Überlegungen', *Jahrbuch der Psychoanalyse* 29: 167–214.

Gutwinski-Jeggle, J. (2003) 'Wenn Zeiträume nicht zu Spiel- und Denkräumen werden. Die Depression als "Zeitkrankheit"', manuscript.

Higonnet, M. (1985) 'Suicide: representations of the feminine in the nineteenth century', *Poetics Today* 6: 104–115.

Hirsch, M. (1989) 'Der eigene Körper als Objekt', in M. Hirsch (ed.) *Der eigene Körper als Objekt. Zur Psychodynamik selbstdestruktiven Körperagierens* (pp. 1–9), Berlin, Heidelberg and New York: Springer.

Hirsch, M. (2003) *Der eigene Körper als Symbol. Der Körper in der Psychoanalyse von heute*, Giessen: Psychosozial Verlag.

Kappert, I. and Gerisch, B. (2004) 'Einleitung', in I. Kappert, B. Gerisch and G. Fiedler (eds) *Ein Denken, das zum Sterben führt: Selbsttötungen: Tabu und Brüche* (pp. 11–17), Göttingen: Vandenhoeck & Ruprecht.

Khan, M.M.R. (1979) *Entfremdung bei Perversionen*, Frankfurt: Suhrkamp.

Kind, J. (1992) *Suizidal. Die Psychoökonomie eine Suche*, Göttingen: Vandenhoeck & Ruprecht.

Klein, M. (1957) 'Envy and gratitude', in M. Klein (ed.) *Envy and Gratitude and Other Works 1946–63*, London: Hogarth Press, 1975.

Laufer, M. (ed.) (1995) *The Suicidal Adolescent*, London: Karnac.

Laufer, M. and Laufer, M.E. (1984) *Adolescence and Developmental Breakdown. A Psychoanalytic View*, New Haven: Yale University Press.

Neumer-Pfau, W. (1987) 'Töten, Trauern, Sterben. Weiblichkeitsbilder in der antiken griechischen Kultur', in R. Berger and I. Stephan (eds) *Weiblichkeit und Tod in der Literatur* (pp. 11–34), Köln: Böhlau-Verlag.

Perelberg, R.J. (1997) '"To be – or not to be – here": a woman's denial of time and memory', in J. Raphael-Leff and R.J. Perelberg (eds) *Female Experience. Three Generations of British Women Psychoanalysts on Work with Women* (pp. 60–76), London and New York: Routledge.

Perelberg, R.J. (ed.) (1999) *Psychoanalytic Understanding of Violence and Suicide*, London: New Library of Psychoanalysis.

Rachor, C. (1995) *Selbstmordversuche von Frauen. Ursachen und soziale Bedeutung*, Frankfurt and New York: Campus.

Rousseau-Dujardin, J. (1987) 'Außer sich', in U. Konnertz (ed.) *Die übertragene Mutter. Psychoanalytische Beiträge* (pp. 53–76), Tübingen: Edition Diskord, 1987.

Segal, H. (1957) 'Notes on symbol formation', *International Journal of Psychoanalysis* 38: 391–397.

Suter, B. (1976) 'Suicide and women', in B. Wolmann and H. Krauss (eds) *Between Survival and Suicide* (pp. 129–161), New York: Gardener Press.

Voigtel, R. (2001) 'Sucht als passiver Selbst-Mord', in B. Gerisch and and I. Gans (eds) *Ich kehre in mich selbst zurück und finde eine Welt. Autodestruktivität und chronische Suizidalität* (pp. 101–118), Göttingen: Vandenhoeck & Ruprecht.

Zwetajewa, M. (1989) *Ein gefangener Geist. Essays*, Frankfurt: Suhrkamp.

Chapter 11

Violence to body and mind: infanticide as suicide[1]

Carine Minne

Working in high security settings

In this chapter I will present the case of a suicidal young woman who killed her baby and was treated in a high security hospital over many years. Patients seen in this type of setting have been violent physically to others, and to themselves, and have a phenomenal capacity to be violent to their own and others' minds. They are considered to be high homicide and/or suicide risks, First, I will provide some background details about working psychoanalytically in secure hospital settings with very ill detained patients. Second, I will offer my attempts to work psychoanalytically with a very disturbed young woman.

It is interesting that forensic psychiatry settings may have embraced a psychoanalytic approach more than any other branch of psychiatry. An increasing appreciation has arisen of the impact on staff of working with highly disturbed and disturbing patients. Institutions that house high numbers of such patients are prone to becoming chronically 'sick' places that require chronic 'treatment' themselves. This is reflected in many ways: high rates of sickness in staff, high turnover of staff, difficulties in recruiting, and all manner of staff/patient, patient/patient and manager/staff enactments of maladaptive scenarios on wards, in corridors and at clinical and administrative meetings. If we consider that many of these patients, suffering from severe personality disorders and/or psychotic illnesses, manifest their suffering through violent enactments, then it becomes clearer what the staff, particularly nurses, are exposed to on a daily basis, and how the patients' disorders inevitably 'spread' to the multi-disciplinary team and throughout the organisation. A psychoanalytic perspective is essential in secure hospitals and units, where the ingredients for institutional ill health are potent and certain mental disorders are, basically, 'contagious'. Psycho-analytic input can provide a degree of immunity to this contagiousness through treatment, supervision, consultation and training by bringing to attention the unconscious aspects.

Working psychoanalytically in such settings necessarily affects how psychotherapists work, and adaptations have to be made. It is a frequent misperception that people in high secure hospital conditions are referred to as prisoners. This is the familiar pull towards a custodial and punitive focus and away from the idea of treatment, often misconstrued by the general public as condoning the awful offences that have been committed. What is required is the right balance for each individual case between, on the one hand, the position of treatment, provided by the mental health professionals, and, on the other hand, loss of freedom within a secure setting, provided by the criminal justice system. Both these positions are essential for the proper care of any patient and the safety of the public. The difficulties in achieving this balance contribute to one of the particular dynamics when working under conditions of high security where providing treatment and security can clash.

For example, all of us working in high security carry an enormous bunch of keys tied to our waists. Simply in terms of adding to the 'them' versus 'us' scenario, or 'envious' versus 'enviable', the impact of this cannot be ignored. Here, straight away, a most concrete split is set up where those present, patients and professionals, are dressed in their respective costumes, ready to enact the familiar sadomasochistic script often apparent in places where so-called 'bad' people are housed. Unless one remains constantly aware of this, one can fall for the magnetic pull of such transference and countertransference phenomena and enact again and again the patients' internal worlds, which they can and do succeed in getting the professionals to sculpt with them.

Another difference compared with 'general' psychotherapy is that within secure in-patient settings we go to see our patients rather than assuming they are able to come and see us. Even if we had enough escort staff and rooms available, this expectation would actually place too much responsibility on many of our patients. Often, a long time passes before a patient we see considers him or herself to be a patient.

Another consequence of working in secure settings is that the balance between confidentiality to our patients and the need to communicate information to the clinical team caring for them needs to be constantly reviewed. Regular discussions with colleagues are necessary, for example, in terms of anticipating and managing risk situations or addressing team splits that arise. In that sense, this work resembles child psychoanalytic treatments where some discussion with 'parental' figures is necessary. Indeed, many of the patients, due to the unbelievably traumatic events they were exposed to, have interrupted developmental aspects, and in their way of functioning can appear at times like babies or toddlers, but in adult bodies.

The physical security of such treatment centres can appear sinister and inhibiting, but in fact it provides a necessary, firm, external boundary for these patients, who have often had no containment before, and this can offer them an opportunity to engage with treatment. Some of us are involved in providing long-term continuity of psychoanalytic treatment across decreasing levels of security until the patient is back in the community, if this is feasible and ongoing psychotherapy treatment is recommended. This can provide the patients with the chance to continue to work through the various transferential situations that arise during several years of treatment. Continuity is all the more important at the times of transition between levels of security, when anxieties are at their highest, regressed states of mind are common and patients are at higher risk of acting out, in particular of suicidality. At these times, patients have to manage losing all previous fragile new attachments as well as a familiar environment as they move geographically to another unit and to a completely new team, often repeating for them earlier experiences of a multitude of carers and homes. It can also be terribly shaming for patients to indicate anxiety about leaving and, even worse, for their trial leave from high security to fail.

Treatment issues

In the context of the preceding considerations regarding high secure forensic settings, I will address treatment issues. A major task of this kind of treatment is to enable an awareness of the mind and its functions to become available to the owner of that mind, the person known to us as the patient. This refers to an awareness of who they, the patients, are, what they have done and the impact of this on their minds and on the minds of others. Regardless of their diagnoses, mentally disordered people who have carried out serious violent offences often have a limited capacity for awareness of themselves as people and of the seriousness of what they have done. This absence or avoidance, contributed to by mental structural damage causing defective self and object perception, is also provided by an arsenal of defences, psychotic and non-psychotic. This appears to be necessary for the patient's psychic survival. Indeed, addressing their defences can cause massive anxieties about 'cracking up' and can lead to psychotic breakdown and, perhaps, to suicidality or even suicide. Yet, to allow these defences to remain untouched can leave essential ingredients intact for being violent again. The therapist's task is a delicate and complicated one: first, helping to cultivate awareness in the person's mind without seeming to commit a violent assault on that mind; second, to clinically judge that such awareness is developing, and, third, to continually gauge in what way that person is using his/her new awareness. These are the shifts that we look for in the monitoring of our work. It is also these very shifts, or prognostically positive internal world changes, that can provoke particular negative therapeutic responses, which I will return to. In some cases, the careful and limited use of anti-psychotic medication can helpfully sedate the more intense psychotic anxieties and make ongoing psychoanalytic treatment possible.

Traumatisation

I would now like to refer to how these patients are traumatised threefold because this is so relevant to working psychotherapeutically with them. First, these patients are traumatised by their appalling background histories, second by the offences they committed, and third, by their gradual discovery, during treatment, that they have a mental disorder. Dr Leslie Sohn and I believe that these traumas can lead, in the course of treatment, to the development and manifestation of a post-traumatic stress *type of* disorder, which in our view should be seen as a positive prognostic indicator. In other words, as awareness and understanding develop, patients begin to suffer the consequences of this. Despite the distress which 'getting better' causes, some of these patients can make tentative shifts towards a healthier internal world. These are the shifts that can provoke a particular negative therapeutic reaction, the aim of which is to try to return the patient's mind to its previous disturbed but familiar state – because a return to oblivion is more desirable than managing the burden of awareness.

A case example

I will now illustrate these treatment dynamics by presenting the case of a young woman whose prognosis is very poor and who could not maintain those positive shifts. I have found her a more difficult patient than many of the very violent young men I also see. I have often dreaded going to her sessions and welcomed being 'sacked' by her – which I was frequently. The clinical team and I have had to work hard together to manage the patient's regular provocations to re-enact her trauma in which she, or we, are like her mother. This trauma was reproduced in her offence, the killing of her baby, and in her chronic suicidality, a state in which she is identified with the mother who 'killed' her.[2]

Ms B is a 28-year-old woman who killed her 9-week-old daughter and, later, seriously wounded a professional. She comes from a large and highly dysfunctional family where trans-generational incestuous relationships have resulted in no one being sure of who is who in the extended family. Violence between different sets of parents, mother with father and mother with stepfathers, was the norm. There was no experience of consistent mothering. This young woman developed a tic disorder around puberty which was eventually treated with medication. She met a young man when she was 18 years old and made a conscious decision that he was the man for whom she would leave home, and whom she would marry, and have children with. Prior to this, she had no serious boyfriends and one could speculate to what extent Ms B was attempting to undo some of the chaos she had been raised in by having a 'white wedding'. Following their marriage, she and her husband lived together with his alcoholic mother.

Ms B was soon delighted to discover she was pregnant. However, the stress of this event on an ill-equipped young couple led to the breakdown of their marriage late in her pregnancy, at which point she returned home to live with her own mother. Within days of delivering a healthy baby girl, her mother asked her to leave and go to live elsewhere because she could not stand the crying baby. This behaviour was quite typical of the mother who later, for example, frequently told Ms B that she would be better off committing suicide than causing all this trouble. Ms B and her newborn baby subsequently moved in with a family friend.

Ms B developed concerns about her baby soon after she was born. She was convinced that the baby was sick and called her health visitor and general practitioner on a regular basis, but she could never accept reassurance. On one occasion, she stated that the baby had started to manifest facial tics which were similar to her own and of such severity that the baby's breathing was affected. The mother and baby were admitted to hospital for the baby to be monitored. Initially, the baby was found to be well, but after two days, the baby's condition began to deteriorate. No cause for this deterioration could be found. The baby became critically ill and needed to be looked after in intensive care but then died.

Ms B, bereft, went home with her mother. Soon after the baby's death and post-mortem, laboratory reports showed toxic levels of Ms B's medication in the baby's blood, which were considered to have caused the death from poisoning. Ms B was arrested and charged with murdering her baby. In view of her fragile mental state, her remand period was spent in psychiatric hospital. She denied any wrongdoing for over a year, until the end of the trial, when she admitted having given the baby her medication, not to kill the baby but out of concern that the doctors and nurses were not looking after the baby properly. Retrospectively, it could be suggested that she had projected her own bad experience of being mothered twice over, once into her own baby, by identifying with her mother, and then again by projective identification with the nurses and doctors, who became the bad parents for not noticing what was going on within the sick baby, herself, as well as the actual sick baby.

Ms B was finally convicted of infanticide and admitted under a hospital order from the court to a locked ward. Attempts were made gradually to give her increasing responsibility for herself with, eventually, short unescorted leave periods to go to her mother's home. Following an overnight home visit, she seriously attacked a nurse with a knife, whose injuries were only limited due to wearing thick clothes. The nurse was in the patient's room and had suggested that Ms B begin thinking about taking down all the photographs of her baby in order to try to 'move on'. Perhaps Ms B felt that she was being asked to give up her failed attempts to mourn and this precipitated a catastrophe in her mind which could only be managed through a violent enactment due to an inability to 'mind' it. Ms B was consequently transferred to high security and began twice-weekly psycho-analytic psychotherapy.

The first two years of treatment

During the first few months of treatment, Ms B presented as a model, compliant patient who did as she imagined was expected of her in that situation, which is no more than one can expect from someone with such a history. She presented as a distressed patient who spoke about what a dreadful thing she had done, but all of this had a pseudo-feel to it. This way of presenting to me was gradually shown to her and interpreted as one way she had of avoiding feeling traumatised or victimised by her own disturbed state of mind, at the time of her offences and now in the room with me. This led to suicidality and a further increase in her dangerousness towards herself for a period of time.

In some sessions during these early months of therapy, she was more able to speak to me about what she did to her baby, how she crushed her tablets and secretly fed them to the baby, over and over again. At these moments, her real distress was very apparent. She described her preoccupation at the time with her belief that the baby was not being looked after properly by the nurses and doctors. I said to her, at these moments in her sessions, how she wished to be the baby that could be looked after properly. This was a highly ambivalent situation for this patient where she was faced with the problem that to be looked after properly negated her view of what proper looking after within *her* family structure meant. A sense of her betraying her family could be created therefore if she followed the trend of her therapy. I had to be kept as someone who was bound to harm her in some way and her history and offence were once more re-enacted.

The pathological mother–child dynamic present in this patient's mind could also be seen in her therapy when, unbeknown to anyone, she took an overdose before a session and then came to her session appearing with glazed eyes and bilateral hand tremor. She denied several times that any-thing was the matter when her physical state was commented on, became angry and shouted that there was no point in all this and insisted that she wanted to be with her baby, another reference to her suicidality. She kept me in a concerned state and, after considering the likelihood of her having taken an overdose (because of a particular constellation of symptoms that became more apparent), I told her that I thought she wanted me to be a good mother and guess what was the matter with her. This was followed by a long silence. I then said that I believed she would be relieved if I guessed. I proceeded to tell her that I thought she wanted me to know that she had taken an overdose. If I did not notice this, then she could congratulate herself that she was right, no one notices she is serious (about suicide). If I did notice, she would get something from me but it would feel spoilt because of how she got it. In this situation, the patient did finally admit to having taken an overdose, which then urgently had to be dealt with medically. In this session, the offence is repeated again: a baby, herself, is harmed, again with medication, but this time the baby is saved. Indeed, the 'being saved' actually led to a manic outburst of profuse thanks from the patient which diluted the seriousness of what had just happened and avoided the experience of guilt that such a saving could provoke.

In those first two years of treatment, Ms B's perception of me was of someone bound to harm her and, in that situation, trying to 'poison' her with my words. She was frequently placed on continuous observation due to the episodes and threats of self-harm. On other occasions, which could last for several weeks or months, she would become manically freed from all her difficulties and claim to be cured and no longer in need of any treatment from anyone, especially from me. During these phases, she could become extremely hostile and even violent – indeed, she is the only patient for whom I have ever had to press the emergency alarm. These were the occasions when she would 'sack' me, which, to my shame, I welcomed. Discussions with the nurses and regular consultations with Dr Sohn enabled me to remain as a non-retaliatory and non-abandoning object, an experience she had never had before. Eventually, her manically 'cured' state of mind would crumble when, once more, she would self-harm and enter a withdrawn and even less receptive state of mind. Breaks in therapy often triggered deteriorations in her mental state and the consequent need to increase her levels of observation due to risk of self-harm. Any attempts to show her links between her feelings and the presence or absence of those around her were totally negated – the idea of being affected by such things was too frightening, impossible to 'mind' and therefore manifested in her behaviour. The nurses were invaluable during these phases in enabling the therapy to be maintained and in avoiding the temptation, present in therapist and nurses, to enact what was being provoked, a violent retaliation or a permanent rejection.

Treatment from two to five years

In the third year of treatment, Ms B's mental state deteriorated into a more overtly psychotic presentation when she appeared perplexed and had paranoid delusions of being poisoned by staff as well as experiencing hallucinations. She stopped eating and drinking and required transfer to the medical ward where she seemed relieved and gratified at being tube fed, which she never refused, as though delegating her need to torture herself to those around her, including her therapist. What emerged from this more psychotic presentation several months later was a patient who appeared depressed and who complained of flashbacks and nightmares, the content of these always being about her daughter's last hours attached to life-saving equipment and then in the morgue with a damaged, dead body. Many sessions were brief and consisted of the patient slowly shuffling into the room and reporting the following with her head down, no eye contact and in a monotonous voice: 'I can't keep going like this, I want to be with my baby, I don't deserve to live, I don't deserve to die.' Eventually, she would ask a nurse to come and liberate her from me. I would try to take up with her how she mercilessly punished the baby's mother, herself. I would also take up with her how I was felt to be the punitive one, punishing the baby's mother. She was the baby as well who was being harmed by me and who needed to be rescued from me by the nurses. There appeared to be a clash in Ms B's mind between the part that killed her baby (or herself), and knew it, and the grieving part that experienced the flashbacks and that longed to be an ordinary grieving mother (or person).

A basic struggle at this time in the therapy was whether she could face up to knowing who she was and what she had done and therefore be able to change, or whether she needed to go back to, or stay in, a state of not knowing. In my view, there is a link between these positions in terms of her dangerousness. In the situation of remaining unaware, she remains a chronic risk to her babies, actual ones or symbolic representations of them. The pathological mother–child dynamic remains intact. In the situation of getting to know herself and being helped to deal with this knowledge, the risk to these babies diminishes but, without treatment, the risk of dangerousness to herself rises. Both these dangerous attitudes could be considered suicidal, indirect or direct.

In parallel with this conflict, Ms B fluctuated between three main states of being: first, being distressed, withdrawn, experiencing flashbacks and self-harming; second, being psychotic with delusions of being poisoned; or third, being manically freed of all problems, hostile towards carers and claiming to be 'cured'. These three states recurred alternately over the following two years of treatment.

During these first five years of treatment, Ms B had two relationships with male patients at the hospital. The first lasted for one year until he was discharged, subsequently re-offended, was convicted of rape and attempted murder and incarcerated in prison. This was a particularly difficult time for Ms B as she attempted to address her pathological attachment to this man in his absence and to distance herself from him. Given her history of perceiving herself as betraying her family by behaving differently (decently), exploring this was extremely difficult for her. Her mother further complicated the situation by repeatedly telling her, when she broke off this relationship, that she should 'stand by your man'. Indeed, her mother began to visit this man in prison, which further confused the patient.

Ms B subsequently began another relationship with a man in the high security hospital, whom she married whilst they were both in-patients. This occurred during one of her phases of being manically 'cured' and any attempts on my part to show her how she was repeating aspects of her troubled family history were to no avail. Indeed, in the context of a system that could be described as colluding with delusions of normality, psychotherapeutic work around this was rendered almost meaningless. He was discharged and they kept in contact. After one year, she was informed by him that he was seeing another woman. She phoned her mother to tell her the awful news and, after listening, her mother then told her that *she* was the other woman. She phoned her sister in a distraught state and her sister then complained to her for not wishing her mother happiness. Given this constellation, it is not difficult to see just how much the impact of Ms B's current situation, as well as that of her history, continues to jeopardise the chances of getting better.

Ms B managed to break off contact with her mother for over two years after learning about this affair. She also began divorce proceedings. During this period of time, a more receptive involvement in her psychotherapy developed and her mental state was more stable. Her relationships with the nurses also improved during this time and it was felt that there was just a glimpse of the beginning of change possible in her way of relating. In particular, there seemed to be the start of giving up the usual sadomasochistic way she had of relating with her 'internal' mother, but this was only possible by simultaneously breaking off contact with her actual mother. However, her mother eventually resumed contact with Ms B after the affair ended. She told her daughter, my patient, that she should be grateful to her for saving her from being with such a terrible man. In an instant, the idealised mother resurfaced in Ms B's mind and her therapist once more became the 'bad' person or object. Ms B's progress was halted in its tracks. This development was a further clear indication to me and the team that contact with her mother was truly detrimental to her mental health, and if she had been a child (which she was emotionally but not in real terms), child protection laws could have been invoked to prevent contact with her mother for the sake of the well-being of that child.

Unfortunately, the patient has remained stuck and often now somatises her unbearable mental experiences or risks developing overt psychotic symptoms. Both these positions prevent her from being able to engage in a regular dialogue about the contents of her mind with her therapist. She has also maintained the idealised mother in her mind, with the implication that the pathological and dangerous mother–child dynamic remains. The reason for Ms B's lack of sustained progress is most likely due to a damaged mental structure leaving her unable to maintain or further develop the slight shift of healthier relating of which we only caught glimpses. The main responses in therapist and staff are hopelessness or fury, both of which are, of course, prominent within the patient. Interestingly, the main responses towards Ms B of other patients vary between hostile hatred towards her when she is at her most suicidal and despairing and, on the other hand, ignoring her when she is in her manically 'cured' states. Evoking such negative and neglectful reactions guarantees that Ms B can feel mother's presence on the ward.

It is very likely that Ms B will require permanent institutional care. The psychoanalytic input has perhaps not ameliorated her situation but it has at least helped her carers to understand her and to keep trying to give meaning to her life as it has been and continues to be. A therapist who is able, with the help of nursing staff, to tolerate the spectrum of mental states with which she presented and not retaliate may also have contributed something to her internal world which may only become apparent in later years.

Conclusion

One aim in providing this kind of input is to enable the nurses to carry out their difficult task of being the recipients of powerful projections and to manage the other patients who, likewise, are deeply affected by each other. Another aim in providing therapy to patients like this, as part of the overall treatment, is also to attempt to bring about a gradual realisation within themselves, regarding what they have done and what kind of mental life they lived before that allowed these awful events. These previous mental lives or mental states are those that the patients resume when in regressed states of mind. The process of treatment appears to require a complicated and lengthy transition period from not knowing anything about themselves to becoming more aware and dealing with the consequent profoundly traumatic effects of this. The objective is to help them gain understanding and, optimistically, some change in their internal worlds. This may involve a change from a more pathologically defended personality disordered or psychotic presentation to one reminiscent of a post-traumatic stress disorder type of presentation. If such a change could arise, the patient might feel much worse early on but they would have a healthier internal world where thoughts and feelings about what happened, as well as their predicament in relation to this, could be experienced in the mind without the need to get rid of their mental experiences in the familiar ways of acting them out violently.

A major difficulty that arises, as these patients make progress with treatment, is that of a negative therapeutic reaction, provoked by 'getting better'. With consistency over a long period of time, it is possible for these patients to make tentative shifts towards the depressive position and this is something that needs to be worked through over and over until the negative therapeutic responses, triggered by the positive shifts, lessen in severity and frequency.

How much further one can go in Ms B's particular case remains a question. The traumatic developmental interruptions which caused mental structural damage have affected her mental functioning in several areas.

Her capacity for self-reflection is limited. Her ability to regulate her affects is seriously impeded, and leads to impulsive, violent behaviour. Her main defence mechanisms are primitive and have been seen to be stable but inflexible. Her mind is populated with objects that devalue or punish and this leads to a dependence on external others onto whom she projects her distorted view of them as good or bad. Ms B's central fears revolve around the eternally intrusive presence of the bad object or, just as awful, the always impending loss of the good one she never quite had. These fuel her suicidal and self-harming tendencies.

Long-term continuity of treatment throughout patients' transitions to different levels of security is necessary to enable real shifts to arise that could be maintained. The hope is that the 'muscles' of the mind strengthen and can tolerate and contain what previously needed to spill out of the mind into bodily action.

Notes

1 This chapter is also to be published in J. Gordon and G. Kirtchuk (eds) (2008) *Psychic Assaults and Frightened Clinicians: Countertransference in Forensic Settings*, London: Karnac. We are grateful to the editors for their agreement to publish this chapter.
2 I have the consent of the patient and her consultant psychiatrist's agreement to use anonymised case material from my work with her. I am grateful to Dr Leslie Sohn for providing regular consultations about the treatment which could not have been sustained otherwise. I am also grateful to Dr Estela Welldon, whose work on the perversion of the maternal instinct (Welldon 1988) has been invaluable.

Reference

Welldon, E. (1988) *Mother, Madonna, Whore. The Idealization and Denigration of Motherhood*, London: Free Association Books.

Chapter 12

Suicidal thoughts during an analysis[1]

Elmar Etzersdorfer

Introduction

The aim in this chapter is to explore the meaning of suicidal thoughts that emerged in the clinical material of a psychoanalysis of a severely disturbed patient. In this analysis, suicidality is projected into others, but there are also times when directly expressed suicidal thoughts appear. In the discussion of this case I focus on understanding the underlying psychic mechanisms. I describe the transference and countertransference situation and thereby demonstrate the complexities in the process of analytic work and the embedded nature of suicidality within the patient's relatedness to himself and others. Through this exploration, the purpose of suicidality can be recognized as representing a fear of a psychotic breakdown.

Although I have developed my own thinking in relation to the tradition of understanding suicidality as a narcissistic crisis (Henseler 1974), or as having a regulating function in the psychic economy (Kind 1992), I suggest that this framework needs extending to provide understanding of patients such as the one I discuss in this chapter.

The case history

The patient, whom I shall refer to as Mr A, is at risk of committing suicide and has been recurrently suicidal over his lifetime; however, up to now, this has not led to suicidal action. Working with the threat of suicide is not limited to those who are acutely suicidal but includes what is often very difficult work with patients who pose anxiety about future risks.

Mr A is an employee in his mid-fifties. He sometimes gives the impression of being very arrogant and condescending, but at other times comes across as quite friendly and engaging. He is well-groomed, tanned and in good physical condition. He appears to be a prime example of an active, engaging professional person. He used to organize free-time events at his place of work, is friends with many former business partners and used to be a club leader in his free time. Over time, he got into increasing difficulties at work: he felt that a group of colleagues at work had broken him down and undermined him. They constantly asked him if he was married and implied that there was speculation that he was homosexual, which was in fact a question he had been contemplating for decades. Recently, he had became almost convinced that everyone thought that he was gay, and felt he had come near to going insane. On one occasion he lost control, banging upon a table, whereupon everyone fell quiet with embarrassment. He eventually let himself be referred to a psychiatric hospital by a psychiatrist, as he was at a loss and could not bear the situation any longer.

Much remained unclear about his biography, even after a long time in his analysis. The picture emerged that his mother was very taken with outward appearances. She placed an aristocratic 'von' in front of the family name, without any legitimacy, and he had found this out only after her death. The family must have gone through a social decline, living very much on the social prestige of his grandparents' generation. His father died early when Mr A was about 7 years old. He then became doubtful if this really had been his biological father; and wondered if his father was a homosexual and his uncle was his biological father. He spoke of evidence that he had later found, that for the first half-year of his life he had lived in an orphanage, before coming into the family. He grew up with his mother and partly at boarding schools. All this remained unclear in his narration, which was often difficult to comprehend. In fact, much about Mr A and his story had an air of film or theatre, of being staged and, in fact, in some ways he lived as if in a motion picture. This was the case even in his childhood, when, for example, because he would have liked a sister when he was a child to make an 'ideal' family, he had simply made one up and talked about her, but then got into trouble when the school's priest enquired when the sister would finally be coming to First Communion.

Mr A later completed an academic education and took a responsible job. He had been 'everybody's darling' for a long time, always loved and at the center of attention. However, he had hardly any long-term romantic relationships, and had never lived with a woman. He described a short homosexual episode as an attempt to discover if he really was homosexual. He found no answer for himself and the relationship soon broke up. For the past few years he had been with a woman whom he helped out of another relationship. They did not live together, however. At first glance, Mr A appears narcissistic, in the sense of having a strong self-centeredness and a poor ability to perceive other people as being autonomous. He is of above average intelligence and he repeatedly gave me the impression that he put every effort into the treatment within the scope and limits of his potential.

I began to see him in a high frequency setting during his in-patient treatment. After a period of treatment on a day ward, he began an out-patient treatment with me consisting of four sessions a week. It took place continuously face to face; Mr A would hardly have tolerated treatment lying on the couch, without visual contact and direct possibility of optical feedback.

From the beginning, the treatment was very difficult. Very often I felt inundated by his stories and frequently had the feeling that I understood none of it. When I felt I understood something and gave an interpretation, Mr A could often only apply this very vaguely to himself and his experiences. As I have mentioned, Mr A had never up to this point attempted suicide; and suicidality had also not been the main reason for the in-patient admission. But there had been earlier crises, once even an in-patient treatment. Although he never attempted suicide, there had been times of strong suicidal ideation, where he seriously thought about committing suicide, leading him repeatedly to drive around the countryside, searching for the highest possible bridge from which he could jump.

The following material from the analysis derives from the period after Mr A had been in out-patient treatment with me for just over a year. A superficial stabilization had occurred for the time being, as he had moved into an apartment with his female partner for the first time in his life. Then, the situation again intensified and in recent weeks he had repeatedly considered breaking off the analysis. In a few weeks' time a request for a treatment extension would have to be made to the insurance fund; he was constantly thinking that he must break up with his partner, was ready to relinquish the apartment, and a few weeks previously he had received a notification about temporary disability payments.

It is rather obvious from this initial account that Mr A suffered from a severe disturbance, which strongly affected sexual and emotional areas as well as questions about his own family background and his biography, and this disturbance also quickly showed up in the therapeutic relationship. Although the question of suicidality seemed to be somewhat in the background, it did, as will be shown in the clinical material, appear recurrently, pointing at the need for the analyst to remain aware of the threat of suicidal behavior in patients like this.

Clinical material

In a Monday session – he comes every day from Monday to Thursday – Mr A speaks of stopping his analysis. In the end he concedes that 'we can talk about it'. In the Tuesday session he begins by taking a letter out of his backpack and laying it on the table in front of him; he wants to stop coming. He had written it down but the words wouldn't work; it would make no sense. The atmosphere immediately becomes tense. I say that he must write it down because it would be too difficult to discuss it with me here. After that, Mr A says that he cannot say what is inside him, it would be too much. There is a pause, which I eventually interrupt. I say that Mr A fears that it could become too much for me, if what was inside him could become clear and spoken about; I relate this situation to earlier, similar perceptions of this kind. I then attempt to name the dilemma, which I say arises from Mr A's wish to leave and his wish to stay. Mr A becomes more relaxed after this and speaks of an apartment that he has had a look at and would like to take. He describes the apartment in detail and it has many particulars that resemble the consultation room: it is situated on the ground floor and is rather dark. Then he says that the landlords were very taken with him, and he thinks he will certainly get the apartment. He quickly adds that it is located in a cul-de-sac. As he had looked at it, two women immediately came by and noticed him. One cannot simply be unnoticed there, going in and out, as one pleases.

I understand his description of the apartment as an illustration of the dilemma – how he wants to retreat into a dark, narrow and terrible world. He experiences me as perceptive – I am someone who notices him and what is inside him – however, I am also persecuting – one could not simply go in and out unnoticed. These are considerations that I am not able to make in the session itself, as I formulate them only afterwards and in discussion of the session's material. In the session itself, I only make what is certainly too general a comment when I say that the situation for him is difficult and unclear. Upon this, Mr A gives another narrative and I reproduce this in his own words.

'There was this woman in Munich, I don't know if I have spoken about her. . . . We had met for a weekend and she eventually said to me "I love you, don't you understand that." We then attempted to have intercourse, but it didn't go very well, she was too nervous. I then spent the night at her place in the living room, sleeping on the sofa. I woke up in the night and then lay around for two hours becoming more and more disgusted by her. I was then pacing around the room for two hours and I pictured myself going to her, telling her how much she disgusts me. At six o'clock in the morning I was at her bed, woke her up, and told her "You disgust me." Before this, I had strong fantasies that she would become angry, that she would take my suitcase with my things and throw them out of the window. But she did nothing like that; she was completely silent, just sad. She went into the kitchen and drank a glass of milk. Then she said "You are sick." She even made me breakfast, and then told me that I could go now, if I wanted to. I then packed my things and left, but I couldn't leave; I walked up and down the street for two hours and suddenly had a great concern that she would harm herself. I went back to the house and tried to enter again. . . . That was not successful for very long, first, people going into the house wouldn't let me enter, "What do you want here, what are you looking for here?" . . . Then I got inside and went upstairs, the apartment was on the top floor, with a glass door. . . . I scrunched myself down in front of the door and saw nothing, fearing that she could have done something to hurt herself. . . . When I saw a shadow I knocked and she let me enter. She then said: "You are really sick."'

Mr A recounts this episode thoughtfully, with pauses. After another pause he begins to cry. He sobs: 'What is wrong? . . . I don't molest children!' Then he speaks of the time when he went in search of the highest bridge, which I have already mentioned. He speaks about how he repeatedly considered jumping, also having written goodbye letters which he destroyed when he came back home. Later in the session he recalls a film that had to do with love letters and he speaks about his confusion as to whether love letters are absurd or, in contrast, very essential.

Commentary

This is a difficult clinical situation, but not unusual with this patient. He is, in his relationship with me – as he is in other relationships – in a terrible state, torn apart. He must leave but cannot leave. He brings a letter and cannot speak about what is written in it. It is a frequently recurring situation that Mr A repeatedly recounts, often in speech and rebuttal, as if in a drama. It is, in a way, typical of sessions with this patient. It is an example of a treatment where suicidality, although not in the foreground, does play an important role and imposes a threat not only to the treatment, but to the life of Mr A. It is crucial to keep this danger in mind and I try to address it by interpreting the transference features as they are evolving.

The incident with the woman in Munich describes a situation in which Mr A cannot stay and cannot leave. I try to address this dilemma in the transference. What is Mr A describing with this scene in Munich? Apparently, a dreadful confusion arises for him. He gets close to the woman and he cannot bear it. He is troubled; he awakes in the night and becomes angry. He becomes angry with the woman, not at himself, he who cannot bear the situation. Upon that, he becomes fearful that she will throw him out. Her remark that he is sick apparently does, then, affect him. He cannot go away from someone who can give such a diagnosis ('You are sick'). No sooner has he left than he is immediately concerned about the woman. His concern is that she is suicidal and his suicidality emerges located in the woman. When she turns out not to be suicidal, the suicidality re-migrates back to him, and at this point he travels to the bridges.

Thus he cannot go away from me, although, at the same time, he must go away, because I recognize, at least sometimes, how sick he is. Suicidality occurs here in the session as an expression of terrible anal-genital confusion in Mr A that he must project. There is an attraction followed immediately by an intense disgust. He projects the confusion into the woman in Munich and also attempts to project it into me. I do not become desperate myself, but there are, however, in the countertransference, feelings of confusion and irritation, of not understanding, of being at a loss, and I experience myself as being of no help to Mr A.

If one considers the situation further, it is to be suspected that within Mr A there are probably unconscious phantasies that he attacked me, like he had attacked the woman in Munich. I often had the impression that for Mr A, it is not clear what is in him and what is in me. This confusion gives rise to the assumption that the suicidality expresses a fear of a psychotic breakdown in this situation. Perhaps I was not able to contain Mr A's despair enough in this situation; in the scene with the woman, Mr A described a fear that he would have to walk around with the despair and would not be able to get rid of it. He speaks, however, also about the woman letting him inside again, and I let him again in for the next session and I am not destroyed, not angry and I do not throw him out.

Mr A describes as well a hidden perverse scenario. He takes for granted that the woman must know what a terrible person he is; for if she loves him, she must be pleased by this, and she herself becomes disgusting. This scenario repeatedly emerges in the sessions. With the desperate statement that he does not molest children, perhaps he expresses that he does not want to destroy his objects, does not really want to damage them, although he unconsciously knows about his attacks. So, the letter that he brings to the session is, at the same time, a notice of termination as well as a love letter to me. In a way it is also a hidden suicide threat – or suicide note – which has to be understood as such, as well as a wish to be helped to be able to stay alive.

Perhaps it makes sense to emphasize that I could not recall these thoughts during the session itself. Especially when the material turns to his suicidality, it is difficult to recognize this at the time. This seems to me a particular difficulty in treating patients with suicidal risk, and particularly when suicidal thoughts emerge in a session. Also, a difficult technical situation occurs: the massiveness of his threat and his distress are not easy to tolerate. On the other hand, Mr A makes it clear how very much he will feel persecuted with each of his comments of 'you are sick'.

Further clinical material

In the Wednesday session, Mr A reports at length about the suicide of a former patient of the hospital, with whom he had contact after his discharge. Suicidality emerges again, manifest in the idea, though dealt with through another person. He gets to talking directly about his own suicidality and says, 'I am not going to kill myself.' He expresses thoughts that the balcony of the future apartment would be too low, that it would not work at all. Then it occurs to him that he once drove to a bridge, with thoughts of jumping off it, when he read a sign: 'Mortal Danger, High Tension Wires'. As he read this, he had to laugh and he then drove away. The incident could be understood as a description of the high tension that Mr A perceives within himself, and the mortal danger with which the tension is linked, but it is also the high tension between him and me that can become life-threatening.

In the following sessions, suicidality continues to come up, partly hidden and, as earlier, mostly projected. When he treats his girlfriend badly and she does not call the next day, as he expected, immediately the thought emerges that she could have committed suicide out of loneliness. He expresses his fear, that he could have driven her to her death through his bad behavior. An overtone of triumph lies in this phantasy. In these sessions, too, there are repeated attacks to be found, often subtle and difficult to grasp. I often feel helpless and affected by my own defenses and hope for the possibility of recovering from such attacks – for example, through supervision.

In the following sessions, thoughts repeatedly manifest around death, murder and suicide, and whether I am allowed to notice this. Or if Mr A is terribly afraid, I could not only perceive it, but also articulate it. Again and again a sadomasochistic entanglement emerges that circumvents attempts to obtain clarity. This compulsive defense is an attempt to keep a structure and the impression is, to emphasize it once again, that Mr A must try to prevent not only a suicidal action but also a psychotic breakdown. I repeatedly get the impression that addressing the threat perceived by Mr A would be experienced by him to have a massive impact – in a very concrete way. Sometimes the impression emerges that Mr A gains structure through speaking and not so much through interpretations. Through talking to him, I myself remain alive, overcoming his affronts. At the same time, talking remains both threatening and persecuting. He is terrified of a horrible truth, that I might be able to know this truth, and talk to him about it. This also relates to the destructive way Mr A treats his analysis. He has perceived that, at some moments, I am able to think, and could come close to him, and this was more than was tolerable for him. His turning away from knowing and experiencing this is his protection, that is, protecting him from having to commit suicide. He again expresses this in the depiction of the high bridge with the high-tension wires, which are mortally dangerous.

Mr A did eventually break off the analysis. It appeared that in fact he could not find it tolerable to be more forthcoming and to talk more about these issues in the analysis. However, he visited me a few months later, to my surprise, shortly before Christmas. He suddenly appeared, standing at the secretary's desk, and wished us a Merry Christmas. The impression emerged that he wanted to show that he was still alive, that he was able to survive in his very limited way. Perhaps he also wanted to see if I am still here, if I survived the attacks.

Discussion

I would like now to take a step back from the material and consider how to understand it. With regard to Mr A's suicidality, the material remains fragmentary. The treatment could not be taken very far; much could not be sufficiently understood. Nevertheless, it did become clear that this is a patient with very severe difficulties. The inner world of Mr A is full of horrible phantasies, full of threat and persecution, and he constantly rids himself of these by very violent projective and introjective means.

The relationship is dominated by massive projective identifications that aim to get rid of those persecuting inner aspects, at the same time controlling them in the object. The object sometimes can be perceived as someone knowing or noticing some of those horrible emotional processes in Mr A, and then quickly becoming persecuting and dangerous itself. Characteristically in this patient, his suicidality often emerges in his objects, sometimes described as fear that the object might kill itself. It has been suggested that suicidality represented the fear of a psychotic breakdown, of being overwhelmed by a confusion that Mr A cannot get rid of by projective means, and of losing a sense of boundaries of the Ego, of what is inside or outside.

I also tried to describe how difficult it was in the sessions with Mr A for me to maintain a capacity to think about what was going on, often being confronted with a countertransference that was hard to tolerate. It seemed to me, however, that the ability to stay alive psychically, with important help from supervision and colleagues, also had an important impact on the patient. He experienced that I survived his attacks on feelings and processes that were hard to bear for him as well.

Nevertheless the question arises: how can we understand his decision to break off the treatment? Can it simply be understood as too great an amount of destructive forces, keeping him from experiencing his need to project unbearable feelings and fantasies? I think that at the point of breaking off the analysis he had glimpsed more than was tolerable for him about the severity of his difficulties. In a practical sense he had to face these difficulties through applying to his insurance for a treatment extension, and receiving a notification about disability payments. In the treatment itself, he came closer to acknowledging more of his confusing and horrifying fantasies that were also connected to his suicidal thoughts.

We cannot describe this as a successful treatment, leading to recognized improvements in the patient's psychic functioning. However, it remains an open question as to how his experience of an object, that to some extent was able to tolerate his inner world, may have had a stabilizing effect, although on a labile and rather poor level of functioning. Thus it is possible that this may have had an impact in respect of his suicide risk as well. This fits with the point made by Perelberg (1999) that suicide as well as violence against others may be viewed as attempted solutions to the experience of feeling overwhelmed by the object. Remaining in the therapeutic relationship at this point might have put an intolerable pressure on Mr A by an object filled up with his violent projections that threatened to overwhelm his capacity to keep them away from himself. It may also relate to Moses Laufer's (1995) view that suicidal acts can be seen as attempts to regulate distance in relation to internal objects, which are experienced as identified with the body, particularly in adolescents with suicidal behavior. Tilman Grande (1997) has also highlighted how suicidal behavior can be understood as an attack and attempt to destroy the self as well as the object(s) (or parts of them) through attacking the body. Thus Mr A's breaking off the analysis may have been a desperate attempt to avoid an even more destructive threat of being overwhelmed by his own violent and suicidal feelings, which he had mainly projected into his analyst.

For Mr A no secure object exists, as there is also no good inner object to be found that gives him sufficient protection and security. They are predominately part-object relationships that occur here, not relationships with complete external or internal objects. The situation is complicated by the quality of these part-objects and the feelings associated with them. With Mr A, the entire process of thinking and feeling is attacked and is threatened by a total disintegration, and his thoughts of suicide are closely linked to that.

If suicidal impulses are in the ascendant, for whatever reason, with patients like Mr A, it becomes very hard to think and to function as an analyst. One could speculate that these complications in the analytical situation have contributed to why some analytical theories of suicidality have remained either schematic or very theoretical. A retreat into theory in such a clinical situation can also be a defense for the analyst.

In this situation, I do not primarily see the suicidal danger as a narcissistic catastrophe, as Heinz Henseler (1974) described it. He had assumed that the suicide attempt would correspond to a regression to a harmonic primary state. With Mr A, such a harmonious primary state itself would be an illusion, a defense to escape the horrible inner truth.

More recently, Feldman (2000) has added a clinical – and therefore practical – perspective to the theory of the death instinct. He suggests that the goal of the death instinct is the destruction of liveliness and of meaning as well as, or rather than, psychic destruction. It is also an attack on the thinking of the analyst, his ability to understand and to function. Feldman writes that, 'In a certain sense, of course, these activities are murderous and suicidal, but I am suggesting their primary aim is not totally to destroy life, but to take the life out' (Feldman 2000: 55). With Mr A, therefore, following this line of thought, a suicidal action would not be the immediate goal of a death instinct, as understood here, but rather would have actually been an 'accident' of the death instinct. In this context, a suicide attempt would then appear, when the therapeutic relationship cannot contain these attacks any more, but forces their reintrojection. This might be the case when the analyst is unable to provide containment any longer or withdraws himself. Such withdrawal may manifest itself in a decision to end the treatment, or more subtly by withdrawing emotionally, and thereby creating too much distance between himself and the patient.

We repeatedly see patients like the one illustrated here, Mr A, in analytical treatment, and presumably they are more frequently seen than decades ago. No patient can be sufficiently understood with the analytic theories of neuroses as Freud formulated them. Also, analytical theories of suicidality, at least in the German language areas, have explicitly excluded such patients for a long time, as has been pointed out by both Heinz Henseler and Jürgen Kind (Henseler 1974: 95; Kind 1992: 20).

Towards the end of his life, Freud wrote about suicide, and this was posthumously published in 'An outline of psychoanalysis'. He assumed suicide required a defusion of instincts with release of a large quantity of the destructive drives, and then added: 'But we must confess that this is a case which we have not yet succeeded in completely explaining' (Freud 1940: 180). We must still concur with this view; the question of suicidality is surely, even today, more than sixty years after Freud wrote these words, in many respects not yet sufficiently illuminated.

Conclusion

In this chapter I have discussed some detailed clinical material from a man in analysis whose suicidality was a major factor in the treatment, even though he had not in fact made any suicide attempts. Partly his suicidality was projected into others, but it also appeared as suicidal thoughts and ideas. Though understanding of his suicidality remained unclear and fragmented in the clinical material, I suggested that suicidality was embedded in some complex and disturbed patterns of relatedness to himself, particularly associated with a fear of psychotic breakdown. The analysis was terminated prematurely without explicit improvements in the patient's psychic functioning, but it can be speculated that the analysis did offer some stability through withstanding his destructive attacks.

Feldman's thinking about the death instinct as aiming to attack meaning and liveliness appears to provide a way of beginning to understand how, for Mr A, a suicidal act might be an 'accident' of the death instinct whilst his underlying preoccupation with suicide was pervasive.

Note

1 The work presented here draws on inspiration from exchanges with my former colleagues at the Department for Psychoanalysis and Psychotherapy at the University of Vienna Medical School, Melitta Fischer-Kern, Katharina Leithner-

Dziubas, Henriette Löffler-Stastka, Eva Presslich-Titscher, Kitty Schmidt, and Peter Schuster. It is a main emphasis of research activities there to examine analytical therapy of severely disturbed patients, along with the support of British psychoanalysts, especially Patricia Daniel who comes to provide supervisions. I am particularly grateful for her support as well. Translation of an earlier version has been provided by Robert Lightner.

References

Feldman, M. (2000) 'Some views on the manifestation of the death instinct in clinical work', *International Journal of Psycho-Analysis* 81: 53–65.

Freud, S. (1940) 'An outline of psychoanalysis', in J. Strachey (ed.) *The Standard Edition of the Complete Psychological Works of Sigmund Freud, Vol. 23* (pp. 139– 207), London: Hogarth.

Grande, T. (1997) *Suizidale Beziehungsmuster*, Opladen: Westdeutscher Verlag.

Henseler, H. (1974) *Narzisstische Krisen. Zur Psychodynamik des Selbstmordes*, Opladen: Westdeutscher Verlag.

Kind, J. (1992) *Suizidal. Die Psychoökonomie einer Suche*, Göttingen: Vandenhoeck. *Suicidal Behaviour: The Search for Psychic Economy*, London: Jessica Kingsley, 1999.

Laufer, M. (ed.) (1995) *The Suicidal Adolescent*, London: Karnac.

Perelberg, R. (ed.) (1999) 'Psychoanalytic understanding of violence and suicide: a review of the literature and some new formulations', in R. Perelberg (ed.) *Psychoanalytic Understanding of Violence and Suicide* (pp. 19–50), London: Routledge.

Part 3

Applications in practice, prevention and postvention

On suicide prevention in hospitals: empirical observations and psychodynamic thinking

Frank Matakas and Elisabeth Rohrbach

Introduction

A suicide prevention strategy aiming to identify real risks of suicide in patients in treatment is described in this chapter. It was developed in a psychiatric hospital and based on the results of a longitudinal study of patients who committed suicide over twenty-one years. This study was able to compare suicide rates before and after a change of policy in the hospital for the treatment of depression. Since 1999 the treatment of moderate to severe depression has been based on the principle of meeting the patient's regressive needs, and the rates of suicide have declined. This model of treatment and the implications for understanding the role of depression in suicide are discussed in this chapter.

Suicide risks in psychiatric hospital settings

A suicide prevention strategy would be at its most effective if it could identify patients with a real suicide risk. We are aware that we do not use the term 'prevention' here in the traditional way. It is neither primary nor secondary prevention in a strict sense, because we are considering patients in treatment, and patients of known risk. But it seems to us still an appropriate phrase to apply to the situation where clinical science cannot refine the risk prediction any further. Although some factors are known to increase the suicidal risk – such as a diagnosis of affective disorder or schizophrenia (Sharma *et al.* 1998; Martin 2000), hopelessness (Fawcett *et al.* 1987), and previous suicide attempts (Powell *et al.* 2000) – these factors do not narrow down the number of high risk patients sufficiently to allow targeted preventive measures (Appleby *et al.* 1999; Eagles *et al.* 2001). In addition, many if not all patients with moderate to severe depression have suicidal thoughts but do not openly express them (Gladstone *et al.* 2001).

Consequently, as far as therapeutic practice is concerned, one must assume that any patient with moderate to severe symptoms of depression is at risk of suicide. What is required, therefore, is a suicide prevention treatment strategy that is applicable to the many patients with symptoms of depression.

However, searching for such a strategy, one should bear in mind that suicide is a rare event, even in psychiatry. The suicide rate at psychiatric hospitals in Germany is given as approximately 250 per 100,000 patients (Wolfersdorf et al. 2003). The probability that a patient who is admitted to a psychiatric hospital because of a psychic disorder will commit suicide is therefore p = 0.0025. This probability rate suggests that there is no causal link between suicide, hospital admission and the psychiatric diagnosis. Consequently, the search for factors linked with suicidal behavior must be extended beyond the psychiatric disorder itself.

The suicide prevention strategy was developed in a psychiatric hospital after all the patients who had committed suicide were analyzed with respect to their psychic condition and the corresponding efforts of the doctors to relieve them (Matakas and Rohrbach 2007).

The hospital setting and its treatment procedures

The hospital referred to here (Matakas 1992) has three in-patient wards, one of them a secure unit, with a total of forty beds. The hospital also has four day-patient wards, each with a capacity of fourteen places. The treatment program for the patient consists of daily appointments with the physician or consultant, contact with the family, and an individual treatment plan drawn up in consultation with each patient which specifies the social and, if appropriate, psychotherapeutic objectives as well as the type of drug therapy. There are group sessions which cover communal life on the ward, patients' social problems, art and motion therapy, and psychological problems. In-patients are often unable to participate in the group sessions owing to their mental condition. Sometimes they cannot even take part in the group walks or joint meals, and thus receive individual care. The average duration of treatment is twenty-five days for in-patients and approximately fifty-five days for day patients.

From October 1, 1999, the treatment rules were altered for patients in a depressive condition. The treatment method distinguished between regressive and progressive measures. Under the 'regressive' treatment strategy, the patient was temporarily relieved of his responsibility for himself and others. 'Progressive' treatment, on the other hand, was based on measures that gave back the patient his responsibilities or aimed to reintegrate him into his normal life.

Regressive measures were initiated for all patients in a depressive condition. Progressive measures were gradually introduced only when all symptoms of depression had disappeared. A depressive condition was diagnosed

Regressive treatment	Progressive treatment
in-patient care	permission to go out of the hospital
an ordered daily routine	visits home
no leaving the ward without supervision	discussion of the patient's social situation
no discussion of family conflicts with the therapists	contact with employers if appropriate
no dealing with the patient's social problems	planning the patient's life after completion of hospital treatment
no contact with his work environment	conflict-oriented rather than purely supportive psychotherapy
	day-patient treatment or out-patient treatment

if moderate to severe depressive mood was present. 'Moderate' or 'severe' means that the patient is able only with great difficulty, or totally unable, to continue performing social or domestic activities. If depressive symptoms recurred under the progressive measures, these measures were discontinued and another attempt was made once the patient's depressive condition had disappeared again. This procedure was repeated until there was a sustained improvement.

Day-patient treatment was possible for patients with a mild depressive episode, with dysthymia, or whose symptoms of a moderate or severe depressive episode had subsided. If, however, depressive symptoms worsened for two weeks or more, treatment was continued on an in-patient basis. If, under day-patient treatment, depressive symptoms developed in patients who originally had neither a depressive episode nor dysthymia, and if these symptoms persisted for longer than two weeks, day-patient care was broken off and treatment was continued on an in-patient basis where appropriate. These rules applied to all patients, irrespective of the primary diagnosis. The treatment concept described above remained otherwise unaltered.

Treatment before and after October 1999 did not differ fundamentally as regards administration of antidepressants, which followed the usual rules. The difference was that before this date it was the doctor's decision whether the patients' interpersonal conflicts and social difficulties were discussed and worked on with them, and patients were granted generous leave to visit their families, even if they were still in a depressive condition. After October 1999, a 'regressive' and a 'progressive' treatment method were defined in detail, and there was a criterion – the presence of moderate or severe depression – that determined which form of treatment should be used.

Table 13.1 Patients and diagnoses, January 1984–December 2005

	January 1984– September 1999	October 1999– December 2005
Admissions	6,891	5,149
Of which: men	35%	35%
women	65%	65%
18–44 years of age	76%	73%
45–64 years of age	22%	25%
> 64 years of age	1%	2%
day patients	3,514 (51%)	1,802 (35%)
in-patients	3,377 (49%)	3,347 (65%)
Schizophrenic disorders	21%	18%
Affective disorders	42%	48%
Addiction (alcohol)	6%	10%
Dementia	1%	1%
Others (mainly severe personality disorders, in particular borderline disorder)	33%	23%

The patients

The study covers all patients admitted to the hospital between January 1, 1984 and December 31, 2005 (Table 13.1).

The period before the approach differentiating regressive and progressive treatment was introduced covers fifteen years and nine months and 6,891 patients. The period after the change in therapeutic strategy covers six years three months and 5,149 patients.

Diagnoses are defined at the hospital according to the DSM III, III-R or IV and, in addition, since the year 2000, the ICD-10 criteria. Before October 1999, 21 per cent of patients in the study were diagnosed with schizophrenia, 42 per cent with 'affective disorder', 6 per cent with 'addiction', meaning addiction to alcohol and/or prescription drugs (patients addicted to illegal drugs are not treated at the hospital), 1 per cent with dementia, and 33 per cent with other disorders (mainly severe personality disorders, in particular borderline disorder).

There was no fundamental change in the distribution of sexes, age groups and diagnoses. The only difference was the ratio of day patients to full in-patients, which changed from 51:49 per cent to 35:65 per cent. The reason for this is that a third in-patient ward was opened in July 1996.

Results

From January 1, 1984 to September 30, 1999 there were 6,891 patients admitted, of whom 22 (13 women, 9 men) died as a result of suicide. This represents a total suicide rate of 319 suicides for every 100,000 admissions.

Table 13.2 Suicides

	January 1984– September 1999	October 1999– December 2005
Suicides	22	5
In-patients	14	5
Day patients	8	0
Schizophrenia	5	1
Depression	16	3
Alcoholism	1	1
Suicide rate*	319	97

* for every 100,000 admissions or discharges

Of these suicides, five patients had been diagnosed with schizophrenia, sixteen with depression, and one with depression and chronic alcohol abuse, although the primary diagnosis was depression (Table 13.2). Eight of the twenty-two patients had been treated on a day-care basis and fourteen as in-patients.

In nineteen of the twenty-two cases, the patient records clearly indicate that the depressive condition had not improved in the week prior to the suicide. There are references to a continuing depressive mood, paranoid thoughts or severe agitation. The psychic condition of the remaining three patients was unclear. All of the twenty-two patients who died by suicide were on progressive treatment measures at the time of death, by retrospective assessment. All but one of the twenty-two cases denied any suicidal intent in the last few days before their suicide.

From October 1, 1999 to December 31, 2005 there were 5,149 patients admitted, of whom five in-patients (two women, three men) died as a result of suicide. This corresponds to a suicide rate of 97 suicides for every 100,000 admissions. Three of the patients were allowed to leave the ward, although they were in a poor condition. This was a clear contravention of the treatment rules described above.

Comparison of the suicide rates before and after October 1999 reveals a significant difference.[1] Figure 13.1 shows the suicide rate as a rolling average over three years. The trend line is a logarithmic function of the values for 1984–1999. The difference between the values of this logarithmic function and the actual values for the period from October 1999 to December 2005 is significant at a level of $p < 0.001$ according to the Wilcoxon test.

Accounting for the changing suicide rate

The first and decisive question is whether the change in the suicide rate from 319 to 97 can be attributed to the change in the treatment strategy.

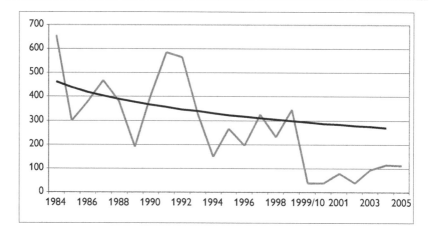

Figure 13.1 Suicide rate (per 100,000 admissions per three years as rolling average), 1984–2005. The trend line (logarithmic) represents prediction of suicides based on values for 1984–1999

This question was discussed in detail in our original paper (Matakas and Rohrbach 2007). All evidence would indicate that the difference in the suicide rate before and after the change in treatment is not a matter of chance. The authors think it reasonable to speculate that the treatment intervention accounted for the decrease.

The second question is whether we can draw from our findings conclusions about the possible reasons for the suicidality. The rarity of suicides by patients in psychiatric hospitals would indicate that the suicide is brought about through factors independent of the primary mental disorder, as mentioned above. It would therefore be wise to broaden the search for factors that can cause suicide into other areas and not just the psychological disorder.

Our investigations have not led to a direct identification of factors that cause suicide. We have, however, discovered a strategy for better protecting the patient from suicide. Owing to the nature of the hospital, it was precisely the severely and persistently depressive patients who often received intensive treatment, as was borne out by the analysis of the suicide cases. In particular, if the depression was deeper and longer, the doctors showed a tendency to go to great lengths to work out the conflict which they saw as the cause of the depression, with the patient and consequently their families. However, this approach apparently increased the suicidal tendency. In comparison, the opposite approach had more success. Heavily depressive patients need peace and regressive forms of treatment, as other authors have called for (Clark 1995). In extreme cases this can mean that the patient is looked after for a long time, and, apart from medication, does not undergo any specific rehabilitative or psychotherapeutic process. This demands patience and strength from the therapists to endure the prolonged depression of their patients.

In a paper about the psychodynamics of depression (Matakas and Rohrbach 2005) we have been able to show that there is a close connection between depression and regression. Depression is always connected to regression. Mature mental functions are given up. The depressive has great difficulty making decisions, often about the simplest things, and cannot take any responsibility, even for himself. Work becomes difficult, if not impossible. Eventually the depressive arrives at the position of not being able to do the vital things for himself. The regression manifests itself in egocentric behavior, referred to by Freud (1917) in 'Mourning and melancholia'. The depressive becomes totally preoccupied with himself.

These are the symptoms that are observed. They are based on the fact that the depressive needs a person who guarantees his narcissistic stability. He needs someone who will relieve him of particular ego functions. A situation occurs which is similar to that of a child who is dependent on the relationship to mother and father.

Our research has shown that the typical symptoms of depression – i.e. the depressive mood, the reduction of drive, and the resulting feeling of worthlessness – derive from a situation whereby the needs of the depressive after regression are not accepted. Or it is they themselves who will not allow regression. (These two possibilities, that the depressive does not find the conditions for regression or does not allow it himself, correspond to the distinction of 'anaclitic' and 'introjective' depression of Blatt (1998).)

Typical depressive symptoms are brought about when mature ego functions are demanded from the depressive – they make such demands on themselves and do not accept help from others to regulate their mental functions, that is to support their narcissistic stability. According to our research it is this constellation that may bring about the suicidal urge. Leenaars, in his account of psychotherapy of suicidal persons, summarizes: 'Suicide is . . . an outcome of frustrated attachment needs (wishes)' (2004: 74).

When, through admission to a hospital ward, for example, the depressive has the opportunity for regression or, in the case of introjective depression, this is brought about through compulsory admission, then the anguished symptoms, the depressive mood, lack of drive, and vegetative symptoms will improve if not disappear completely. The reduction of the suicidal urge is a special effect of this general efficacy of regression on the depressive. However, the depressive process is not stopped through regression. It is just less visible. The depression-connected urge to regression and typical depressive symptoms such as the depressed mood, reduction of drive, and so on, are two distinct features. Regression can be separated from depressive symptoms by appropriate treatment procedures. This is the most important finding of our research.

An effective strategy for the prevention of suicide is to allow the patient a regressive state for as long as they are depressed and to the extent that is needed. The regressive treatment must take the ego function, which cannot be handled, away from the patient. This differs according to the depth of the depression and there must be someone to take the responsibility away from the depressive for a considerable time. Both requirements can be well fulfilled in a psychiatric hospital. The regression protects the depressive from suicide because the negative symptoms of depression will be diminished by the possibility for regression.

Interpersonal factors in suicidality

Regression means, as stated above, that the depressive needs an object that will help with the regulation of her/his narcissistic stability. If this is not available, then, in extreme cases, she/he will become suicidal. It seems to us to follow from this that we should be looking for the reason for a suicide not so much in the patient alone as in the relationship of the suicidal person to the people in his surroundings.

There is a considerable amount of empirical data that would indicate that suicide is in fact a problem of the relationship between relatives or professional helpers and the depressive. A suicide creates a feeling of guilt among the relatives and the professional helpers. As this is a common enough occurrence, one could assume that the feeling of guilt is not totally unjustified. The reason is that there may have been a failure in the treatment by the therapists. This seems to be no seldom occurrence. In our study, for example, three suicides occurred after the treatment strategy had been changed in 1999 and the therapeutic rules were not adhered to.

Heller and Haynal (1997) made a video documentation of the initial interviews between the doctors and the patients who had been admitted to hospital because of attempted suicide. Some of these patients attempted suicide again later. An analysis of the videos revealed that indications for the second suicide attempt were found not in the way the patient represented himself during the interview, but in the doctor's face 'The doctor displayed longer activation of facial muscles around the eyes, longer eyebrow lowering, and more time spent facing and looking at patients' with re-attempter patients (Heller and Haynal 1997: 49). Could we surmise that there exists a subconscious death wish on the part of the participants which would then be the reason for the malfunctioning of the treatment, leading to the subsequent feeling of guilt? Menninger (1938) had voiced such suspicions many years ago.

Staff of the hospital were asked in an interview what thoughts they had about treating depressive patients. They answered more or less unanimously that they had the fear of never getting rid of the patient. These ideas correspond to the feeling of the depressives that their depression would never disappear. From our dynamic perspective this means that the depressive fears never being able to find someone who can help them with their narcissistic problem. This belief stems perhaps from childhood in the form of traumatization, namely, that they did not receive the supporting physical or emotional care they needed. To the mind of a child this means 'never'. This is possibly the cause of the countertransference on the part of the staff, who may have feelings like those of a mother who doesn't know what to do with her child and perceives the child as a burden she can't get free of.

The results of our investigations and findings present no surprises. The suicidal person needs good care for as long as the depressive process lasts, and needs a person who is there for them. There seems to be nothing more dangerous than to push a depressive into a situation that they cannot handle. This arises all too easily out of a countertransference situation. The suicidal person's need for protection and care is refused.

This interpretation also better explains the characteristic role that aggression plays in suicidality. Those who have to deal with a person who is suicidal or has attempted suicide perceive the suicide threat as aggression and often react correspondingly aggressively. But all efforts to make the depressive person aware of aggressive urges fail. The depression deepens and the suicidal tendency rises (Matakas and Rohrbach 2005). Our findings strengthen the supposition that a suicidal tendency is itself a paradoxical situation. The depressive needs the close contact of another person. When this vital dependency is put in danger, then the depressive may try to obtain independence by an act of force and will commit suicide (Fonagy 1999). Thus the aggression that comes out is, in the suicidal person's experience, a way of saving him or herself. Therein arises also the phantasy that in death he will be re-united with the object of his needs (Schachter 1999). To the persons concerned their aggressive feelings may have also the unconscious meaning of saving identity.

But the question of what finally leads to a suicide is still not answered by this. Our empirical findings do not allow any further conclusions. However, we would like to add another conjecture. When it happens that the narcissistic support is not forthcoming, suicide may follow. It would lead one to speculate that everyone, in order to live at all, needs a certain social acceptance. This doesn't simply mean social recognition but a kind of attachment similar to the attachment we find in children to their mothers. Children may die if they are separated from their mother at an early age and do not find a replacement within a short time. The research by Spitz and Wolf (1946) bore this out. This attachment seems to be different from the love which a mother may feel towards her baby. Babies can live without love but not without being attached to a person. In the case of a suicide this would mean that this vital attachment has been severed by the people around or by the depressive person themselves. These are, however, theoretical conjectures that can only be borne out by empirical observation.

It is often the patients themselves who ask for their responsibilities to be gradually returned to them, explaining that it makes them feel better, or it is their families that push for patients to be given back their responsibilities. The physician, who feels obliged to alleviate his patients' distressing symptoms and is determined not to miss any opportunity to help them, feels forced to take action and gives in to their demands (Maltsberger *et al.* 2003). But the physician should not encourage patients to be more active as long as there are no objective indications that it improves a patient's condition. In particular, discussions with the family that touch on family conflicts do not appear helpful for at least some patients while they are still in a depressive condition (Matakas *et al.* 1999). The family contributes significantly to the development of depression. However, this is not fully understood yet. As long as we cannot identify this connection it would seem the best course to relieve both, the patient and the family.

Regressive treatment does not mean that patients are left alone to deal with their problems in the family or at work. But they should not work on these problems until they have largely overcome their symptoms of depression if these are more than moderate. Severe depression, therefore, should be treated in two stages: first of all the depressive symptoms should be treated, and then the patient should be helped to deal with his social, family and work conflicts.

Conclusion

In this chapter we have shown that, in the context of a psychiatric hospital, it is important to base a suicide prevention strategy on the appropriate treatment of moderate and severe depression. The essence of this treatment is regressive, through which approach the patient is temporarily relieved of social stresses, and her/his regressive needs are met through offering to guarantee her/his narcissistic stability. Under this treatment model, suicides in the hospital have decreased and this can be satisfactorily explained by understanding how the regressive approach is crucial when working with moderate and severe levels of depression.

Acknowledgement

The authors are grateful to Dr John T. Maltsberger and Dr David C. Clark for their substantial help in revising the manuscript.

Note

1 Comparison of the suicide rate before and after October 1999 in a cross table according to the two-sided version of Fisher's exact test reveals a significant difference at a level of 1 per cent ($p < 0.01$). A one-way ANOVA of the suicide

rate before and after October 1999 yields a value of p = 0.038 based on the suicide rate per admissions per year (1984/1-1999/9: mean 396; 95 per cent CI: 217, 574. 1999/10-2005/12: mean 82; 95 per cent CI: 2, 162). If one takes a rolling average of three years, then p = 0.001 (1984/1–1999/9: mean 391; 95 per cent CI: 295, 486. 1999/10–2005/12: mean 103; 95 per cent CI: 46, 160).

References

Appleby, L., Shaw, J., Amos, T., McDonell, R., Harris, C., McCann, K., Kiernan, K., Davies, S., Bickley, H. and Parsons, R. (1999) 'Suicide within 12 months of contact with mental health services· national clinical survey', *British Medical Journal* 318: 1235–1239.

Blatt, S.J. (1998) 'Contributions of psychoanalysis to the understanding and treatment of depression', *Journal of the American Psychoanalytic Association* 46: 723–752.

Clark, D.C. (1995) 'Epidemiology, assessment, and management of suicide in depressed patients', in E.E. Beckham and W.R. Leber (eds) *Handbook of Depression* (pp. 526=-538), London and New York: Guilford Press.

Eagles, J.M., Klein, S., Gray, N.M., Dewar, I.G. and Alexander, D.A. (2001) 'Role of the psychiatrists in the prediction and prevention of suicide: a perspective from north-east Scotland', *British Journal of Psychiatry* 178: 494–496.

Fawcett, J., Scheftner, W., Clark, D., Hedeker, D., Gibbons, R. and Coryell, W. (1987) 'Clinical predictors of suicide in patients with major affective disorders: a controlled prospective study', *American Journal of Psychiatry* 144: 35–40.

Fonagy, P. (1999) 'Final remarks', in R.J. Perelberg (ed.) *Psychoanalytic Understanding of Violence and Suicide* (pp. 161–168), London and New York: Routledge.

Freud, S. (1917) 'Mourning and melancholia', in J. Strachey (ed.) *The Standard Edition of the Works of Sigmund Freud, XIV* (pp. 237–258), London: Hogarth.

Gladstone, G.L., Mitchell, P.B., Parker, G., Wilhelm, K., Austin, M.P. and Eyers, K. (2001) 'Indicators of suicide over 10 years in a specialist mood disorders unit sample', *Journal of Clinical Psychiatry* 62: 945–951.

Heller, M. and Haynal, V. (1997) 'The doctor's face: a mirror of his patient's suicidal projects', in J. Guimón (ed.) *The Body in Psychotherapy* (pp. 46–51), Basel: Karger.

Leenaars, A.A. (2004) *Psychotherapy with Suicidal People. A Person-centred Approach*, Chichester: John Wiley and Sons, Ltd.

Maltsberger, J.T., Hendin, H., Haas, A.P. and Lipschitz, A. (2003) 'Determination of precipitating events in the suicide of psychiatric patients', *Suicide and Life-Threatening Behavior* 33: 111–119.

Martin, B.A. (2000) 'The Clarke Institute experience with completed suicide: 1966 to 1997', *Canadian Psychiatry* 45: 630–638.

Matakas, F. (1992) *Neue Psychiatrie*, Göttingen: Vandenhoeck & Ruprecht.

Matakas, F. and Rohrbach, E. (2005) 'Zur Psychodynamik der schweren Depression und die therapeutischen Konsequenzen', *Psyche* 59: 892–917.

Matakas, F. and Rohrbach, E. (2007) 'Suicide prevention in the psychiatric hospital', *Suicide and Life-Threatening Behavior* 37: 507–517.

Matakas, F., Schmitt-Voss, T., Rohrbach, E., Vogtt-Kempe, A. and Churan, J.

(1999) 'Effect of the family relationship on in-patient treatment of severe major depression: is family therapy always appropriate?', *Family Therapy* 26: 201–211.

Menninger, K. (1938) *Man Against Himself*, New York: Harcourt, Brace and Co.

Powell, J., Geddes, J., Deeks, J., Goldacre, M. and Hawton, K. (2000) 'Suicide in psychiatric hospital inpatients', *British Journal of Psychiatry* 176: 266–272.

Schachter, J. (1999) 'The paradox of suicide: issues of identity and seperateness', in R.J. Perelberg (ed.) *Psychoanalytic Understanding of Violence and Suicide* (pp. 147–158), London and New York: Routledge.

Sharma, V., Persad, E. and Kueneman, K. (1998) 'A closer look at inpatient suicide', *Journal of Affective Disorders* 47: 123–129.

Spitz, R.A. and Wolf, K.M. (1946) 'Anaclitic depression. An inquiry into the genesis of psychiatric conditions in early childhood', *Psychoanalytic Study of the Child* 2: 213–242.

Wolfersdorf, M., Klinkisch, M., Franke, C., Keller, F., Wurst, F.M., Dobmeier, M. (2003) 'Patientensuizid – Ein Kontrollgruppenvergleich Suizidenten versus nach Behandlungszeitraum parallelisierte Patienten eines psychiatrischen Fachkrankenhauses', *Psychoanalytic Praxis* 30: 14–20.

Chapter 14

On being affected without being infected: managing suicidal thoughts in student counselling

Ann Heyno

> Students and suicide have come to represent something heavily symbolic in our collective psyches. Young people who kill themselves, particularly if they are students, face us with the perennial and discomforting question, why did he do it when he had everything to live for?
>
> (Coren 1997: 89–90)

A Royal College of Psychiatrists' report (2003) on the mental health of students in higher education said that students 'are at no higher risk of suicide than the general population, and may be at lower risk'. The report went on to say that 'the significance of reported suicidal ideation requires urgent evaluation'. While intense public scrutiny, particularly from the media, continues to surround student suicide, the prevalence of suicidal ideation in our universities has not yet been addressed.

This chapter will focus on that gap. It will ask why completed suicide, which is relatively rare in universities, receives more attention than suicidal ideation, which is relatively common. It will consider the effect this attention has on universities, student counselling services and the clinical work of counsellors.

The emphasis of the chapter will be on suicide prevention within a university setting, looking first at the counsellor's role, in terms of organisational expectations and projections, and then at the clinical aspect of prevention. It will show that if a connection can be maintained between a counsellor and the suicidal part of a student by constant vigilance of the countertransference, then the risk of suicide may be reduced. It will demonstrate that if counsellors can bear the projections that surround suicide, they can do a great deal to prevent suicidal thoughts from becoming suicidal acts.

Finally, it will suggest that the current expansion in higher education and the rapid growth in technology are amongst the factors that have led to a depersonalisation of the learning process which may leave today's students more vulnerable to depression and suicidal thoughts.

The institutional role of the counselling service in a university

Student suicide has attracted interest and concern for almost a century. In 1910, the Vienna Psychoanalytic Society (VPS) symposium 'On Suicide' made particular reference to suicide amongst students, and there are many clinical examples of students in the literature on suicide. In his book, *A Psychodynamic Approach to Education*, Alex Coren comments that, 'While there is an increased vulnerability to suicide in adolescence and young adulthood, a seemingly disproportionate amount of attention is paid to students who kill themselves' (1997: 90). He does not say why this is the case but he does imply that it may be because they are seen as a privileged group with apparently everything to live for. However, alongside the privilege, come great expectations, both from society and from students themselves. If these expectations cannot be met on either side, psychological problems can ensue.

Currently there are no figures on the number of student suicides in universities, and researchers on the RaPSS project (2006/2007) agreed that it would be difficult for universities to produce these figures. Nevertheless the pressure to do so remains and, despite the objective reality that students are no more likely to kill themselves than anyone else in their age group, student suicide remains under constant scrutiny.

Coren (1997) notes that psychoanalysts, including Freud, who attended the 1910 symposium in Vienna debated whether the severity of the Austrian education system had a causal effect in student suicide. Coren also refers to Wilhelm Stekel's suggestion at the VPS symposium that suicide is linked to anger and can be an aggressive attack on the parents. He quotes Stekel's well-known suggestion that 'No one kills himself who has never wanted to kill another, or at least wished the death of another' (Friedman 1967: 87).

'Our difficulty in viewing suicide as a communication often involving hostile or negative thoughts may be an attempt to deny that these troublesome feelings exist or existed', says Coren.

> The nature of the suicidal act is then denied, and the students who kill themselves are turned into innocent 'murder' victims. The hunt for the 'murderer' is then instigated, with education immediately becoming a suspect. That education is a prime suspect in this investigation is alluded to in a contribution by Freud to the VPS discussions, in which he suggests that '. . . schools ought to do something more than drive their pupils to suicide.'
>
> (Coren 1997: 90)

Similar implied criticism of the educational system persists today. When a student kills themselves, there is normally intense media interest and a wish to find someone or something to blame. This scrutiny, in terms of blame and projected guilt, is problematic for universities, as it is for prisons and other public institutions. It makes universities very cautious about talking and thinking about suicide and it creates a climate of fear in which suicide can become a taboo subject. If this happens and a university becomes infected by the fear that it will be blamed if a student commits suicide, then suicidal risk and suicidal thoughts also become difficult to talk about. Confusing actual death by suicide with suicidal thoughts gets in the way of thinking about what can be done to help the many students who feel suicidal. It also creates a situation in which omnipotence and denial are used as defences against the realistic anxiety that there are always some students who are at risk of killing themselves.

As Coren implies, the relatively privileged position of students may contribute to the attention they attract when they kill themselves, but what is less clear is why the significance of suicidal thinking in the student population is denied. One possibility may be that it is simply too difficult to accept that many of our students, with apparently everything to live for, have self-murderous thoughts they are in danger of acting out. If the incidence of these self-destructive thoughts is perceived to be increasing in the student population, it may feel safer and more manageable to focus on completed suicide. In this way the unthinkable aggression and despair, associated with suicidal thoughts, can be located outside the individual and projected into universities, who can then be blamed for failing their students. It may be easier to accept that organisations drive people to suicide than to think about the level of despair students experience when they have suicidal thoughts.

In his chapter, 'Who is killing what or whom? Some notes on the internal phenomenology of suicide', David Bell (Chapter 4, this volume) acknowledges that 'no one can be absolutely prevented from committing suicide'. Nevertheless, he continues, 'it is easy for staff to become identified with an omnipotence which dictates that it is entirely their responsibility'. If universities fear they will be publicly blamed when a suicide happens, this can lead to this omnipotent fantasy that all suicide is preventable and the entire responsibility for keeping students alive lies with the university. In other words, universities can become infected by the fear of being blamed for suicide, rather than being affected by the realistic anxiety that some students may act out their suicidal thoughts.

Because it is an impossible task for universities to prevent student suicide, the omnipotent fantasy that they can, gets projected onto student counselling services. These services are then expected to protect the institution from all the unwanted publicity, perceived ignominy and psychic pain of a student suicide. This organisational projection can have an effect on the clinical work of counselling services. If the counsellors become infected by the fantasy that universities are responsible for student suicide, they can identify with the projection. They may then find themselves in a position where the 'determination to save the patient acquires a religiosity, the staff believing themselves to be specially selected for this mission' (Bell, Chapter 4, page 55). Alternatively, if counselling services try to protect themselves from the uncomfortable projection by refusing to be affected by it, they are in danger of denying the seriousness of suicidal risk in the student population. Either way, the fear of an actual student death may prevent universities and student counsellors from being alert to the many students who are experiencing suicidal thoughts and who can be helped.

Previously (Heyno 2004) I have suggested that there are both conscious and unconscious reasons why universities employ counsellors. Consciously they do so out of genuine concern for the welfare of students. At a less conscious level, they may employ counsellors because they are afraid that the disturbed and disturbing parts of the institution cannot be managed within their everyday structures. Hence, in part, universities need counsellors to provide a receptacle for all the unacceptable, disturbing and unwanted aspects of the institution and the uncaring parts of themselves that they cannot consciously bear.

In their book *Organisations, Anxieties and Defences*, R.D. Hinshelwood and M. Chiesa (2002: 210), talk about the psychological function of psychiatric hospitals in society. They refer to the work of Elizabeth Bott Spillius who says patients are often admitted on the basis of the assumption

> that madness cannot be contained and accommodated as part of ordinary personal and social life. It is beyond the pale, or it should be beyond the pale. If it is kept inside it will destroy the individual, the family, the fabric of society. At all costs it must be separated off and sent somewhere else, and the main task of a mental hospital is to be that 'somewhere else'.
>
> (Bott 1976: 121)

I think there are exact parallels in education. At an unconscious level, student counselling services are expected to be that 'somewhere else' that Bott refers to in relation to psychiatric hospitals.

Hinshelwood and Chiesa (2002: 212) describe the position of a psychotherapist in a psychiatric hospital as representing a 'counter-culture' which is both feared and denigrated. The position of a counsellor in a university is similar. Counselling is counter to the culture of teaching and learning. Hinshelwood and Chiesa (2002: 213) talk about the way a psychotherapist is seen in a prison as 'a soft, gullible, weak point in the system'. At other times, a psychotherapist in a psychiatric hospital 'may be idealised and turned to for magic – an attitude that the psychotherapist may himself be tempted to encourage'. This is certainly true of student counsellors who are often invested with the power to deal with mental health problems and situations no one else can manage, including potential suicide.

The projections that student counsellors receive add up to what Donald Meltzer (1967: 20, 23) calls the 'toilet-breast' into which all the excrement is dumped, to be flushed but not processed. It is important that counsellors do not get infected by this excrement because the projections are not personal and they in no way reflect the quality of a counsellor's work or the value of what she is providing. They are simply part of the institutional role of being a counsellor in a university. When a former financial controller greeted me by saying, 'here comes the soft face of the university', it jarred. At the same time it would have been pointless to challenge him. Institutions need counsellors who can carry and survive their projections without retaliating or being infected and contaminated by them.

The way in which student counselling services manage organisational projections has implications for the management of suicidal students. Counselling services need to be aware that the organisational expectation is that they carry all the worry and responsibility for suicide risk. They have to accept this expectation but they don't have to act it out. They need to be affected by the projections that are coming their way but not persecuted or infected by them. If counsellors carry too much unprocessed anxiety about organisational pressure, or too much fear about being blamed if a student dies, or if they are too worried about being wholly responsible for keeping students alive, this can infect the therapeutic relationship and contaminate the clinical work.

The use of the countertransference in managing suicidal risk in students

So far I have been suggesting that the fear of being blamed gives rise to an omnipotent fantasy that universities are responsible for preventing all student suicide and this omnipotent fantasy is projected onto counselling services. We will now turn from the organisational dynamics involved in student suicide and look at work with individual clients. We will focus on how vigilance in countertransference gives counsellors important information about suicide risk.

At the University of Westminster in London, where I work as a student counsellor and Head of the Counselling and Advice Service, we see around 700 students a year and, in line with national trends, by far the highest presenting problem is depression (33 per cent). A significant proportion of these depressed students have suicidal thoughts and between 5 per cent and 10 per cent of the students seen each year are considered, by counsellors, to be at risk of acting out their suicidal thoughts.

In the twenty-seven years I have worked at Westminster, there have been relatively few suicides, and we are fortunate that not many of our students have made suicide attempts while in counselling. However, despite this, I always have in mind that a suicide attempt or a suicide could happen. At times colleagues have perceived me as over-anxious about suicide risk. However, I am now convinced that rather than being something negative, the healthy, rather than the omnipotent anxiety that suicidal students evoke in counsellors plays a useful part in managing risk. If we take a cue from Laufer's idea that suicide is always 'carried out in a disassociated or transient psychotic state' (1995: 115), we also need to note that suicidal thoughts can be split off from conscious reality but their disappearance may only be temporary. A useful analogy can be made with the Alcoholics Anonymous concept of 'once an alcoholic always an alcoholic'. Once a student has had suicidal thoughts or been a suicide risk, counsellors need to be aware that the risk is always there, even when it appears to have vanished or there is very little evidence that suicide is still a danger.

If counsellors can allow themselves to be affected but not infected by the uncomfortable projections they receive from suicidal students, just as they do in an organisational context, they can use these feelings to stay connected with the suicidal part of the client. This active connectedness by the counsellor with the split-off bit of the student can help prevent acting out even when the objective assessment of suicide risk is relatively low. If a student perceives that a counsellor is not keeping in mind the ongoing risk of suicide, then the danger of acting out may be increased. Clinical material from a student counselling caseload and my experience as a manager of a counselling service will be used to illustrate this countertransference state and how it can be used in working with students.

The countertransference comes to be so important in working with suicidal students because those students who contemplate suicide are considering an act that bypasses words as a way of dealing with unbearable feelings. Instead of being able to use words to bring relief to these feelings, they revert to a pre-verbal, paranoid-schizoid state in which they project their anger, despair and anxiety outwards in an attempt to communicate. If these communications are not heard, then the unverbalised feelings are in danger of being acted out. With clients who are contemplating bypassing words to express what they feel, counsellors have to be even more alert to countertransference feelings to pick up cues that cannot be communicated verbally. That puts being constantly vigilant about the countertransference into a central position in relation to working with suicidal students.

The following is an example of a student who made his counsellor very anxious in a way that was helpful in containing the client's suicidal thoughts. In this case, the counsellor made use of the countertransference to stay connected to the suicidal part of a student in his final year at university. The student had suffered a family trauma in adolescence. At the peak of his suicidal ideation the counsellor was seeing him twice a week. For several weeks she had been acutely worried about this student, who was very isolated, severely depressed and consistently saying his life was not worth living. During this period the student had affected the counsellor so deeply that at times she woke early in the morning worrying about him. At one point the counsellor felt she was the only human contact the student had. Her countertransference feeling was that she was handling a very fragile baby who might not survive without her.

At this point the counsellor was in danger of being infected by her client. In reality she was not responsible for this student's survival, unlike the mother of a real baby. Once she realised that the anxiety she was feeling belonged to the countertransference she was able to use it appropriately. In this way, the counsellor was able to turn her feelings into 'useful anxiety', an example of being affected without being infected.

For the counsellor to stay internally connected through her counter-transference with the student's suicidal depression while at the same time maintaining professional boundaries was uncomfortable and difficult, especially as her anxiety peaked whenever the student was late or missed an appointment. However, instead of becoming overwhelmed by her anxiety, she recognised it as a projection of the client's state of mind and a vital way of staying in contact with the client's deepest suicidal feelings. Slowly over the months and with the help of psychiatric intervention, the danger of the student acting out lessened. One day, following a missed appointment, in this objectively less dangerous period, the student came to a session saying he was on his way to see a friend who would give him some pills so he could take an overdose. He had spent the missed session getting drunk with this friend in an attempt to disconnect himself from normality, but by this time the pull to connect with the counsellor was also strong. The student had come to the session to stop himself acting out by telling the counsellor what he was planning to do. 'If I tell you that I'm going to get these pills from my friend', he said, 'then I won't do it because I've told you.'

The earlier life and death communications that had been picked up through the countertransference had provided a lifeline for this student. It had helped him to believe that the counsellor was connected to his suicidal part and was taking this very seriously. This helped him to move to a position in which he could begin to use words to communicate the depth of the despair he was feeling. Although he was still at risk and the counsellor continued to be very anxious about him, the danger of acting out was reduced.

This example shows how anxiety in the counsellor made the student feel connected to the counsellor and reduced the risk of acting out. 'I won't do it because I've told you.' The anxiety also served to remind the counsellor that the risk had not gone away and could re-emerge at any time. With some students the actual risk of suicide is objectively less likely than it was in this case. However, this does not necessarily stop anxiety-provoking feelings about suicide risk being projected into the counsellor.

The next example is of a student who only caused serious anxiety about suicide risk several months into the counselling. This 23-year-old international student used anger to defend herself against her depression and in this way managed to keep her suicidal thoughts at bay. However, when she got more in touch with her depression, the counsellor had to be alert to her suicidal part and actively connect with it. The student came to counselling during her second year at university. The previous spring she had taken an overdose following a family crisis, in her home country, that brought up memories she found unbearable. On the surface this student gave the appearance of being self-confident and self-assured. At times she came over as aggressive and hostile, particularly in relation to the conditions in her home country and the problems within her family. As the end of the year approached, she became less angry and more reflective. She became worried about her coursework and her exams and one day she said she felt empty, isolated and lonely. She was afraid that if she was not angry, she would become very depressed. When she was saying this the counsellor became overwhelmed by a feeling that she must not get in touch with her depression at any cost. She questioned herself about how helpful counselling had been and whether the student would have been better off without it. The student had not mentioned suicidal thoughts for a long time but because of constant vigilance about suicide and because she had taken an overdose in the past, the counsellor asked her if she felt suicidal again now. The student responded by saying that that was what she feared. She feared that if she got depressed she would feel suicidal and she didn't want to feel like that. She didn't want to die because of the grief it would bring to her family. By using countertransference feelings and constant vigilance about suicide risk it was possible to help the client put into words what she might otherwise have felt impelled to act out.

The third example is of a student who failed to arouse any useful anxiety in his counsellor. Despite saying, in the first session, that he was afraid he would put himself in dangerous situations in traffic, where he might get killed, the counsellor failed to pick up on the seriousness of this. The suicidal part of him was so split off that both counsellor and client lost sight of it until counselling was about to end. This student explained straight away that his girlfriend had just told him she was having an affair. He was devastated by this unexpected news and said that he was afraid of what might happen to him because he kept riding his bicycle through red traffic lights. Superficially this was a very together young man who came for counselling in his final term at university because his girlfriend had rejected him. The main focus of the brief work was the relationship break-up and how he felt about it. The extent of his suicidal thoughts and his depression were not explored. It was only when the sessions were coming to an end that the counsellor realised properly that there was something seriously wrong. In her mind he had used the sessions well and he planned to continue counselling when he returned to his home town. However, what was surprising was that he didn't seem to mind at all that he was finishing counselling despite having formed a good attachment.

At this point, it was clear there was something that hadn't been understood. This was confirmed when the student said he was upset because his mother hadn't taken his problems with his girlfriend seriously. The counsellor wondered whether he felt she hadn't taken his self-destructive thoughts seriously either and took this up with him. He confirmed this was how he felt. The counsellor also wondered why she hadn't suggested he saw a doctor when he had first told her about his self-destructive thoughts. This is something she would normally have done. When it was, at last, suggested he might like to see the university psychiatrist, he jumped at the idea. The following week, before he had even seen the psychiatrist, he came back saying he felt a lot better. The fact that his fear, that he would harm himself and possibly kill himself, was eventually taken very seriously was an enormous relief to him.

Despite the various warning signs being there, they were missed. There was the relationship break-up, the fact that he felt his parents didn't love each other, the statement that he felt he would never be able to love anyone, his hopelessness about the future – all signals of depression – and yet this bright young man did not cause any worry until the work was nearly at an end.

Keeping anxiety about risk constantly in mind helps to contain suicidal thoughts and reduce the danger of these thoughts being acted out. In 'Mourning and melancholia', Freud (1917) suggests that where ambivalence and hostility towards the lost object dominate, mourning is impeded and a melancholic state ensues. He introduced the idea of the object being incorporated inside the self and the self being attacked as though it were the object. Experience of working as a student counsellor has shown me that it is not only the attack on the object that is a risk factor in suicidal ideation, but also the loss of hope of connecting with an object. At some level the suicidal part of these students has lost hope of connecting with an object.

This student felt empty inside. Rejection by his girlfriend was concrete confirmation to him that he was unable to connect. His socially adept manner disguised a part of him that felt isolated, alone and suicidal. The absence of anxiety in the countertransference was the signal that the suicidal part of him had become split off and disconnected. It was the realisation that this didn't feel right that enabled the counsellor to re-connect with the suicidal part of the client. This was an example of the counsellor not being infected enough.

In this case the objective risk of suicide, confirmed by the psychiatrist, was not high, but the danger of this student acting out his suicidal feelings may have been greater if the seriousness of how he felt had continued not to be registered. By referring him to the psychiatrist it had been acknowledged that his fear was real and his suicidal thoughts had been taken seriously.

Ironically the weak signals he was giving unconsciously put him at greater risk of acting out than the first two clients. It was only when the counsellor thought about why she wasn't anxious that she was able to be in touch with the suicidal part of him.

With the first two students the uncomfortable projections in the counter-transference provided the useful anxiety needed to keep in contact and to contain the suicidal part of the student. In the third case, attention had to be paid to the way the suicidal feelings were being split off and to what was missing in the countertransference. In the first two cases the counsellor had to be careful not to be infected by the projections. In the third case, she had to ask herself why she wasn't being infected.

In none of the cases described was the university or the counselling service responsible for the student's self-murderous thoughts. Universities do not cause students to kill themselves or to feel suicidal. Nevertheless there are aspects of the way organisations and systems operate that can put students at greater risk of feeling isolated, lonely and de-personalised. If this is the case, then their suicidal feelings can come to the foreground and students can be at greater risk of acting out their suicidal thoughts. The more personal a university is in terms of numbers and the one-to-one contact it offers students, such as personal tutoring, good induction systems, mentoring schemes, and well-resourced student support, including counselling, the more likely it is that students will feel connected and able to ask for help when they experience negative and self-destructive thoughts. The more impersonal the institution, the more lost and disconnected the individual will feel. In this situation students are at a higher risk of acting out their suicidal thoughts, possibly accidentally, as a way of trying to make contact and communicate with someone.

Conclusions

If universities and counsellors are to be in the right state of mind to address the growing problem of students with suicidal thoughts, they need to accept that they cannot carry the omnipotent fantasy that all suicide can be prevented. All they can do is to try to minimise the risk of suicide by accepting that that risk is always there. If they can bear this level of 'useful anxiety' they can do a great deal. Because of the psychotic nature of some suicidal thoughts and the fact that they can be split off, counsellors cannot rely on words alone to pick up suicidal risk. If the cues are picked up in the countertransference then risk may be reduced. If counsellors can resist being infected by the organisational fantasy that requires them to be responsible for all student suicide, this will free them to be affected by the 'useful anxiety' that accompanies students with suicidal thoughts.

This non-verbal aspect of suicide risk means that counsellors must be constantly vigilant in ways that might not be immediately obvious. For example, all students who say they are depressed should be asked if they are suicidally depressed; all disclosures of suicidal thoughts should be brought into the open and discussed in detail; every mention of suicidal thoughts should be taken very seriously, whatever the objective risk, and once these thoughts have been mentioned, the risk must continue to be held in mind even when it has apparently disappeared. In this way suicidal thoughts are less likely to become a source of shame, isolation and aggressive acting out.

In this chapter it has been suggested that a disproportionate amount of attention is paid to completed student suicide, which is relatively rare, compared with suicidal thoughts, which are relatively common. We have seen how universities come to be blamed for students who kill themselves and consequently adopt the omnipotent fantasy that suicide can be prevented. This fantasy then gets projected onto student counselling services. Counsellors have to manage these organisational projections as well as metabolising the sometimes terrible states of mind of their clients. We have seen how attention to the 'useful anxiety' aroused by students with suicidal thoughts and constant vigilance about countertransference may reduce the risk of suicide. We have noted that the non-verbal aspect of suicide risk means that counsellors need to be pro-active in picking up cues about risk and helping students put their unbearable thoughts into words.

Finally, I have suggested that it may be too difficult to accept the idea that increasing numbers of students, with everything to live for, have self-murderous thoughts that could be acted out in our universities. It may feel safer to deny that the aggression and abject loss of hope, involved in suicidal states of mind, belong to the individual. It may be preferable to locate the cause of these feelings in the universities, who can then be blamed for failing their students.

However, while this complicated institutionalised mindset is in place, it is difficult to unravel and debate which social and external forces may, in reality, put students at risk, and what measures, if any, universities can take to alleviate these. One such difficult debate is centred on widening participation and the expansion of university places. On the one hand this has been an excellent development away from the elitism of previous generations. At the same time, it leads to a situation in which universities are such big places that students can easily feel de-personalised and known to no one. For students, vulnerable to suicidal thoughts, this lack of personal contact with academic staff is unhelpful and may exacerbate suicide risk. It resonates with the depressed and empty part of their internal worlds and their lack of hope of ever making a connection, giving rise to suicidal thoughts.

References

Bott, E. (1976) 'Hospital and society', *British Journal of Medical Psychology* 49: 97–140.

Coren, A. (1997) *A Psychodynamic Approach to Education*, London: Sheldon Press.

Freud, S. (1917) 'Mourning and melancholia', in J. Strachey (ed.) *The Standard Edition of the Works of Sigmund Freud, XIV* (pp. 237–258), London: Hogarth.

Friedman, P. (ed.) (1967) *On Suicide*, New York: International Universities Press.

Heyno, A. (2004) 'The counselling service as a container', presentation at the Counselling in Educational Settings Course, London, British Association of Psychotherapists.

Hinshelwood, R.D. and Chiesa, M. (eds) (2002) *Organisations, Anxieties and Defences: Towards a Psychoanalytic Social Policy*, London: Whurr.

Laufer, M. (ed.) (1995) *The Suicidal Adolescent*, London: Karnac Books.

Meltzer, D. (1967) *The Psycho-Analytical Process*, London: Heinemann.

RaPSS Project (2006/2007) 'Responses and prevention in student suicide' conducted by Papyrus, University of Central Lancashire and King's College London.

Royal College of Psychiatrists (2003) 'Report on the mental health of students in higher education'.

Chapter 15

Suicidality in later life

Reinhard Lindner, Astrid Altenhöfer, Georg Fiedler and Paul Götze

Introduction

Suicidality in later life is relatively neglected in the literature as a whole and in psychoanalytic thinking in particular. The particular issues arising in working psychotherapeutically with older people have been insufficiently addressed. Suicidal people in later life find it hard to access therapeutic help. In this chapter we discuss findings from interviews with people aged over 60 years who were suicidal but who felt unable to talk about this in a professionally helping relationship. We aim, through addressing the transference and countertransference patterns in these interviews, to explore issues that contribute to difficulties in achieving engagement in helpful therapeutic relationships, and thus to assess how therapists can approach this work more effectively.

Suicide in later life: an overview and therapeutic considerations

Suicidality among the elderly is a mental health and socio-political problem needing serious attention. In Germany, like so many other western countries, suicide rates rise significantly with advancing age. Rates of *attempted* suicide in old age are clearly decreasing compared with committed suicide – that is, in contrast to young people, the elderly are more likely to commit suicide without previously attempting to do so. Suicidality in old age has a particularly high mortality rate. In psychodynamic psychotherapy suicidality of the elderly seems to be a neglected topic.

Teising (2001) mentioned the growing importance of the body in old age, which again becomes the organizer of the psyche. Suicidal psychodynamics are characterized by unbearable affects concerning the ageing process, which are projected into the body and split off in a rescue fantasy, a process which also occurs in adolescence. Based on the widespread tradition in Germany of conceptualizing suicidality as a symptom, a fatal ending of a narcissistic crisis (Litman 1969; Henseler 1974; Henseler and Reimer 1981;

see also Etzersdorfer, Chapter 12 this volume), Teising described a potential suicide beginning with the loss of a narcissistic object or an important ego function, which diminishes the ego ideal. The most threatening and feared potential aspect of becoming very old is that of needing care. If this cannot be tolerated because dependency on another person, both physically and emotionally, has to be avoided and the internalized parental object is felt to be unable to bear and detoxify the wishes for dependency (Martindale 1989), then suicide can feel like the only option: 'What is most important is not the real physical limitation or the fact of dependency on care, but the related intrapsychic individual significance for the narcissistic experience' (Teising 2001: 4).

There are special developmental psychodynamics concerning elderly suicidal men, who, due to psychosocial and physical triggering events, reactualize vulnerability in male identity. This vulnerability is the outcome of the stage of disidentification from the mother, which was not facilitated by the development of a stable relationship with the father. These theoretical assumptions have important implications for the transference when working with older suicidal patients. The transference is challenging where the patient unconsciously projects parts of his relationship with his own children onto the younger therapist – for instance, the (German) patient, who vehemently shouted to the therapist: 'You were not a soldier in the war!' Here the patient may want to make unconscious murderous impulses real, which the younger therapist has to ward off because of his own aggressive feelings towards his parents. This could result in feelings of anxiety and guilt, and may lead to withdrawal and not accepting the patient for therapy, or acting out with an offer of real social help instead of psychotherapeutic understanding.

It is evident that the suicidal elderly benefit from psychotherapeutic and psychiatric treatment. In western countries there is a noticeable discrepancy between the increased risk of completed suicide in old age, and a low take-up of professional help for their suicidality by the elderly. This discrepancy is particularly high among older and old men (Canetto 1992, 1994). At 38 per cent, people over 60 are proportionally over-represented in overall suicide mortality figures. However, in the group seeking help in Germany and the USA, they are clearly under-represented at 10 per cent at most of all out-patients in crisis facilities (Erlemeier 2002). Factors associated with this discrepancy are – as mentioned above – to be found on both sides of the therapeutic relationship.

A study of suicidality in elderly people: sample and method

As part of a larger study on the intrapsychic and psychosocial situation of the suicidal elderly we carried out thirty in-depth interviews with people aged over 60 who judged themselves to be suicidal and who felt unable to talk

Table 15.1 Characteristics of the sample

Items	Total (%)	Women (%)	Men (%)
Total	30 (100)	18 (60)	12 (40)
Age			
60–69	16 (53)	8 (44)	8 (66)
70–79	8 (27)	6 (33)	2 (17)
80–89	5 (17)	3 (17)	2 (17)
> 90	1 (3)	1 (6)	0 (0)
Education			
Not given	7 (23)	6 (33)	1 (8)
Primary school	7 (23)	1 (6)	6 (50)
Secondary school	9 (31)	8 (44)	1 (8)
A levels/university	7 (23)	3 (17)	4 (32)
Marital Status			
Single	5 (17)	2 (12)	3 (25)
Married	11 (36)	6 (33)	5 (41)
Separated	1 (3)	1 (6)	0 (0)
Divorced	4 (14)	2 (12)	2 (17)
Widowed	8 (27)	6 (33)	2 (17)
Not given	1 (3)	1 (6)	0 (0)
Lives			
Alone	18 (60)	10 (56)	8 (66)
With spouse	10 (33)	6 (33)	4 (32)
With friend	2 (7)	2 (12)	0 (0)
Children	22 (73)	15 (83)	7 (58)
Grandchildren	15 (50)	10 (56)	5 (41)

about this in a professionally helping relationship. The participants were recruited in a variety of ways – for example, through newspaper articles about the research project in Hamburg's daily papers, or after psychiatric examinations following suicide attempts, or in homes for senior citizens where their carers had noticed their suicidal intentions and behaviour, or in a geriatric clinic. All participants were initially given the opportunity to enter into a detailed conversation about their life situation and their suicidality but without any offer of psychotherapeutic treatment. The interviewers, both of whom were experienced psychodynamic psychotherapists, had to perform a complicated balancing act in their dual role of psychoanalytically oriented researcher and potential therapist. Some participants explicitly took part in the study because it was *not* a therapeutic relationship. At the end, only two of the thirty participants actually entered psychotherapy. The characteristics of the sample are set out in Table 151.

The aims of the interview were, first, to investigate the outer edges of an area that psychotherapy can reach, and, second, to track typical transference/ countertransference patterns that can hinder the older suicidal persons and their potential therapists from achieving psychotherapeutic contact and helpful therapeutic relationships.

The qualitative method used in this research project is described elsewhere (Gerhardt 1990, 1994; Stuhr and Wachholz 2001; Lindner 2003, 2006). In a process of qualitative condensation and group discussion, five psychodynamically trained researchers (including the two interviewers) systematically developed ideal typical constellations from the thirty interviews. According to Max Weber (1904), these ideal types are not illustrations of reality but are thought extensions of clinical material with which the respective reality of each case can be compared. For each ideal type there is a prototype – that is, the case which best describes the ideal type. In this study only the three ideal types are presented, which portray a typical transference and countertransference pattern. Other typical aspects concern patterns of biography, and patterns demanding concrete psychosocial assistance.

This method enables the identification and elucidation of typical, overall significant dynamics from a larger collection of material (in this case thirty in-depth interviews) with the aim of generating the possibility of greater potential for generalizations than a single clinical case presentation. Thus the aim is to describe the process and through this method make it more understandable, verifiable and falsifiable.

Ideal typical constellations of transference relationships

'Under pressure and aggressive'[1]

A strong negative transference offer[2] experienced as 'overwhelming' (for example, in being accused of never experiencing help, or of offering 'evil' help) serves to ward off painful experiences of being uprooted, threatened and excluded. An unconscious fear with pressing feelings of being left alone can only be warded off with suicidal fantasies. An impulse to reject the person is experienced in the countertransference.

The prototypical case of this ideal type is Mrs A, a 64-year-old married woman, an economist, who wanted to remain anonymous. In the very first telephone call in reply to a newspaper article about the research project, the participant made it quite clear that she did not expect any type of help and was, in fact, particularly annoyed by and disappointed in psychiatry. She had always been disadvantaged. This had started with her father's enforced kinship imprisonment in a punishment battalion in 1942 (an aunt and uncle were put to death for hiding Jews), followed by the family's post-war odyssey when they were not permitted to leave the Soviet zone. Adding insult to injury, her husband's occupation as a railway worker provoked feelings that the kind of work was contemptible and led to neglect of the family, because he was away for long periods. Finally, she felt the psychiatrists had failed her, leaving her completely on her own with her seriously psychiatrically ill and suicidal husband, plus a lack of medical help for herself. She described a life filled with experiences of uprootedness, exclusion, of having to assert herself, and rejection; a life in which not even the fantasy of creating a 'happy family' needing protection from the threatening outside world had been possible. Quite the contrary, the burdened family members acted in a despicable and destructive manner towards her. She therefore developed a suicide fantasy corresponding with her experiences, of bleeding or choking to death, or of her heart simply stopping – she suffered from asthma and cardiac insufficiency. Suicide was, so she said, 'no longer my own choice. Politics, the health reform will take care of that. I already cannot afford all of the medication.'

She spoke at length, so the interviewer had no choice other than to listen. She even felt the need to correct short comments by the interviewer. But she was increasingly able to speak openly about herself. However, the accusing, angry and disappointed emotions remained the whole time. She did not come up with any ideas as to how she could be helped, although she did say that public places of peace and quiet, such as churches, where one did not have to explain anything or fear control, were of help, as well as cafés, where one could just sit and see normal people. She could not imagine that a therapeutic relationship could be of any help.

'Turns himself off'

A superficially averted transference offer serves to defend against conflictive experiences of an urgent desire for a dyadic relationship and/or fears of being overwhelmed, consumed, and cast out afterwards. There is a partially warded off wish for dependable, effective and concrete support. The ambivalent struggle for independence is experienced in the countertransference, as a feeling of self-ineffectiveness in the relationship.

Of all of the men examined, 41 per cent fell into this category of ideal type. Five of the seven participants allocated to this type were men. This supports the hypothesis that this object-averted transference pattern shows a gender-specific dominance in favour of men.

The prototypical case for this ideal type is Mr S, a 62-year-old widower. The appointment for Mr S was made from a psychiatric department where he was being treated after a suicide attempt some days earlier. He had slashed his wrists with a knife after receiving news that the life support machine, which had been keeping his wife alive since her intake of a toxic amount of medication a few days before, had been turned off. When he talked with the interviewer about six weeks later, he said with bitterness that he had not wished her to be resuscitated. It had been a great mistake to call for an ambulance when he found his wife lifeless in another room. She had been ill for many years, was dependent on alcohol and repeatedly seriously depressive. They had both promised each other to leave this world together and now she had left him.

From the start, Mr S was rejecting, stressing many times that he did not need any help, he had been thinking about life and death for as long as he could remember. Dying was something beautiful for him. Life was merely an episode, an unimportant part of existence. He and his wife had had a strong harmonious bond, he said, although this was said with an accusing under-tone. The interviewer felt like an intruder, unwelcome – totally different from the previous telephone conversations in which Mr S had sounded quite willing and interested, also intimating that he would probably 'need to talk' for quite a time. When he did talk about his life it came as a surprise to the interviewer. He was a refugee child, and should have lost his life at $3\frac{1}{2}$ on boarding a refugee ship in Pillau/East Prussia. He remembered low-flying aircraft attacks, corpses at the side of the road and hunger. The war was far away from the village in Sauerland (West Germany) where he, his mother and his two older siblings finally found a new home. They remained outsiders because of their Protestant religion. His father was missing but returned in 1947. He had been unable to build a real relationship with him. But, he interrupted himself at this point, his biography was too long to recall here, as though he had already said too much about himself. He ended the interview almost abruptly: he wanted to wait a while, he could always get in touch again. The interviewer felt thrown out, and left with a feeling of irritation, a mixture of annoyance and worry.

'Disappointed'

A superficially positive, unconsciously aggressive transference offer acts as a defence against a failed search for an idealized, identity-providing loving relationship with a frequently absent father. The unresolved ideal-ization leads in the professional relationship to a non-verbalization of unconscious aggression (like disappointed anger), which is felt by the interviewer as a countertransference, and is manifest in the suicidal acting out and enactment.

The prototype for this ideal type is Mrs D, a 63-year-old married pensioner. The interview with Mrs D took place in a closed admissions ward at a psychiatric hospital. A few days earlier she had attempted suicide by ingesting a large amount of morphine-containing pain-killers. She said she had 'been tempted to commit suicide, which was so surprising, even for me'. It was not her first attempt: since jumping from a bridge thirteen years ago she had been paraplegic and in a wheelchair.

The interview began in a very friendly atmosphere. Mrs D seemed to be happy that someone was interested in her and her story. Her hair was carefully groomed and she sat very upright, almost enthroned on her bed.

The room was tidy, everything in its place ready for her. She felt a pain in her legs, phantom pains, simply unbearable, and she was so ashamed to be always dependent on someone's help, to 'be a burden to everyone', she said. When she said that she had a 'splintered fracture L1', the worst thing anyone could have, she began to cry. The interviewer gave her a handkerchief and experienced a sudden vehement inner contradiction: 'She shouldn't make such a fuss, there are far worse things', he thought. The strength of this emotion somewhat shocked and silenced him.

Mrs D continued. She had received so much support from her husband of forty-three years, he was her 'greatest treasure'. She had actually had thoughts of suicide constantly since then, although, in fact, she could not 'complain in the slightest' as, she said, her husband practically read every wish from her lips. But often the feeling of being at someone's mercy was so terrible and unbearable. But she did not show her anger at all; she was, she said, 'always nice and friendly'. In answer to the interviewer's question whether this had something to do with her biography, she willingly told him that she was 4 years old when her father was killed in the war. Since then she had always missed him and had felt bad and inferior to others. She had always looked for him to come back, although she knew he was dead.

Born in Breslau, she was her parents' only child, and as a refugee with her mother finally ended up in Westphalia. She was very often alone when her mother was working as a caretaker in the household of a teacher. Mrs D was very emotional while she talked and it appeared to be important for her that the interviewer was included in the drama: 'Were you ever alone until eight in the evening as a child?', she asked. At the end of the interview, Mrs D said it might be wrong of her to feel so disadvantaged, because her husband had made up for everything by being so good to her, and she started to cry again. The interviewer left with an annoyed feeling of having been the recipient of a frequently told story.

Understanding the interactions

How can psychoanalysis contribute to the understanding of these inter-actions? The ideal types presented here with their prototypical descriptions point to three interpersonal dynamic patterns.

In the first ideal type, the interviewer finds himself overwhelmed and accused. He has neither the chance to think nor to speak. This interaction serves as a defence against experiences of being uprooted, threatened and excluded. In the second ideal type, there is an overt turning away from objects and currently from the interviewer, which serves to ward off wishes for independence, effective help and support. In the third ideal type, the contact appears positive, friendly and open on the surface but in fact generated feelings of annoyance, contradiction and rejection within the interviewer. This interaction serves to ward off wishes for an identity-providing parental object.

These three ideal types could be understood as encapsulating different qualities of first contacts with suicidal people who, because of their suicidality, were very ambivalent regarding the possibility of psychotherapy. These could be thought about as reflecting three forms of psychic retreat (Steiner 2002), first from paranoid anxieties, second from experiences of destructive dependency, and third from the reactualization of an experience of loss of a central parental object. Depending on the functional psychic level, these retreat scenarios contribute significantly to the avoidance of contact, relief and understanding and preclude the integration of unconscious anxieties and traumatic experiences.

The psychic retreat defence dynamics described by Steiner (2002) serve the withdrawal from an internal and/or external reality when paranoid anxieties become too threatening (Weiß 2002). Such dynamics are generally described in enactments in long psychoanalyses and less so in the course of a first contact or conversation, and one which is not even defined as a psycho-analytical first interview. Nevertheless, these dynamics are also identifiable elsewhere and, according to theory, are central moments of the suicidal person's general avoidance of helpful psychotherapeutic relationships.

The theoretical background has its basis in a phenomenon that has been described as enactment in English literature by Jacobs (2000), and synonymously in German literature by Klüwer (2001) as 'dialogue of action' ('Handlungsdialog'). In enactment, unconscious material crosses from the patient to the therapist, who immediately experiences a psychic change, although this all occurs incidentally, that is, unconsciously, and leads to what Klüwer (2001: 350) and Feldman (2002) call an 'engagement', that is, a partial enactment of archaic object relationships in which the patient has reached and touched the therapist so deeply that he must surrender. Only then can understanding and interpretation begin. This occurs by means of language giving rise to the symbolizing third and leads to a changed view of the patient (Carpy 1989). In the meantime it is general knowledge that such engagements, marked by avoidance and destructive attacks on dependency on the object, are typical in the treatment of the suicidal. They are, however, also central psychic elements which make the *beginning* of a professional helping relationship with the suicidal elderly person more difficult.

Conclusion

Contrary to the idea that suicidality in the elderly can be explained merely by age-related 'actual conflicts' (Heuft *et al.* 2000), our results suggest that long-term, dysfunctional object relationships and traumatic experiences in childhood and youth, as well as how people coped with these experiences, are the causes of suicidality in old age, and that they are directly linked with enactments occurring when setting up contact or, more to the point, avoiding contact. The first prototypical participant overwhelms because her whole life she has defended herself in this way against an outer world that she experiences as evil, and one which bears deathly neglect. She can only expect and accept help of a very distanced and uncommitted type. Throughout his whole life, the second participant withdraws from a battlefield of death, although he appears to have lived a dyad in his relationship with his wife which supported him temporarily – but at the cost of feeling incapable of surviving independently. The third prototypical participant retreats to a 'splendid isolation' of friendliness and apparent openness in which the true story of not being seen and being indignant can only be read in countertransference.

We must acknowledge the bitter truth, as must some of our patients: it is not always possible to recognize such 'engagements' in the first sessions of treatment and to use them to inform the therapeutic position or an interpretation which identifies and engages with the core of the person's unconscious experiences and also aims to avoid confirming that person in his projections and causing a renewed retreat. Being alert to these interaction patterns is a step towards recognizing them and addressing them in the actual clinical situation.

Notes

1 The prototypical participant of this ideal type called herself a 'human lemon', meaning that she feels constantly under external pressure and therefore 'sour', meaning hurt and angry. The ideal type is called 'human lemon' elsewhere (Lindner et al. 2006). The name is changed to avoid a potentially pejorative meaning.
2 The term 'transference offer' means that there is always an unconscious 'subtle pressure' from the patient into the therapist, which Stuhr (1992) described in four steps: (1) the patient projects unbearable experiences into an outer object; (2) the patient tries to hold an empathetic connectedness with this object; (3) in this connectedness the patient tries unconsciously to control the object; and (4) the projected experiences are revitalized in the outer object. The 'transference onslaught' is the most aggressive form of suicidal transference offer (Maltsberger and Buie 1973).

References

Canetto, S.S. (1992) 'She died for love and he for glory', Omega 26: 1–17.
Canetto, S.S. (1994) 'Gender issues in the treatment of suicidal behavior', Death Studies 18: 513–527.
Carpy, D.V. (1989) 'Tolerating countertransference. A mutative process', International Journal of Psycho-Analysis 70: 287–294.
Erlemeier, N. (2002) 'Stand und Perspektiven ambulanter Krisenhilfe bei

Suizidgefährdung im Alter – Ergebnisse einer Befragung', *Suizidprophylaxe* 28: 158–164.

Feldman, M. (2002) 'Zum Umgang mit Projektionen: Formen der Verwicklung', in H. Weiß and C. Frank (eds) *Pathologische Persönlichkeitsorganisationen als Abwehr psychischer Veränderung* (pp. 19–46), Tübingen: Ed. Diskord.

Gerhardt, U. (1990) 'Patient careers in end-stage renal failure', *Social Science and Medicine* 30: 1211–1224.

Gerhardt, U. (1994) 'The use of weberian ideal-type methodology in qualitative data interpretation: an outline for ideal-type analysis', *Bulletin de Méthodologie Sociologique* 45: 74–126.

Henseler, H. (1974) *Narzisstische Krisen: Zur Psychodynamik des Selbstmords*, Opladen: Westdeutscher Verlag.

Henseler, H. and Reimer, C. (eds) (1981) *Selbstmordgefährdung – Zur Psychodynamik und Psychotherapie*, Stuttgart-Bad Cannstadt: Frommann-Holzboog.

Heuft, G., Kurse, A. and Radebold, H. (2000) *Lehrbuch der Geronto-Psychosomatik und Alterspsychotherapie*, München and Basel: Ernst Reinhardt Verlag.

Jacobs, T.J. (2000) 'Unbewusste Kommunikation und verdeckte Enactments in analysischen Setting', in Ulrich Streeck (ed.) *Erinnern, Agieren und Inszenieren: Enactments und szenische Darstellungen im therapeutuschen Prozess* (pp. 97–127), Göttingen: Vanderhoeck & Ruprecht.

Klüwer, R. (2001) 'Szene, Handlungsdialog (Enactment) und Verstehen', in W. Bohleber and S. Drews (eds) *Die Gegenwart der Psychoanalyse – die Psychoanalyse der Gegenwart* (pp. 347–357), Stuttgart: Klett-Cotta.

Lindner, R. (2003) 'Gegenübertragungsdiagnostik in der Psychotherapie suizidaler Männer', *Psychotherapeut* 48: 230–239.

Lindner, R. (2006) 'Suicidality in men in psychodynamic psychotherapy', *Psychoanalytic Psychotherapy* 20: 197–217.

Lindner, R., Fiedler, G., Altenhöfer, A., Götze, P. and Happach, C. (2006) 'Psychodynamic ideal types of elderly suicidal persons based on countertransference', *Journal of Social Work Practice* 20: 347–365.

Litman, R.E. (1969) 'Psychotherapists' orientation towards suicide', in H.L.P. Resnik (ed.) *Suicidal Behaviour*, Boston: Little, Brown & Co.

Maltsberger, J.T. and Buie, D.H. (1973) 'Countertransference hate in the treatment of suicidal patients', *Archives of General Psychiatry* 30: 625–633.

Martindale, B. (1989) 'Becoming dependent again: the fears of some elderly persons and their younger therapists', *Psychoanalytic Psychotherapy* 4: 67–75.

Steiner, J. (2002) 'Fortschritte in einer Analyse, Verlegenheit und Empörung', in H. Weiß and C. Frank (eds) *Pathologische Persönlichkeitsorganisationen als Abwehr psychischer Veränderung* (pp. 67–88), Tübingen: Ed. Diskord.

Stuhr, U. (1992) 'Überlegungen zum Verhältnis, Übertragung/Gegenübertragung und projektive Identifikation. Ihre Bedeutung für die therapeutische Beziehung in der Psychoanalyse', Inaugural lecture, University of Hamburg, Medical Faculty.

Stuhr, U. and Wachholz, S. (2001) 'In search for a psychoanalytic research strategy: the concept of ideal types', in J. Frommer and D.L. Rennie (eds) *Qualitative Psychotherapy Research – Methods and Methodology* (pp. 153–169), Lengerich: Pabst Science Publishers.

Teising, M. (2001) 'Suicidality in the elderly', lecture at the 1st International Congress, 'Suicidality and psychoanalysis', Hamburg.

Weber, M. (1904) 'Die "Objektivität" sozialwissenschaftlicher und sozialpolitischer Erkenntnis', in *Gesammelte Aufsätze zur Wissenschaftslehre* (pp. 146–214), Tübingen: Mohr, 1988.

Weiß, H. (2002) 'Diskussion des Vortrags von John Steiner', in H. Weiß and C. Frank (eds) *Pathologische Persönlichkeitsorganisationen als Abwehr psychischer Veränderung* (pp. 89–96), Tübingen: Ed. Diskord.

Chapter 16

Skin toughening and skin porosity: addressing the issue of self-harm by omission

Maggie Turp

My subject in this chapter is the phenomenon of 'self-harm by omission' and its relationship to disturbances of psychic skin functioning. The term 'self-harm by omission' refers to avoidable injury or damage to health arising from significant lapses in self-care, rather than from acts of self-directed violence. The term is not without complications, since *perfect* self-care is neither normal nor desirable. Living a full life involves a readiness to take risks and, where appropriate, to prioritise emotional self-care over physical self-care. It is not my intention to pathologise behaviour that falls within the normal domain in this regard. Nevertheless, I have encountered in my clinical work lapses in self-care that go far beyond the usual compromises associated with endeavours to find and maintain a workable balance. It is in relation to such examples and their serious consequences for health and functionality that I employ the term 'self-harm by omission'.

To give an example, I worked at one time with a patient, 'Kate', whom I saw on a once-weekly basis. Kate came to me saying that her life 'had been turned upside down' as a result of repetitive strain injury (RSI). It soon became clear that her neglect and overriding of painful and worrying symptoms had resulted in permanent disability. She was unable to work and it was very difficult for her to carry out everyday activities such as shopping or cooking, as she could not lift 'heavy' items such as a bag of groceries or a pot of water. Kate told me she had been advised by one of her consultants not to have children, as she would not be able to carry a child or push a pram up a hill. In addition to her extreme physical weakness, she experienced constant pain in her arms, shoulders, neck and back. Kate, who had worked for years on a keyboard, let me know about her own part in bringing about this situation, telling me she had *always known* that her pain was at its worst on a Friday night and better again by the time Monday morning arrived. I said that she seemed to want me to know about her way of 'carrying on regardless', overriding her symptoms and not taking her pain seriously. To this, she responded simply that she had not wanted to 'make a fuss'.

Reflections on encounters such as these have led to changes in my perception of the phenomenon of self-harm. These changes, in turn, have brought into view questions about how we conceptualise the underlying dynamics involved in self-harming behaviour and how we relate to individuals who self-harm.

Self-harm as a multifaceted phenomenon

Self-harm may take the form of self-directed violence, directed either towards the interior of the body, as in overdosing on prescribed medication, or towards the exterior of the body, as in self-cutting and self-scalding. These behaviours are widely recognised examples of self-harm. Readers will no doubt be familiar both with the behaviours themselves and with some of the conceptual frameworks that have evolved in relation to them.

Self-harm may also take the form of self-harm by omission and this has been the subject of less discussion. Self-harm by omission may likewise affect the interior of the body and lead to ill health, or the exterior of the body and lead to injury or disability, as was the case with Kate. An example of self-harm by omission resulting in ill health is sexual risk-taking, which can of course have serious and lasting consequences as in the case of AIDS and herpes. A further, perhaps more contentious, example is prolonged overworking, which often ushers in ill health and is sometimes fatal. (In the UK, the country with the longest working hours in Western Europe, we may wish to take note of developments in Japan that led to the emergence at the start of the new millennium of the word 'karoshi', meaning 'death by overwork'.) Examples of self-harm by omission resulting in injury and/or disability include failures of self-care that lead to frequent accidental injury, neglect of serious bodily symptoms, and placing oneself in dangerous situations and coming to harm through being assaulted or involved in a physical fight. The possibilities are not mutually exclusive, hence an incident of self-harm by omission – for example, neglect of serious symptoms – may result either in ill health or in injury, or both.

As well as thinking in terms of self-harm by commission and self-harm by omission, I have found it useful to introduce the term 'cashas' – culturally accepted self-harming acts/activities – as an aid to distinguishing between clinically relevant phenomena and those that belong to the domain of the everyday (Turp 2003). The term 'cashas' refers to acts and omissions that result in some level of health impairment or injury but are, as the acronym suggests, widely culturally accepted. Examples include nail-biting, eating poorly, drinking too much alcohol, getting too little sleep, smoking, and engaging in sports and outdoor activities involving a significant level of risk. Cashas are commonplace and occupy a border area between health and pathology. However, when a particular casha is used to excess or in particular circumstances – for example, when a person smokes heavily even though he or she has been previously treated for cancer – we may feel that the meaning and significance of the activity have changed, indicating a shift out of the border zone of the casha and into the domain of clinically relevant self-harm.

A study undertaken into the health status of looked after children (Stein *et al.* 2001) suggests a significant level of co-variation between active self-harm, self-harm by omission and reliance on cashas, with levels of all three appearing to be well above average among those taking part in the research. The researchers noted:

> Serious and widespread mental ill health, including self-harming and attempted suicide
> High levels of smoking and substance abuse
> Elevated levels of risk-behaviour
> Uncompleted courses of medical treatment
> Chronic and neglected health conditions, including poor and uncorrected eyesight, weight problems, glue ear, asthma and eczema

All of these problems were particularly pronounced between the ages of 15 and 18 when the majority of the young people involved were leaving care.

It can be argued that, since difficulties of many different kinds are over-represented in the population of looked after children, this particular clustering of active self-harm and suicidality, self-harm by omission and heavy reliance on cashas is without significance. The case for a link is strengthened, however, by the frequent appearance of co-variation in the consulting room.

For example, I worked at one time with a patient, 'Linda', who actively harmed herself by picking her skin, particularly in the bath, causing sores that formed scabs, which she then picked off. She told me that, underneath her clothes, she was a mass of sores and small bleeding wounds. Over time, I noticed that Linda also suffered an apparently never-ending succession of colds and sore throats. Although she always attended her session, she was never really well. I commented on Linda's apparent lack of concern for her well-being and her assumption that I too would take it for granted that she should not expect to feel well. In drawing attention to Linda's failure to attend to her health problems, my intention was to decline the invitation to collude with her self-harm by omission. Over time, Linda began to eat better, take vitamins and generally take care of her health. Her nose and throat problems abated. Increasingly, the material Linda brought to the sessions indicated the development of an internal object characterised by concern for her well-being and a sense of entitlement to proper care.

Another patient, 'Lorraine', had a long history of self-cutting and suicide attempts. She eventually found her way to once-weekly psychodynamic counselling with a practitioner working with a voluntary organisation and I supervised the work. We learned that, in addition to her obvious self-harm in the form of attacks on herself, Lorraine had other significant difficulties in the arena of self-care. She described being unable to allow herself to rest. When she went out for a drink with her boyfriend, she busied herself collecting and washing the ashtrays from the tables in the pub. At home she tidied and cleaned obsessively. She assumed excessive responsibility for a sister and two nephews, 'rescuing' them by having them to stay for long periods in her one-bedroom flat.

Lorraine's primary defence emerged as one of pseudo-independence in the context of a childhood marked by chaos, violence and periods in local authority care. An apparent self-sufficiency was expressed in many ways, including her preoccupation with the needs and difficulties of others and her arrival at each session with a carton of sweet drink and an attached straw, which she sucked upon intermittently. I have suggested elsewhere (Turp 2004) that the emergence of a capacity for self-care is by no means automatic. It is dependent upon the internalisation of sufficiently frequent and adequate experiences of maternal care. Lacking such experiences, Lorraine had responded with skin toughening, as a defence against, to use Bick's (1986) term, the terrifying experience of 'liquefying' and leaking away. This defence, so vital to her survival as an infant, now manifested both as an obstruction to the therapeutic work and an indication of exactly where the work needed to be focused.

Difficulties with issues of dependency and trust are characteristic of cases where psychic skin issues form a major part of the clinical picture. Therapeutic progress in the work with Lorraine required that these issues be recognised and repeatedly addressed. In response to this approach, Lorraine's episodes of active self-harm diminished in frequency and intensity and so also did her incessant activity. In parallel, her capacity for self-care gradually improved. Towards the end of her two-year period of counselling, she told her counsellor that she and Michael, her boyfriend of seven years, had never taken a holiday together. She was delighted that they were now able to make plans to do so.

Co-variation and clustering of self-harm by commission and omission suggest that the underlying dynamics involved in different forms of self-harming behaviour may be broadly similar, and yet the differences between self-harm by commission and self-harm by omission are striking. The pleasure/relief afforded by, for example, self-cutting features as a highly significant aspect of the aetiology of the disturbance and the meaning of the act of self-harm. In the case of self-harm by omission, however, this element is missing, or at the very least difficult to discern. To take the example of somebody who fails to seek urgently needed medical help, how possible is it to think in terms of pleasure or relief arising from either the inaction itself or the ensuing harm? There is no obvious 'reward' element, such as the rush and relief of the blood flow described by individuals who cut themselves. We may, however, discern the avoidance of psychic pain achieved by putting oneself on hold and turning away from contact. Meltzer (1975) describes how the autistic child on the brink of being overwhelmed by forceful emotions is drawn to allowing his mental organization to passively fall to pieces. Clinical experience suggests that, as Mitrani (2001) describes in her work on 'ordinary people and extra-ordinary protections', understandings such as these may be relevant also to the non-autistic population.

Psychic skin issues

A conceptual framework that readily encompasses self-harm by commission and self-harm by omission is that of psychic skin functioning, introduced in the context of a post-Kleinian framework by Bick (1968, 1986). It is beyond the scope of this chapter to detail the many and valuable contributions, emanating from France, Italy and the USA as well as from the UK, that have been rendered since that time. A theme that runs through the body of relevant work is the role of 'psychic skin' in mediating the relationship between inner and outer worlds.

In health, the physical skin allows messages from and to the external world to be received and transmitted, while at the same time maintaining a boundary between what is inside and what is outside the individual. Physically speaking, these 'messages' come in the form of different touch sensations and of cold and warmth. In the case of 'psychic skin', the reference is to a degree of psychological sensitivity and permeability. Where there is a suitable degree of permeability and resilience, the individual is able to sense and take on board the emotions of others without becoming swamped, and at the same time effectively communicate his or her emotions without losing the sense of a private inner space. It is the skin, both literal and metaphorical, that holds the individual together, safeguards coherence and yet permits the inter-penetration of internal and external worlds of experience.

Bick (1968) describes how the skin is not at first experienced as having a sufficient binding force to hold the infant together. The infant relies on maternal care, including being wrapped in clothes and being held and fed at the breast, for a sense of proper enclosure and embodiment. Where maternally provided skin containment is adequate, it becomes internalised and the infant gradually develops the capacity to continue to feel held together, in one piece, during periods when the mother is absent. No infant enjoys continuous provision of maternal skin containment and an infant has an inherent capacity to defend against the threat of psychological disintegration. Bick (1968) gives examples of intense anxiety relating to skin issues, such as that expressed by her 5-year-old patient 'Jill' whose shoes and clothes must always be tightly fastened, and identifies a primary defence of 'toughening', involving an intense focus and concentration on a non-human object, for example a moving curtain or a patch of light on a wall, or 'muscularity' in the form of constant activity, arching the back or holding the breath.

While such defences are to some degree normal and necessary, Bick observes that repeated failures of maternal care force an infant into excessive reliance upon them. A continuing situation of this kind ushers in a more entrenched distortion of psychic skin functioning, described as 'second skin' formation. Where 'toughening' defences are predominant, a 'hippopotamus hide' develops which protects the infant against the threat of disintegration but at the same time impairs his or her capacity for relationship. This state of affairs, a clinical version of which has been briefly described in relation to 'Lorraine', may be expressed in a number of different ways including a tough confrontational stance, incessant activity, self-caretaking, the avoidance of relationships, or 'adhesive' relating, expressed in clinging and over-dependent behaviour.

In a later paper (1986), Bick includes a clinical example of adhesive identification, a theme developed in the meantime in Meltzer's writing (1974). Bick describes her work with 'Mary', who suffered from eczema and told her analyst that she was 'spilling out'. Bick noticed that Mary both clung to objects and parroted her phrases, leading to the reflection:

> The desperate clinging for survival was mounted in the face of an experience of lacerating separation which would let her life leak away like a liquid substance. It therefore seemed likely that identification and mimicry of my phrases was due to her sticking on to my surface, and I came to think of it as an adhesive identification rather than a projective one.
>
> (1986: 62)

Stephen Briggs (1998) extends Bick's work in this area, exploring the possibility of psychic skin that is 'porous' rather than 'toughened'. In a discussion of feeding difficulties in infancy, he describes two infants, both experiencing poor skin containment. 'Hester' resorts to skin toughening, 'fights the spoon', refuses to allow food into her mouth and becomes embroiled in a battle of wills. 'Michael', on the other hand, adopts a stance of 'porosity'. He is a 'leaky' infant who freely allows the food into his mouth, only to allow it to dribble out again at the sides, or to regurgitate it shortly after it has been ingested. He is failing to put on weight and his cognitive development seems to also be affected. 'Slack and open, with his tongue pushed forwards, he developed a distinctive almost "stupid" expression' (Briggs 1998: 49).

Discussing the issues involved, Briggs writes:

> Alongside the idea of different infantile responses to problems in the relationship with mother, is the question as to which kind of infant has the greater capacity for resilience; is it the more impervious or the more porous infant who is more able to develop and maintain internal

resources which enable, despite difficult and adverse circumstances, the capacity to maintain relationships and relatedness to others? In both cases there is a disturbance to the central, dependent relationship to a primary object, and defensive formations such as withdrawal or a vigorous kind of muscularity are seen, developing as defensive alternatives to maintaining a relationship with another person and confirming problems in the processes of internalisation.

(1998: 48)

Skin porosity and self-harm by omission

The concept of 'porosity' has proved particularly helpful to the development of the account offered here of self-harm by omission and the nature of its relationship to self-harm by commission – that is, self-harm involving self-directed violence.

Patients who engage in self-harm by commission frequently demonstrate modes of relating that epitomise the 'toughened second skin' defences described by Bick. They may be hard to reach and seem impervious to bids for contact, which they resist through an apparent absence of neediness, silent resentment or verbal muscularity in the form of tough, confrontational speech.

A parallel connection may be made between self-harm by omission and skin porosity. The 'porous skin' patient gives the impression of being meek, cooperative and unadventurous. The narrative that unfolds speaks of an individual who lacks an appropriate sense of agency and has an impaired capacity to take care of him or herself. There may be neglect of health issues, or accident-proneness or a marked failure to protect oneself from mistreatment by others. The patient usually appears to be open to contact and able to take something in. However, material emerging in subsequent sessions suggests that what was taken in has leaked away again, without any contribution to the development of an internal object having taken place.

To illustrate these themes, I will return to the example of Kate, who seemed initially to be the 'perfect patient', amenable to anything I suggested. Kate's RSI had resulted in referrals to a number of consultants in the field. The severity of her symptoms and the inefficacy of the treatments led to recommendations of more extreme, experimental interventions, to which Kate submitted without complaint. At the same time, she told me she was being used as a 'guinea pig', that she did not believe these treatments were helping her and that physiotherapy was the only physical treatment of value to her. I felt that, like the infant 'Michael' described by Briggs, Kate was allowing any kind of food to be spooned into her, including the psychotherapeutic food I was offering. Because she was retaining none of it inside, her acceptance was indiscriminate. It did not really matter what she allowed in. The possibility of putting a boundary around herself and hence of exercising discernment seemed remote.

I became aware also of an adhesive quality to Kate's relating, a tendency to unconsciously mimic my gestures and intonation. Early on, my countertransference response was characterised by a strong inclination to intervene and protect Kate from her doctors. At times, I would catch myself thinking of them as her 'assailants' rather than her 'consultants'. In a striking example of 'total transference' (Joseph 1989), it became clear to my supervisor that I felt Kate was being bullied. In earlier work (Turp 2003), I describe how this led indirectly to the revelation of repeated incidents of cruel bullying in Kate's childhood. Kate had not 'made a fuss' about these incidents, which were perpetrated by younger twin brothers with serious behavioural problems. She told me her mother had been overwhelmed by the demands of six children, including these difficult twin boys. With no one to turn to and no way of defending herself, Kate seems to have survived through withdrawal and resignation, allowing everything to come in on her but nothing to take up residence inside her.

The story Kate had at first related to me was full of gaps and holes. I surmised that her 'narrative skin' – her sense of enclosure within her own experience and story – had been damaged by a long period of trauma, characterised by the central features of traumatic experience – a sense of helplessness and abandonment by one's good objects (Garland 1998). As an adult, Kate continued to be passively subject to whatever circumstances came her way. Hence, under pressure to spend long hours on a keyboard, she continued to do so, in spite of increasing pain and growing disability. Likewise, she meekly submitted to the experimental treatments to her hands that she so resented. In the analytic work, I found it important to move slowly, with a minimum of interpretive intervention, since it became clear that Kate would readily subject herself to interpretations, apparently taking them in and finding meaning in them but then quickly allowing them to leak away.

The containment provided by the therapeutic setting, together with my supervisor's valuable insight into the nature of the early trauma, enabled Kate to begin to tell me about the parts of her story associated with feelings of terror and despair. She remembered Christmas Day scenes, where the meal her mother had painstakingly cooked would be fought over by the twins, with turkey bones and potatoes being thrown across the table; and toys would be stolen and broken as soon as they were unwrapped. She described episodes of hiding in a cupboard or under a table, sometimes watching her younger brother being hit or tormented by the twins. This piecing together of Kate's childhood experience, which I have described elsewhere in terms of 'narrative skin repair' (Turp 2003), formed a major part of the therapeutic work. Details were remembered, reflected on, narrated and re-narrated between us. As a result, Kate began to experience a sense of coherent and boundaried self. With this accomplished, she began to be able to 'make a fuss'. She told her consultants what did and did not help her RSI symptoms and refused to participate in further experimental treatments. She asserted that it was her place, not theirs, to decide whether or not to have a child.

Returning to Briggs's question regarding the relative capacities and vulnerabilities of 'impervious' and 'porous' individuals, it is interesting to note that Kate's development had in some respects been quite stunted. During the course of the therapeutic work, it emerged that she was intellectually capable of far more than the well paid but routine position she had held in an office in the City. It seemed fitting, therefore, that towards the end of her time with me, she returned to study with a view to becoming an English teacher. As she could not write continuously for more than a few minutes, she was unable to sit examinations in the usual way and had to argue quite forcefully for special dispensations appropriate to her disability. The fact that she was able to do so provided further evidence of the efficacy of the psychoanalytic work we had undertaken together.

In terms of the physical consequences of her self-harm by omission, Kate's disabilities were of a serious and probably permanent nature, with no hope being held out of a full reversal. When a move of house precipitated the end of Kate's period of psychotherapy with me, the work of mourning the serious losses she had suffered was far from complete. In terms of the work we had undertaken, Kate's account of her childhood experiences strongly indicated to the role of trauma in her failure to develop an adequate capacity for self-care, one that would have served to protect her from the physical abuses she allowed. Freud (1920) noted that the literal meaning of the word trauma is 'wound' or 'piercing'. In the case of physical skin, good functioning involves strength, flexibility, resilience and a certain degree of permeability. Understandings emerging from the field of neuroscience are also interesting and significant to this theme, attesting as they do to the centrality of affect regulation to adequate psychological functioning (e.g. Schore 1994). Although there is insufficient space to explore the relevant findings here, we may note that the physical skin is the organ of regulation *par excellence* and surmise that the psychic skin, in parallel, is the 'organ' of affect regulation.

When all is in order, the skin has an elastic quality. It cannot be easily pierced and, if it is pierced, then the damage will heal. The time required for healing will vary, depending on the severity of the wound, the care given and the individual's capacity for recovery. The same may be said of psychic skin, the point of negotiation of connectedness and separation between self and others. The physical skin is often the site of damage inflicted in acts of self-harm. Similarly, distortions of psychic skin functioning involving 'porosity' and 'toughening' are frequently in evidence among individuals who self-harm. In some individuals one or the other may be emphasised, while in others, or in the same individual at different times, porosity and toughening may be equally apparent.

Theoretical issues

Bick identifies in her work an early stage of development that precedes the achievement of the paranoid-schizoid position. She notes that: 'Until the containing functions have been introjected, the concept of a space within the self cannot arise. Introjection, i.e. construction of an object in an internal space, is therefore impaired' (Bick 1968: 56).

Bick was in no doubt that she had identified in her infants characteristic modes of relating and defending prior to and more primitive than those characteristic of the paranoid-schizoid position. Andrew Briggs states:

> Klein drew our attention to the fact that in the paranoid-schizoid and depressive positions the infant has an internal object at the core of the ego. In drawing our attention to severe difficulties in the development of a capacity to introject, Bick took us to a stage prior to this.
>
> (2002: 10)

Judith Mitrani (2001) cites Winnicott, Ogden, Meltzer and Tustin as other writers who reached similar conclusions. Each of them refers to an inchoate infantile state characterised by non-integration and associated with an autosensual orientation to the container-object. Each suggests that, in the context of repeated skin-to-skin experiences, the infant develops his or her own sense of a serviceable skin boundary and is thereby enabled to differentiate inside from outside.

The idea of a constellation of concerns and defences and associated countertransference experience that is distinctive, that does not belong to either the paranoid-schizoid or depressive constellations, continues to develop in the contemporary literature. Ladame and Perret-Catipovic (1998) and Waddell (2006) have noted the ways in which adolescent 'toughening' in the form of narcissism can operate in the service of development. Stephen Briggs (2006) describes suicidal adolescents being able to make use of containment when it is offered, and identifies a distinct, less hateful, countertransference response to an adolescent patient's omnipotence when it emerges as operating in the service of development.

With the exception of Ogden (1989), who coined the term 'autistic-contiguous position', writers have not formally identified the constellation observed as a separate 'position'. This may have limited the range of influence of these theoretical developments, which are, on the whole, not well addressed in adult training and are only rarely referred to in the adult literature. In the light of this situation, I believe it would be helpful to identify clearly a *precarious skin position*, a term that makes explicit the link to Bick's groundbreaking work, the centrality of psychic skin issues in the early weeks and months of life, and the relevance of the specific concerns, defences and countertransference experiences to our clinical work with adults, as well as with children and adolescents. In a continuation of the passage cited above, Andrew Briggs alludes to the need for further discussion and theoretical development: 'The relationship of this earlier stage to the paranoid-schizoid and depressive positions is obviously an important question, the answer to which is not readily available in Bick's papers' (2002: 11).

I have come to think that 'precarious skin' moments feature to a greater or lesser extent in every clinical encounter but are particularly prevalent in work with individuals who self-harm. Hence in relating to individuals who self-harm, whether by commission or omission, we may meaningfully enquire whether the key issues emerging speak primarily of precarious skin or paranoid-schizoid preoccupations. In any one particular session, are the predominant concerns intolerance of dependency, adhesiveness and terror of liquefying? Or are we more aware of envy, greed and fear of fragmentation emanating from the projection of the patient's own destructiveness? As described by Heimann (1950), Britton (2003) and others, countertransference experience is our most reliable indicator of the underlying state of mind shaping the patient's thoughts, words and actions. In the situation where a patient is self-harming, consideration of experience in the countertransference can usefully be combined with an understanding of the possibilities of precarious skin, paranoid-schizoid or depressive concerns predominating at any one time.

References

Bick, E. (1968) 'The experience of the skin in early object relations', *International Journal of Psychoanalysis* 49: 484–486.

Bick, E. (1986/2002) 'Further considerations on the function of the skin in early object relations', in A. Briggs (ed.) *Surviving Space: Papers on Infant Observation*, London: Karnac, 2002.

Briggs, A. (ed.) (2002) *Surviving Space: Papers on Infant Observation*, London: Karnac.

Briggs, S. (1998) 'The contribution of infant observation to an understanding of feeding difficulties in infancy', *Infant Observation* 1, 3: 44–59.

Briggs, S., Maltsberger, J., Goldblatt, M., Lindner, R. and Fiedler, G. (2006) 'Assessing and engaging suicidal teenagers in psychoanalytic psychotherapy', *Archives for Suicide Research* 10, 4: 323–338.

Britton, R. (2003) *Sex, Death and the Superego*, London: Karnac.

Freud, S. (1920) 'Beyond the pleasure principle', in J. Strachey (ed.) *The Standard Edition of the Works of Sigmund Freud, XVIII* (pp. 1–64), London: Hogarth.

Garland, C. (ed.) (1998) *Understanding Trauma: A Psychoanalytic Approach*, London: Duckworth/Tavistock Clinic Series.

Heimann, P. (1950) 'On countertransference', *International Journal of Psychoanalysis* 31: 81–85.

Joseph, B. (1989) 'Transference: the total situation', *International Journal of Psychoanalysis* 66: 447–454.

Ladame, F. and Perret-Catipovic, M. (ed.) (1998) *Adolescence and Psychoanalysis: The Story and the History*, London: Karnac.

Meltzer, D. (1974) 'Adhesive identification', in A. Hahn (ed.) *Sincerity and Other Works: The Collected Papers of Donald Meltzer*, London: Karnac, 1994.

Meltzer, D., Bremner, J., Hoxter, S., Weddell, D. and Wittenberg, I. (1975) *Explorations in Autism*, Strathtay: Clunie Press.

Mitrani, J.L. (2001) *Ordinary People and Extra-ordinary Protections: A Post-Kleinian Approach to the Treatment of Primitive Mental States*, Hove: Brunner-Routledge.

Ogden, T. (1989) *The Primitive Edge of Experience*, London: Karnac.

Schore, A. (1994) *Affect Regulation and the Origin of the Self: The Neurobiology of Emotional Development*, New York: Lawrence Erlbaum Associates.

Stein, M., Sufian, J. and Hazlehurst, M. (2001) *Supporting Care Leavers: A Training and Resource Pack for Young People Leaving Care*, First Key, Oxford Chambers, Oxford Place, Leeds LS1 3AX.

Turp, M.D. (2003) *Hidden Self-Harm: Narratives from Psychotherapy*, London: Jessica Kingsley.

Turp, M.D. (2004) 'The capacity for self-care', *International Journal of Infant Observation* 7, 1: 108–125.

Waddell, M. (2006) 'Narcissism – an adolescent disorder?', *Journal of Child Psychotherapy* 31, 1: 21–34.

Chapter 17

Psychological safety: a missing concept in suicide risk prevention

Martin Seager

The concept of risk is inextricably interwoven with its opposite concept of safety. Together both concepts create a system of thinking. However, when it comes to looking at risk in mental health services our thinking has traditionally been very concrete and focused almost exclusively on physical danger. Very little conscious attention has been given to the relational and social context that gives rise to dangerous feelings, thoughts and acts, and even less attention to the relational and social factors that give rise to an atmosphere of safety and security.

Traditionally, attempts to use psychoanalytic thinking to address the task of preventing suicide and self-harm in our mental health services have been focused at the purely clinical level. This has largely meant spreading psychoanalytic skills to a wider group of clinicians, improving methods of clinical risk assessment and improving therapeutic interventions for individuals, couples, families and groups. Whilst this has been valuable at this level, it also arguably represents a failure to exploit psychoanalytic thinking and wisdom at a wider level. In this chapter I wish to broaden the focus to include the whole culture or ethos in which mental health services are provided. I shall be arguing that it is vital for psychoanalytic and other psychological concepts to be brought to bear in designing our mental health services so that they promote a culture of what I am calling 'psychological safety'. Such a culture for service provision would also entail a much wider concept of risk assessment that goes beyond the 'medicalised' examination of the stability of an individual personality and explores the actual attachments and relationships available to that individual, including those attachments and relationships that the service itself is (or is not) providing. In this way risk and safety in mental health terms can be seen as emerging from an object-relational context in which it is the way that the 'outer world' and 'inner world' mesh, clash or connect with each other that is even more critical than either 'world' alone.

It is not controversial to say that, in the UK at least, we live in an era of unprecedented preoccupation with the notion of 'risk' in our public mental health services. Notions of 'risk' and 'safety' have long been at the heart of government policy on mental health, as epitomised by the guidance document entitled 'Modernising mental health services: safe, sound and supportive' (DoH 1998). This is partly a consequence of the continuing switch of emphasis by both major political parties over the last twenty years or more away from hospital or in-patient care and towards community-based services. However, in psychological terms what really is a 'safe' or 'secure' mental health service? The more I have thought about this question, the clearer it has become to me that the psychosocial aspects of risk and safety have traditionally been overlooked. When we (the generic 'we' of the British NHS) collectively and publicly talk about 'security' in our mental health services, we seem immediately to focus on the 'forensic' end of the scale. The very term 'secure' in our mental health services appears to have been hijacked by associations with criminality and dangerousness, rather than its more natural association to notions of calmness and carefree stability. Indeed, the word itself originally comes from the Latin 'securus', meaning exactly that – 'free from care and worry'. In stark contrast to this, however, the tone of thinking in our mental health service culture, when addressing itself to security, is in essence 'paranoid' and 'concrete' in the Kleinian sense.

In this more paranoid and concrete state of mind, we are persecuted by the threat of a *destructive action* or *outcome* and are defensively attuned to avoiding or escaping any manifestation of 'risk', as if risk was a concrete monster lurking in the shadows. When any 'serious untoward incident' (interestingly abbreviated as SUI, the first three letters of the word **sui**cide) does occur, we 'enquire' into it not in a spirit of genuine curiosity (though we may *say* this), but in a spirit of blame, criticism and persecutory guilt (again from a 'paranoid' position). Conversely, we are far less focused and explicit about what *good* mental health might look like and even less explicit about what a safe *service* might look like. We do not hold formal meetings to mark the positive developments that we may have helped to generate in vulnerable people (including perhaps reclaiming lives from the brink of suicide). In the same way, we do not create guidelines about the processes and conditions under which these life-affirming developments are nurtured.

Generic guidelines constantly talk of the importance of 'teamwork' and 'partnership' but in reality there is still as yet no psychologically (let alone psychoanalytically) informed definition of what this actually means in practice. It is still far too common that there is no genuine meeting of minds between the different professional groups and agencies that may all be dealing with the same individual service user. Sometimes this will even amount to a schism or conflict that emanates from the actual professional ethos even before transference processes are taken into consideration. Our mental health services to this day remain driven by a largely bio-socio-political ethos, but this is a 'default position', implicit, unspoken and in many ways unconscious. There is in essence a 'philosophy vacuum' in which psychological principles, concepts and values (including psychoanalytic ones) are conspicuous by their absence. Where the minds of professionals are not empathically linked to buffer the distress of service users, but instead are linked to a general 'surveillance' mentality (see Cooper and Lousada 2005), deriving from risk-focused government policies and performance-driven managerial styles, anxious, defensive and even 'paranoid' professional practice thrives. This culture or atmosphere will inevitably often echo, collude with and amplify the paranoid states of mind that service users bring to us in the hope of understanding and change.

As the 'love cure' and the original 'talking cure', psychoanalysis can teach us much about the life-promoting properties of attachment, containment and relationship to self and others. It equally teaches us about the deadliness, danger, terror and despair that result when these qualities are perverted or simply not available to the human psyche or spirit. It provides an overall guiding framework for understanding the causes of both good and poor mental health. How strange, then, that the psychoanalytic literature, whilst being prolific on these subjects in relation to the treatment of individuals, couples, groups and families within the specific micro-environment of the consulting room, is relatively silent (with perhaps a few notable exceptions such as the work of Isabel Menzies Lyth (1988), Tom Main (e.g. 1946) and S.H. Foulkes (e.g. 1964)) in relation to the general macro-culture in which these and other clinical services are provided every day in the public mental health sector. As a consequence, psychoanalytic thinking does not sufficiently inform public policy on good practice in generic mental health services, and psychoanalytic concepts have not sufficiently entered the clinical ethos of public mental health services in which all of us, including NHS psychoanalytic specialists, are expected to work.

Suicide prevention – the contribution of psychoanalytic thinking

Psychoanalytic thinking teaches us that suicide is the ultimate act of someone who feels at the complete mercy of one or more 'bad objects' (internal or external) and/or bereft of attachment to any sufficiently 'good object' (external or internal). An object-relational framework helps us to understand how the balance of an individual's mind can be tipped from life to death. It shows us that suicide can be both the murder of an unbearable self because it is identified with a bad object and an escape from an unbearable torment. It is at one and the same time the ultimate communication and an end to communication, the ultimate attack and the ultimate defence.

What keeps any of us alive psychologically? Love is the primal food of the human spirit. For all of us as human beings there is a potential for suicide if we are starved of love and positioned without real hope of escape under sufficient hardship, pain, deprivation, trauma, loss, abuse or torment.

It is the experience through the developmental years of being known, 'held in mind', remembered, loved and cared for that gives our lives an underlying thread of security and meaning. This 'good enough experience' can then be internalised as a foundation for the personality. The root of mental health is in secure attachment. Within different strands of psychoanalytic thought, there are different terms that equally reflect this concept of a healthy, secure, contained and socialised personality or self evolving from infancy to mature adulthood. These include the Freudian notion of 'ego strength', 'psychic skin' (derived from the work of Esther Bick, e.g. 1968), and more recently the attachment-based concept of 'mentalisation' put forward by Anthony Bateman and Peter Fonagy (e.g. 2004). The experience of being externally cared for and emotionally mirrored enables all of us to develop a secure and realistic internal sense of self that can be resilient in the face of external stress and creative in relationship to others rather than being distrustful, defensive or destructive.

In this way psychoanalytic theory provides a very clear foundation for defining what we actually mean by 'mental health'. It provides concepts and language that successfully capture the essence of human joy and human misery at both ends of the spectrum of experience, where love has gone well enough or very badly. The theory teaches us that the human spirit, whilst remarkably resilient, is only capable of bearing so much pain, trauma and grief. It teaches us that overwhelmingly painful emotion cannot be borne without the availability of 'good enough objects' both externally and internally. It teaches us that where pain outweighs the (internal and external) resources to bear that pain, defences will be formed in an attempt to disconnect the pain. It teaches us that the emotional and motivational potential of each human personality develops or flounders over a lengthy period in the context of dependency upon the sufficient attentiveness, love and structure provided by caregivers. It teaches us that a healthy personality will be formed in the context of secure attachment. It follows equally that where secure attachment is ruptured, disrupted, perverted or in other ways depleted or damaged, a healthy personality cannot form.

These are powerful lessons and well known to us every time that we do an individual piece of clinical work. But these lessons are not generally translated into the service ethos in which we all work except in the rare case of specialist institutions designed along psychotherapeutic models such as the Cassell and Henderson hospitals within the NHS in Britain. Our generic mental health culture is full of unconscious breaches and ruptures of attachment and containment. Tentative links that are formed between vulnerable individuals and a variety of mental health staff are broken every day in our services by a *mindless* use of referral/admission procedures and criteria, discharge policies, staff rotations, appointment systems, fixed or prescribed treatment quotas, bureaucratic systems, service cutbacks and reconfigurations. These represent breaches of developmental links and ruptures of containment that invite re-enactments of destructive processes (through the mechanism of transference) but at the same time constitute an environment that is *in reality* psychologically 'unsafe' 'insecure' and at times even 'toxic'.

Discharge from hospital, suicide and psychoanalytic thought

The statistical evidence – for example, King *et al.* (2001) – makes it clear that one of the times of greatest risk for suicide is the period immediately following discharge from a psychiatric hospital. According to a traditional bio-medical view of mental suffering as *illness*, discharge from hospital is based on signs of improvement *in* the patient. The reduced *symptoms* are thought to indicate that the patient is *better* and so can be *safely* allowed to return to the community. This leads to a sense of shock and surprise when the opposite result unfolds and suicide occurs. Within that conceptual frame there is no real capacity to learn from this experience as there is the tendency to see each suicide as a 'one-off', an *exception* to the rule. From a psychological and more particularly a psychoanalytic point of view, however, it is clear that there is a powerful connection between these two events. A hospital is much more than a place where an illness gets treated. It is a place where new attachments are sought out and also resisted, where the hope of being listened to, understood, contained and 'reached' is both re-stimulated and defended against. It is a place where new experience can repeat, reinforce or challenge old experience. In this context, any observed or apparent improvement in symptoms may be the result of nascent, hopeful attachments and containment afforded by the hospital setting. Discharge could then be experienced as a betrayal of nascent trust and the premature severance of tentative attachments that were beginning to develop.

Conversely, a troubled in-patient who experienced no hopeful attachments in hospital and no concerted attempts to reach him or her might well feign signs of 'improvement' as a defence against further humiliation and as a means to accelerate escape from a toxic or unmindful environment. In this case, unmindful discharge could represent confirmation in reality of the patient's worst fears and expectations, expunging all hope that some of the treatment failure might have been due to personal cynicism. The risk of suicide would certainly be increased in such a case by the experience of a further failure to connect with a 'good object' and a rejection at the hands of an unmindful caregiving object, especially one that also had the perverse audacity to *see itself as therapeutic*. This situation could certainly reactivate past patterns of experience through the mechanism of transference re-enactment, but it is my contention that such a situation would also independently involve *really* toxic or *really* unmindful properties of the current caregiving environment. This lack of containment flows from pressures on bed numbers and bed occupancy, staff rotations, staff morale, treatment models, staff training, staff defence systems, *mindless* (or even *soulless*) management systems and equally *mindless* generic care policies. I think it is clear enough that this is not so much about the qualities of individual staff members, although this is clearly also important, as about the *total ethos* of the service as a whole and the impact that this has on the *total* experience of the individual patient.

Suicide, risk assessment and the value of psychoanalytic thinking

In an NHS culture increasingly permeated by a preoccupation with risk, our NHS mental health services are teeming with a plethora of professional and generic guidelines or protocols on *risk assessment of individual patients* – see for example Linke (1997). In all such protocols suicide rightly sits at the top of the 'risk list' alongside dangerousness to others and self-harm. However, in all of this documentation, designed to aid or shape *clinical* judgements about risk, there is little evidence of the influence of psychoanalytic or even psychological thinking. In particular, risk of suicide is treated as if it were an inherent property or propensity of the patient rather than a reflection of that patient's connectedness or relatedness to his or her 'objects' and psychosocial environment. Such generic 'toolkits' consider previous suicide attempts, current intent, diagnostic factors, epidemiological factors and various 'stress' factors, but are relatively blind to the quality of attachment, relationship and containment afforded by the service *as a whole and here and now*. If we were to derive a golden or guiding principle from psychoanalytic theory and practice, however, about what keeps any of us psychologically safe, it would be something ultimately quite straightforward and '*externally* object-related' like the following:

1   To be held in mind and thought about in an empathic way by at least one other person in whom there is at least a basic level of trust (i.e. attachment) and with whom there is reasonably regular contact and the opportunity of rapid support at times of heightened need.
2   To feel connected to other human beings socially in a way that affords a sense of belonging, identity, shared meaning and purpose.

For all of us, if our quality of life were to fall too low in terms of these basic psychosocial standards, the risk of suicide would sharply increase. This is made clear by the fact that people often commit suicide even when they have had a 'good enough' developmental background and are perfectly fit and well physically but have lost all current meaningful psychological and social connections. A striking example of this is provided by a recent fire safety campaign on the radio in which we are invited to imagine a man who has escaped injury in a fire but has lost his wife, children and home and cannot face going to work. The slogan for the advertisement is 'a fire doesn't have to kill you to take your life'. This is a powerful example of how a person's body and their psychological history may be secure but their current 'psychological safety' is destroyed.

Therefore, although it is known that following traumatic incidents those who go on to develop difficulties are those whose previous internal levels of mental health were not good enough even though they may have appeared to be so, I contend that where psychological safety is breached, from without and/or within, physical safety is also at risk. Hence, in these exceptional external circumstances a suicidal or destructive act against the body itself would not be so hard to understand, even in someone whose previous internal level of 'mental health' had always seemed 'good enough'.

When we define safety in these terms, it is clear that it is quite misleading and indeed quite dangerous to split off our own role and the part played by other relationships in the total care system when assessing the risk of suicide. Under this framework, any risk has to be calculated on the basis of the *sum total of containment provided by the totality and quality of attachments available to the individual* at any given point in time. In my experience, it is precisely at those points when the sum of external attachments has been sufficiently cut or impoverished, however temporarily, that the risk of suicide, particularly in those who have little or no internally secure sense of self, is at its greatest. Of course, 'good enough inner objects' do not just have to be developed in life, they have to be *maintained*. Without sufficient continued validation and mirroring from adult relationships and attachments, even the previously 'mentally healthy' individual is capable of extreme regression, breakdown and even suicide. Such an individual could become overwhelmed and tormented (persecuted) by feelings of grief, isolation, despair, guilt and dread. Loss can only be borne if there are other 'available objects' to mitigate that loss. If the lost objects are precisely those that would have been needed for such mitigation, then there is a psychic vacuum in which breakdown and/or suicide become much more possible.

Winnicott (1965) famously wrote that there 'is no such thing as a baby'. If he was right to say this, then our mental health systems (if adequately informed by contemporary psychoanalytic theory) would similarly have to say that 'there is no such thing as a suicidal patient'. In the same way that we can only understand a baby in the context of its reciprocal relationship to a maternal or caregiving environment, we can only truly understand the full meaning of suicide risk in the context of the sum and quality of reciprocal caregiving attachments available to the suicidal individual. A truly psychoanalytically and psychologically minded risk assessment therefore should look not simply at measures of individual 'personality disturbance, vulnerability or mental health' in isolation, nor at measures of social or environmental stress in isolation. What is more critical is the inter-relationship between a given individual's inner 'object world' and the actual external objects that are available (including those represented by the service itself). In the absence of what we might call an 'object-related' or 'reflexive' approach to risk assessment, simplistic clinical errors could be made of two broad types: first, overestimating the risk in a highly internally vulnerable person who has a highly structured and accessible matrix of attachments; and, second, underestimating the risk in a less vulnerable individual who has an insufficient external structure to contain him or her. Very often it is the structured containment provided by the network of attachments (including the other patients) within an in-patient unit that provides the very sense of security that may ironically trigger 'symptom relief' leading to premature discharge and a fundamental rupture of con-tainment that may lead to suicide.

Containment also goes beyond the mindful support available to the patient or service user. There is a world of difference for the service user in being cared for by a carer who is contained and one who is not. This is a well established conclusion from the psychoanalytic literature, based upon years of clinical work and observation of mothers, babies, nuclear families and extended families. Just as the individual patient needs the containment of 'good enough' attachments to a caregiving system, so also do clinicians need the containment provided by good quality attachments to skilled super-visors, supportive managers and meaningful policies. To be 'good enough' parents or carers, professional or otherwise, we all need the support of grandparent figures. Taking this thought to its logical conclusion, the ulti-mate containment for the development of safe and thoughtful therapeutic relationships in a *public* mental health service must be the *state* itself. This need not be the *'nanny'* state in the pejorative sense of an *over-controlling, over-protective* or *interfering* grandmother, but rather what we might call the *'grandparent'* state which 'contains the container', sets a benign and creative tone for clinical work and keeps a respectful distance, but is available when needed to support the primary caregiving relationship. As those of us who regularly work in the NHS know only too well, these wider sources of containment are often lacking. Links to good supervision, management and even to a simple space for reflection are often broken by wider organisational changes and pressures.

In our public mental health services, we are routinely dealing with people described as 'severely mentally ill' and, in terms of the risk/safety frame-work described above, people who would score at the lower end on both domains. What this tells us immediately is the importance of trying to monitor and influence for the better the *sum total and quality of all attach-ments*. Even a good psychotherapy relationship, however skilled and com-passionate, may not always be enough to tip the balance away from suicide in the absence of other available 'good enough' objects or in the presence of other more 'toxic' influences. When we assess the 'risk' of those who consult us for psychotherapeutic interventions, however, we often fall foul of what might be termed the 'medical illusion' that our intervention is somehow *the* treatment and that other influences are relevant but not so central. This might also be termed the 'dyadic illusion' of the perfect mother–infant relationship. The risk analysis model proposed above hopefully shows, however, that this frame of mind may not always be quite as 'safe' as it seems. It is the net total impact of the whole configuration of 'object attachments' (both external and internal) that is critical.

There is a long tradition of acknowledgement that individual psychotherapy is only appropriate when the patient has sufficient internal and external resources to support the treatment. Very often, however, our public mental health services are being asked to deal with just those individuals whose 'complex, severe and longstanding' mental health problems leave them too damaged internally and too unsupported externally to respond to this kind of individual talking treatment on its own. There is still something of a culture even to this day that categorises such individuals as 'not suitable for psychotherapy', as if this deficiency in their psychological mindedness and external support was a badge of disability that somehow rendered them outsiders to the world of good, wholesome talking treatment. This picture is changing somewhat with the advent of specialist 'personality disorder' programmes and services designed to target those who might previously have been excluded from psychoanalytically based and other psychological treatments. However, even this in some respects reinforces a split between a specialist 'psychological treatment' culture and the general mental health service culture. The former may be seen as an oasis within the latter rather than as a part of the whole, thus paradoxically repeating the pattern of 'exclusion' in a different way.

We are still a long way from recognising in our public mental health services that severe mental health problems are all 'personality disorders' of one kind or another, if that phrase is to mean anything substantial. The psychoanalytic approach therefore still gets split off in a concrete way as 'suitable for a select few', whereas the science and wisdom of psychoanalytic theory, as a general theory of personality, should be applied to all in creative ways, particularly those who are the least psychologically minded and articulate. After all, these are the very people whose lack of self-development, profound psychic defences, 'acting out' and lack of emotional literacy *most* need explanation and containment in terms of the pre-verbal and infant developmental concepts that are the hallmark of the psychoanalytic approach. It flows from this argument that one-to-one talking treatment and indeed any modality of talking treatment (including couple, group and family) should really only form one part of the total application of psychoanalytic theory in our public mental health services.

'Psychological safety' and implications for improving service provision

Psychological safety is about the total service ethos and the total experience of the service user. In particular, it draws upon psychoanalytically-informed notions of attachment, containment and object relations. It is less about containment in buildings and institutions than about containment in relationships and social networks, although both may be important.

It is fashionable nowadays to talk about the 'patient journey' and the 'patient pathway'. To the extent that this concept recognises the total, continuous experience of the patient in relation to the system as a whole, this is a welcome development. However, it is not clear that in the UK the NHS has been able to progress very far in building the design of services around this vital concept. Too many other factors get in the way. Some of these are harder to change than others. I will now list below some possible areas for change. These can all be grouped together broadly as an attempt to move away from a concrete, illness-based ethos to a more dynamic, object-related ethos.

(a) Referral systems

Seager (1994, 1999) describes how referral systems can become less concrete and more psychologically and psychoanalytically minded simply by conceptualising the referring agent and the receiving service as parental couple/system needing to work together in the interests of the patient/client/ service user that they share. Equally, referral systems need to place the service user at the centre of this constructive triangle so that 'ego strength' and personal choice or autonomy are developed rather than eroded by the process of referral in itself.

(b) Referral criteria

Within the general ethos and culture of our public mental health services, referral criteria remain highly diagnostic and service-centred (does this person fit into the service framework that we have got?), rather than reflecting the dynamic and developmental aspects of individual need (how can we adapt what we do to help this person develop further from the point they have reached so far?). In this sense all mental health services need to share more of an ethos of 'reaching out' to the different needs of individuals rather than expecting individuals to demonstrate that they 'qualify' for treatment.

(c) Discharge criteria

Still to this day discharge criteria can be based more upon the idea of 'discharging responsibility' rather than linking up to the next stage in the developmental journey of the service user, client or patient. Political and financial pressures increase the tendency that may already be there in the countertransference to 'get rid of' our 'charges' who are somehow felt to be burdensome, difficult or 'challenging' and hand them over to the care of *some*, *any* or even *no* other provider. From a psychoanalytical perspective we know that discharge can only truly be effective if it is a developmental step that offers some kind of link or transition to something new (externally and/or internally) that will promote *continuity*.

(d) Therapy as dosage

Still to this day we talk of 'sessions' of psychological therapy as if these were 'doses' of a drug, and we ration them in our public mental health services in quantitative packages often with specific time frames and time limits. This can often provide a useful boundary within which to do meaningful and useful work. However, our thinking can become concrete and other options can get forgotten. Psychoanalytic theory and practice should tell us that therapy is a relationship rather than a procedure. Our patients improve because they develop a sense of who we are in relation to them and who they are in relation to us, to themselves and to others. They begin to *feel* 'held in mind' because they *are* being 'held in mind'. They need a sense of continuity with us through time and this is not always helped by a rigid focus on the *session* as the key unit of change. As long as therapeutic frameworks are matched to the needs of individuals and as long as psychoanalytic theory is deployed to understand the nature of the relationship and the clinical material being engendered, creative therapeutic developments can be fostered in many different ways. Predetermined clinical therapy contracts with fixed structures can sometimes be detrimental as well as helpful. Where these are based upon the medical assumption of a necessary 'treatment dosage' they are more likely to be detrimental.

(e) Stability and continuity of staffing

If psychoanalytic thinking is truly to penetrate the generic culture of our public mental health services, then it will need to influence the whole frame in which the location and movement of staff are managed. Clinicians of all professions and backgrounds provide the key attachments on which the development of the lives of service users can be built. The whole workforce, including administrative and managerial members, creates a professional family, system, culture or ethos that has a combined net effect on the lives of services users that could promote development, repetition or regression. The health of this professional family depends not just on the connected-ness between professionals across space but also over time. The less that staff movements (including shift patterns, staff rotations, transfers, covering arrangements, etc.) are managed with an eye to the psychodynamics of attachment, object relationships and containment, the less likely it is that the service culture will develop the lives of those that use it. It is a shame that so often the broken attachments of the early lives of our service users are re-enacted or repeated in their experiences of NHS mental health services as a professional family.

(f) Research and the 'evidence-base'

The research picture is evolving – for example, as new psychoanalytically informed research projects attempt to adapt to the new 'evidence-based' culture that is upon us, without surrendering core psychoanalytic principles. This can only help enrich the available data for policy makers. Psychoanalytic theorists equally could be more proactive in influencing and changing the future research culture so that the 'evidence-base' itself becomes more psychologically sophisticated rather than clinging exclusively and concretely to the 'gold standard' of the randomised control trial. There is scope for much more qualitative research, research that captures the subtleties of interpersonal processes and how these relate to development and change in the individual, couple, family or group, and also research that honours subjectivity whilst equally valuing the need for the reality testing of scientific method.

Conclusions

The whole thrust of my argument has been about the value of psycho-analytic thinking at a much wider level than that of the direct clinical setting. By invoking the concept of 'psychological safety' I have tried to demonstrate that risk is perhaps even more a psychological issue than it is a physical one. Moreover, it is not just an individual psychological issue but a systemic or interpersonal psychological issue.

Psychoanalytic thinking can reduce risk in our mental health services not just by the delivery of specific clinical treatments but perhaps even more importantly by informing the design of a 'psychologically safe' service culture that would ensure that our patients are held in mind and contained by the system as a whole. So often the complaint of those who use our mental health services is precisely this, that their personal feelings, needs and their 'stories' get lost, disregarded or rejected by 'the system'. Although those with severe mental health problems come from caregiving back-grounds where their feelings have already been neglected or traumatised, very often these patterns of experience are repeated or reinforced within the UK mental health system. This is not all about transference and counter-transference but also about unmindful and even toxic properties of the mental health system itself. As I hope I have shown, the un-therapeutic and sometimes even anti-therapeutic aspects of the mental health system include 'medicalised' referral systems, appointment systems, discharge systems and team cultures in which the relationship between the service user and the care system as a whole is not held in mind. The experience of caregiving can then be one of fragmentation, depersonalisation, alienation and discontinuity. Putting it simply, people with severe mental health problems generally come from unhealthy, unhappy and unfortunate caregiving environments. Too often the mental health care system in the UK can be experienced as yet one more unhealthy caregiving environment that repeats or reinforces the problems of the past. Changing this is not just about increasing the availability of psychoanalytic and other psychological therapies, but also about supporting, shaping and developing a generic service model that is psychologically minded. In this task psychoanalytic thinking has a vital role to play.

I am not convinced that attempts by psychoanalytic practitioners and consultants to influence decision making and policy making in the wider NHS culture have been as sustained or as intense as they could have been. To this day the psychoanalytic approach still retains an image of being rarefied and of little relevance to the real world, even within the general mental health service culture. It is a shame that whilst this image is a long way from the truth, it is still the image that predominates and it is an image that is perhaps partly deserved. Psychoanalytic thinking continues to be applied too narrowly within the sphere of direct clinical treatments. Attempts to publicise psychoanalytic work in the media may also have reinforced this narrow image as much as challenging it. As a result of this continuing gap in the awareness and application of psychoanalytic theory, core national policy directives about service quality in health care, such as 'clinical governance' and the more recent 'standards for better health', have been created without reference at all to a psychoanalytic or any psychological model. It must be incumbent on psychoanalytically minded leaders at the 'front line' or the 'cutting edge' of service delivery or development to reach out directly to politicians and policy makers, using the simple language of persuasion. It is hoped that the concept of 'psychological safety' as developed here will help in this wider task of translating psychoanalytic principles into improved policies and generic practices within our mental health service culture as a whole.

References

Bateman, A. and Fonagy, P. (2004) *Psychotherapy for Borderline Personality Disorder: Mentalization-based Treatment*, Oxford: Oxford University Press.

Bick, E. (1968) 'The experience of the skin in early object relations', in A. Briggs (ed.) *Surviving Space: Papers on Infant Observation*, London: Karnac, 2002.

Cooper, A. and Lousada, J. (2005) *Borderline Welfare: Feeling and Fear of Feeling in Modern Welfare* (pp. 62–67), London: Karnac.

DoH (1998) 'Modernising mental health services: safe, sound and supportive', HSC 1998/233. http://www.dh.gov.uk/en/Publicationsandstatistics/Lettersandcirculars/Healthservicecirculars/DH_4004567

Foulkes, S.H. (1964) *Therapeutic Group Analysis*, London: Allen & Unwin.

King, E.A., Baldwin, D.S., Sinclair, J.M.A., Baker, N.G., Campbell, M.J. and Thompson, C. (2001) 'The Wessex recent in-patient suicide study 1', *British Journal of Psychiatry* 178: 531–536.

Linke, S. (1997) *Assessing and Managing Suicide Risk, CORE – Mini Guide*, London: British Psychological Society.

Main, T.F. (1946) 'The hospital as a therapeutic institution', *Bulletin of the Menninger Clinic* 10: 66–70.

Menzies Lyth, I. (1988) *Containing Anxiety in Institutions: Selected Essays*, London: Free Association Books.

Seager, M.J. (1994) 'On not leading horses to water: promoting true engagement in psychological therapies by psychologising the referral process', *Journal of Mental Health* 3: 213–220.

Seager, M.J. (1999) 'Three new practical applications of psychoanalytic theory', *Tom Main Memorial Prize Essay*, unpublished.

Winnicott, D.W. (1965) *The Maturational Processes and the Facilitating Environment*, London: Hogarth Press/Institute of Psychoanalysis.

Chapter 18

Postvention: the impact of suicide and suicidal behaviour on family members, professionals and organisations

Stephen Briggs

'Postvention' is a term coined by Edwin Shneidman (1980), to mean the focused provision of help for those bereaved by suicide. Shneidman thought that postvention can also be a form of prevention, since one impact of a suicide is an increased likelihood of suicidal behaviour in a 'survivor'. He wrote that

> the person who commits suicide puts his psychological skeleton in the survivor's emotional closet; he sentences the survivor to deal with many negative feelings and more, to become obsessed with thoughts regarding the survivor's own actual or possible role in having precipitated the suicidal act or having failed to stop it. It can be a heavy load.
>
> (Berman *et al.* 2006: 363)

Professional recognition of the importance of this has followed the upsurge in suicide survivor groups. In the USA 250 groups are listed on the American Association of Suicidology website. In Europe there are 200 similar groups listed by the International Association for Suicide Prevention (Berman *et al.* 2006). Postvention has become a key aim of social policy; in the UK the National Suicide Prevention Strategy for England (NIMHE 2002) included promoting the mental health of those bereaved by suicide as a key objective.

There is an increasing amount of research that has explored the impact of suicide bereavement on family, friends and professionals. Shneidman thought that suicide affected at least six other people, and this led to estimating how many people are thus involved (Jobes *et al.* 2000). The impact of bereavement by suicide and the course of recovery show that the experience is traumatic and difficult, but not necessarily more difficult than the mourning following other kinds of bereavement – especially sudden accidental death (Clark and Goldney 2000). Bereavement by suicide is often followed by a strongly impacting sense of stigma, shame and blame (Barlow and Morrison 2002).

In this chapter I will explore the contribution of psychoanalytic thinking to understanding the impact of suicide and suicidal behaviour on others, families, friends, and work colleagues. I will draw on clinical and research data to look at three particular situations: the loss of a parent to suicide; the impact of suicide and suicidal behaviour of young people on parents; and the impact of suicide on professionals working in mental health settings.

The death of Ophelia

I use Shakespeare's (1607/1997) depiction of Ophelia's funeral in *Hamlet* to provide a model for the impact of suicide on others ('survivors'). On the one hand, Ophelia's funeral scene provides a vivid account of the painfulness of negotiating with the social stigma of suicide, culminating in Laertes' verbal assault on the 'churlish priest'. Ophelia's suicide, like all suicides, occurs in a social and interpersonal context. In the social context Laertes' response represents an attempt to idealise Ophelia and to displace his rage into the societal representative, to blame the priest for failing to understand ('A minist'ring angel shall my sister be / When thou liest howling' (V.1. 233–234)).

In the interpersonal context of the play, its murderousness, betrayal and revenge, Ophelia's suicide is not an isolated event but arises from and is driven by the emotional dynamics of the play. Hamlet attempts to ward off guilt about his contribution, through his rejection of her, to Ophelia's suicide, and to project into Laertes the hatred, murderousness and rage which he has previously recognised in himself ('Yet have I in me something dangerous' (V.1. 255[1])). He makes an extraordinary inflammatory statement after grappling murderously with Laertes, which is competitive, hyperbolic and provocative.

> I lov'd Ophelia. Forty thousand brothers
> Could not with all their quantity of love
> Make up my sum.
>
> (V.1. 264–266)

There are two points that can be developed from this. First, the relational and emotional context, in which, as Shneidman puts it, the 'psychological skeleton' is projected into the survivors, means that others are implicated in the suicide fantasies (Hale, Chapter 1; Campbell, Chapter 2; both this volume). These are dyadic and were active *before* the suicide, often over many years. Ophelia's passive 'giving up on life' (Freud 1923), merging with the waters in which she drowned, conceals aggression from – or more accurately projects it into – others.

Because of this, the experience of a suicide *attempt* also means being in receipt of a phantasied attack, and can have a similar devastating effect.

The difference between a completed suicide and an 'unsuccessful' attempt is that the latter does allow for the possibility of reparation.

For example, Annabel, a young woman of 18, took an overdose, with the unconscious intention of showing her parents, through their remorse at the loss of their daughter, how much they had failed to love her enough. Her father visited her in hospital and told her he loved her. This was the first time, Annabel later told her therapist, he had said this to her (Briggs *et al.* 2006).

Second, a particular difficulty in mourning can be identified in the provocative comments, particularly those of Hamlet but also of Laertes. The problem of bearing guilt and evaluating responsibility is evidenced as a fear of being blamed or punished. In this state of mind the 'survivor' seeks – and sometimes finds – someone, or a part of someone, who will indeed point the finger of blame and criticism. In the aftermath of a suicide or suicide attempt, critical self-observation and realistic reflection are often unavailable and instead we find hypercritical, abnormal superego function (O'Shaughnessy 1999), which projects or points out blame and criticism; it is ego-destructive and strips meaning through processes of splitting and projection.

Suicide is always traumatic for other people connected with the suicidal person, and, in attempted suicide, for the suicidal person (see Ladame, Chaper 6, this volume). The effects of trauma include loss of the capacity for symbolic functioning and increased concreteness of thinking. Identifications are as a consequence more destructive and negative. Mourning is impaired through the aim of narcissistic restoration rather than facing and working through loss (Levy and Lemma 2004). Ophelia's passive, even 'beautiful', death leaves the others traumatised with the mess of it all, and their guilt.

The impact of parental suicide on a child

The death by suicide of a parent is unavoidably traumatic for a child. The death of a parent in childhood or early adolescence is in itself a grievous loss. Death of a parent by suicide can carry a meaning of actively not caring about a child enough to wish to stay alive to be a parent. Mourning the death of a parent is a very difficult experience. Mourning, as Freud (1917) described it, involves facing the reality of the loss and withdrawing one's attachment from the lost object, in a painful process that is accomplished over an extended period of time. Reluctance to face painful reality leads to identifications with the object, denial of the loss and loss of reality. For the loss of a parent in childhood, the child needs the deep support of a loving and containing relationship with the surviving parent and other close relationships. Sense can be made of parental death in childhood only through the prolonged working through of the meaning of death for the child, an accumulated understanding, learned from experience in connection with development and the quality of close relationships. The idea of death, in the unconscious, can take different forms and meanings; but it often involves phantasies of restriction or lifelessness, whilst a part of the self observes one's own deathly state. Elliott Jacques (1965: 507) gives a particularly graphic – and gruesome – example of this kind of self-observation of death in the image from a patient's dream in which she was lying in a coffin and chopped into small chunks, but a nerve ran through every chunk and was connected to her brain.

The sense of self-blame and guilt after bereavement is intensified in childhood and early adolescence by the child's omnipotence. The impact of the death of a parent fits closely with Steiner's view of mourning in which the loss of the object tests the capacity to bear the depressive pain – experienced as desolation, despair or guilt. These follow from the feeling that love and reparative wishes have not been sufficient to keep the parent alive (Steiner 1993: 62). The sense of guilt about the hostile and sadistic impulses and wishes directed to the object, and the consequent sense of being separate from the object, in the establishment of the depressive position, requires the tolerant understanding of the object if these are to be integrated. Without such containment, the child defends against depressive pain, retreats from it and resorts to paranoid-schizoid defences which can cripple development and restrict potential for intimacy. In extreme situations there is the potential for breakdown, defended against by repetitive patterns of relating. Thus, if not worked through, the trauma will be acted out, through identification with an aspect of the lost object (Hale, Chapter 1, this volume). Garland suggests that identification with the dead 'is a means of avoiding unbearable mental pain, the pain that is suffered when it is feared that the damage to oneself and one's internal objects is beyond repair' (2004: 39).

The capacity to cope with the trauma of a parent's death varies. It depends, first, on the quality of relationship that existed between the child and parent, and, second, on the capacity of the surviving parent and/or caregivers to make sense of the loss for the child, to afford them understanding of the meaning of the experience and to work through the loss over time. When the parent's death is by suicide, working through will include understanding the impact of the suicide fantasy in the sense of what this inflicted upon the child.

When a parent dies through suicide, the probability is that this has been preceded by considerable conflict between the parent and other family members. The very notion that suicide is a dyadic concept (Bell, Chapter 4, this volume) in which someone is hurting or killing someone else means that the suicidal person's internal conflicts will be played out through projective and introjective processes in the family, either mediated by containing others, or exacerbated by misunderstanding and the projections of other family members. The family in which a parent dies through suicide may be 'doubly deprived' (Williams 1997). The first deprivation is the loss of the parent and the second is the absence of internal resources that would make such a difficult task of mourning bearable. This is close to what Clark and Goldney (2000: 470) mean when they write that mourning after a suicide is more difficult, not because of the mourning process *per se*, but because suicide identifies vulnerability.

Case example

The following example illustrates the complexities of mourning for a teenager whose father died by suicide when she was 11. Samantha, as I shall call her, discovered her father's body – he had hanged himself in the house. His death occurred at a period when she had not been getting on well with him. She later told me this was partly because she was angry with him – as her parents were always threatening to separate – and also because she felt that he had become critical of her. He had come to demand more from her at school and said he preferred her when she was younger. She had been very close to her father when she was younger.

After her father's death Samantha had been urged to 'go to counselling' (her words) by her family and school, but, perhaps not surprisingly, she had declined. The last thing she wanted to do, she explained, was talk about what had happened. In fact it was not until she was 16 that she agreed to attend the clinic where I work, initially a self-referral counselling service limited to four sessions. Following these sessions she requested further treatment and I then began to work with her.

At the time I began to see her she was preparing for her GCSE exams. She was interested in her school work, but she was very worried by her exams. She lived at home with her mother and younger sister, was bright, attractive and quite energetic. She told me that she had come for therapy because her mother kept telling her she had not spoken about her father's death, and she confirmed that this was true. She pointed out to me that everyone knew about it – at home and at school – and frequently she felt allowances were being made for her at school. She implied that there was no one who could talk *to her* about it and that she experienced as rejecting the way that others expected her to talk about 'it'.

My experience of Samantha in the first few weeks of once-weekly therapy was, first, that she was quite anxious about getting involved emotionally, and though she had agreed to the offer of therapy, she frequently spoke about not wanting to come and wanting to stop. Second, it was particularly noticeable how she appeared to refuse to take in anything I might say to her. Either she would seem to switch off from what I was saying, leaving me feeling I was talking to myself, or she would take what I had said, repeat it and, so to speak, chomp it around as if in a kind of debate with herself, before coming to the conclusion that what I had said was of no use whatsoever and inadmissible. From this kind of interaction, I began to think she might have an eating disorder which she could not tell me about. She seemed to have what Williams has called a 'no entry syndrome', which is a defensive system aiming to prevent a sense of intrusion and a 'terror of "breaking and entering"' (Williams 1997: 118). I thought that the suicide of her father had this meaning for her, of something horrible and awful entering and breaking into her, leaving her rejected, guilty, humiliated and out of control. I used this information to ask her about her eating. Initially she did not respond to this, and I tried to take in, and show her I was taking in, what she said whilst aiming not to overwhelm her with what I put back to her.

After the first holiday break in therapy there was a change in Samantha. She had found the separation difficult and she was fearful that I would reject her. It seemed that in the absence of the object, her hostility rebounded and she became afraid of being treated as she wished to treat me: to be in control of whether she came or not, and to decide what my suffering should be like. As part of her relief that she could come back to her therapy and that I was there for her, she volunteered that she did have eating difficulties. Initially, when she was 12 and 13 she had restricted what she ate, feeling disgusted by meat and rationalising this by 'deciding' to be vegetarian. Then as she entered her teens she found that any substantial meal made her feel sick and she would need to vomit to get rid of the discomfort.

I think that although Samantha felt to some extent relieved that I had continued to be available for her and to think about her, her humiliation and fear about feeling dependent were experienced as a frightening – even terrifying – predicament. This brought about a change in the way she tried to exert control over me. Now Samantha insisted on telling me 'everything' and I found that I experienced this as being held hostage by her imperative and controlling use of the sessions. She appeared to take some power for herself and inflict on me an awful experience that I had no option but to passively endure. In fact, Samantha became more virulently anorexic, losing weight, it seemed, before my eyes, and it quickly became clear she could not continue in out-patient psychotherapy. Along with her weight loss she lost the ability to treat words as words, and there was no longer any way to talk to her. Instead of keeping me out, she now had no defences against words which were felt as missiles that intruded at will. This was a most distressing experience; she became excruciatingly thin, haggard, and tormented. As I arranged her admission to hospital I was confronted with the feeling that I would lose her in a most awful way.

Samantha maintained contact with me during her in-patient treatment and insisted she wanted to return to her therapy when she had recovered. For years after her father's suicide she had avoided any mention of it. Now it was everywhere. She did in time recover, and she returned to her therapy and her school work and took her exams.

This brief and partial discussion of Samantha illustrates the pervasive and pernicious way in which her father's suicide – and probable phantasy in his suicide of punishing his daughter for growing up and becoming separate from him – had invaded Samantha, so that, traumatised by it, she denied the impact of it on herself and tried to shut it out. Behind this lay an overwhelming sense of being invaded, a crucial loss of trust and being able to be dependent on others, which was replaced by a wish and need to stay in control. Her particularly vicious anorexia showed, paradoxically, both how completely out of control she became and also how forcefully she projected her control on to others. This was driven from within by a terrifyingly cruel and destructive aspect of herself, an abnormal superego (O'Shaughnessy 1999) which took no prisoners and was relentless in its pursuit of death and deathliness. My sense of helplessness during this phase of the work with her was complete, as though there was nothing I could do or say that would make a difference and I had to experience in total helplessness her active inflicting on me what she had passively been the recipient of. Garland (2004: 39) calls this a 'projective imperative'. Samantha's utter helplessness and humiliation at the suicide of her father meant for her feeling small for ever. She could only wrest some power and growth through the enactment of her identification with her father, which meant she had 'to shove those awful humiliated feelings back forcibly at and into the agent of the traumatic event' (Garland 2004: 39).

The impact of children's suicidal behaviour on parents

The literature is replete with examples of the impact of a child's suicide on parents (Berman *et al.* 2006; Jobes *et al.* 2000; Clark and Goldney 2000). From a psychoanalytic point of view, Meltzer and Harris concisely express the extent of the vulnerability of parents to the death of a child: 'The great vulnerability of the couple resides in the unique identity of each individual – for the death of a child seems to be the one unbearable stress (Wordsworth's *We are Seven*)' (1986: 161). Gibb (1998: 134), in describing therapy with a mother whose teenage daughter killed herself, shows that the mother's extreme guilt prevented her from being able to use help to find hope. Whenever she did feel more hopeful, the enormousness of the loss and the impossibility of reparation struck her, then the reality of the death of her daughter was denied, and the guilt about her feelings of negligence towards her daughter was projected into her therapist. It is important to bear in mind that the extent of the attack on the parents by a child's suicide was clearly identified by Stekel (1910/1967) when he commented that a child's suicide has the meaning of robbing a parent of their most precious possession.

I shall illustrate the impact of a child's suicidal behaviour on parents through referring to two qualitative research studies. Thrift and Coyle (2005) interviewed a small sample of mothers who had lost a child to suicide. Using a qualitative research design[2] they understood the mothers' responses to the suicide in terms of threats to identity. These parents often reported feelings of failure and stigmatisation. In trying to recover, they found groups of people bereaved by suicide helpful, and they tended to develop accounts of the suicide that did not implicate themselves as having a role in its causation. Rutherford (2005) interviewed a small sample of four mothers using a biographical narrative interview method (see Hollway and Jefferson 2000). This study focused on mothers whose child had attempted, rather than completed, suicide. Despite differences in the methodology and groups being studied, there is a considerable overlap in the findings from the two studies. Rutherford's study is particularly interesting in that it gives detailed biographical accounts of these mothers' lives, it describes the experience of the suicidal behaviour of their teenage children and it captures the intense emotional impact of the interviews.

Talking about the suicide attempt was not easy for these mothers, despite the availability of therapeutic help. One mother said that she had never told anyone about the suicide attempt itself; it was 'very scary' and she did not 'like going back there'. Rutherford noted the impact of the interview:

> Carol's [the mother's] description of her daughter's suicide attempt had, as had all the previous interviews, an intense emotional impact on me. I was aware of needing to be attentive to every gesture and word she said and I had a sense that it was crucial that I recognise and understand how overwhelming and powerful the experience had been for [the mother]. I noticed how exhausted and drained I felt.
>
> (Rutherford 2005: 34)

This was a common feature of these interviews. The parents' shame, humiliation and fear powerfully impact on the interviewer. In another mother's narrative:

> When Helen [the mother] talked about her daughter's suicidal behaviour, I was aware of a feeling of great exhaustion and I felt weighed down and trapped by what she was telling me. I felt protective, even maternal towards her. I was concerned that she was vulnerable.
>
> (Rutherford 2005: 27)

It seems the interviewer is subject to the 'projective imperative' (Garland 2004) of pushing into the interviewer the quite deathly experiences that these parents had known. Helen's account also evokes a maternal response from the interviewer, and this appears from the text of the interview to be connected with the account Helen gave of her own suicidal behaviour in adolescence; the interview suggests a muddle in her mind between two children who had attempted suicide. It was a feature, in fact, of these interviews that three of the four parents had their own histories of suicidality which they had attempted to keep from their children, but who had nevertheless identified with it. This recalls Shneidman's view that postvention can be prevention. Work with those who have suffered the impact of suicide helps to reduce the consequences of suicide including subsequent mental ill health and heightened risks of suicide of the 'survivor' (Jordan and McMenemy 2004). These parents described a cycle of vulnerability, in which their own experiences interacted with the fear of being blamed by professionals, from which they wished to take flight. Rutherford found that these teenagers' suicidality occurred in contexts which included 'a range of disadvantaging factors including insecure attachment, mother's own history of suicidality and the absence of the father' (2005: 48).

Although these interviews took place over a year after the suicide attempts had taken place, parents continued to show traumatised states of mind, as evidenced by the intensity of their feelings, the distortion of time since the event and the continuing need for containment. The terror and indigestibility of the experience are powerfully conveyed, along with a sense of reliving the events through telling the story. The mothers varied with regard to whether they had been able to face looking at the meaning of the suicide attempt. One mother talked of undertaking a 'long journey back to reality' with therapeutic help. Another two mothers found they could not bear to talk about it, could not stay with therapeutic help and could not talk to their children (teenagers). Fear and helplessness were split off from anger and rage. The latter were directed to professionals and separated spouses who were experienced as critical, rejecting and not understanding. There is some evidence that these judgements had some grounding in reality, but they also seemed to serve to protect these parents from facing their guilt and realistically reflecting on the difficulties in their own lives and the impact of these on their children. All four mothers said that they had been taken by surprise and were shocked by their children's suicidal behaviour.

The mothers therefore constructed defensive narratives in which there was a super-critical figure, ready to point the finger of blame. One mother, Carol, said she had telephoned her separated husband after the suicide attempt and he had been unpleasant, he had blamed both her and her daughter and had made no attempt to contact her daughter. Another mother, whose daughter was in care at the time, took an overdose herself when she heard about her daughter's overdose. Another mother remembered her father's response – calling her a 'stupid little girl' – when she took an overdose in adolescence. These blaming and self-blaming punitive responses are aspects of the abnormal, ego-destructive superego, which is, as O'Shaughnessy describes in relation to a patient:

a pure culture of the death instinct; we see its chilling tricks and its installing of repeated cycles of cruelty and punishment and how it aims to detach [the patient] from object relations, personal development, his life and his life instinct.

(1999: 87)

The impact of suicide on professionals and organisations

It is a potentially devastating experience for a clinician to lose a patient to suicide, yet for a mental health professional the risk of suicidal behaviour is common (Jobes *et al.* 2000). Particularly when involved deeply with the patient's internal world and emotional struggles, a patient's suicide can stand for professional failure and have deep personal ramifications. Recently clinicians have been able to write reflectively about the impact and meaning of a suicidal act within a treatment (Campbell, Chapter 2). Studies in the USA show that the suicide of a patient can lead to a loss of professional confidence, and fear of being blamed and of losing the confidence of colleagues. After a suicide clinicians may avoid suicidal patients or alternatively seek to increase their knowledge and skills in suicide prevention (Jobes *et al.* 2000).

There is inevitably a high level of anxiety involved in working with suicidal patients. Partly this anxiety stems from the impossibility of predicting future suicidal behaviour with any degree of certainty. Clinicians can often be taken by surprise by a patient's suicidality; whilst some patients involve clinicians actively in the suicidal struggle, and leave the therapist feeling anxious about them, particularly at the end of sessions and in routine holiday breaks, others do not generate such explicit anxiety in the therapist, but tend to produce an emotional under-reaction. This pattern of understatement has now been recognised as consistent with the patient's dismissing insecure attachment strategy (Wright *et al.* 2005).

The impact on individuals at both personal and professional levels of patient suicide (and suicidal behaviour) occurs within professional, socio-cultural and institutional contexts. In the USA a recent comprehensive study (Berman *et al.* 2006) showed that concern for the bereavement process for the clinician exists alongside the fear of lawsuits for professionals working within individual insurance schemes. In the UK, where the main provision of health is within the NHS, instead of anxiety about lawsuits, the focus is on institutional audit, and the political agenda of scrutiny and targets. This has a mixed impact. It has both generated awareness of suicide as a major issue in mental health, and, through the National Suicide Prevention Strategy in England (NIMHE 2002), prioritised strategy for how this may be achieved. Heightening the need for risk assessment exists in parallel with a drive to meet the targets. There is a risk that a target-setting culture degenerates into omnipotent organisations (Bell, Chapter 4, this volume).

A suicide or serious attempt by a patient usually leads to a tension within the clinician between two parallel and differently motivated strands of reflection. An adolescent patient I saw, who was in the early part of treatment, came to a session and, in a very matter of fact way, told me she had overdosed after the previous session, had been taken to hospital and discharged. It was a very serious attempt and she was saved by vomiting, which her mother heard and responded to. She reported this account to me in a way that made it seem quite unreal and I had to struggle within myself to hold on to the facts. I had two sets of responses, though in practice they intermingled. First, I critically evaluated what I might have missed or misunderstood. This was primarily a depressive response, motivated by concern for the patient and a wish to understand what may have gone wrong and my part in it. The second response, motivated instead from a fear of blame and exposure, and much more persecutory in nature, took the form of a set of highly anxious questions I formulated to myself: were my clinical notes up to date? Had I filled in the right forms at the right time? Had I written to her doctor (GP)? These two different modes of reaction to a suicide or serious suicide attempt represent two different kinds of super-ego functioning: the former is looking for helpful guidance through reflection, the latter is fearing blame from a critical and punishing agency.

Boundaries between reflection and blame and fear of blame become blurred in omnipotent organisational cultures in which there are high levels of anxiety. In these circumstances, institutional defences against anxiety develop which aim to protect the worker from the pain and anxiety of the work (Menzies Lyth 1988). These often take the form of ritualised practices, such as form-filling and completing checklists, generated by the infrastructure of risk management. Anxiety is thus displaced from the pain of work itself on to the 'ritualised' task, the monitoring of risk. Such organisational practices tend to be risk-aversive, and the aim of suicide prevention becomes that of suicide elimination.

The painfulness of exposure to suicide is deeply stirring of personal vulnerability in professionals and potentially traumatising. The point about institutional defences against anxiety and pain, as Menzies Lyth (1988) described these, is that, in seeking to protect the individual member of the organisation from the rawness of painful exposure, they make it much more difficult to recognise, think about and process the unconscious emotional experiences, and thus, paradoxically, expose the workers to a different form of professional danger, that of being unwittingly subject to the projections from distressed and disturbed suicidal people. Although it is now widely recognised that suicidal people are often not treated well in mainstream services (NICE 2004), it is not so well recognised that the often cruel or vindictive responses to people who have attempted suicide constitute enactment of the split-off destructive superego, turning health workers into 'churlish priests'. The way that this kind of dynamic can be played out in organisations can be illustrated by a case example.

Bowley (1996) describes the complex dynamics that developed around a suicidal adolescent, Sarah, who was 14, and in an in-patient unit. Sarah repeatedly overdosed at times of separation or transition. As Christmas approached she refused to leave the in-patient unit, which closed over the holiday period, and when her foster mother arrived at the unit to collect her, staff found she had disappeared. The next contact with her was that she phoned to say she had taken an overdose. Staff in the in-patient unit were furious with Sarah, feeling that she was attacking their work and care for her. They were not able to think about the impact on Sarah of her enforced separation from the unit. This was complicated by the fact that the only professionals still working in the unit were nurses, and they were furious, feeling that their colleagues had abandoned them. With the unit closed, Sarah was admitted to a paediatric ward for the holiday break. Staff on this ward were furious with staff on the in-patient unit for abandoning Sarah.

Thus both groups of staff were aggrieved and pointing the finger of blame at other professionals and, in the case of the in-patient unit staff, at Sarah. These reactions are, at one level, representative of staff dynamics where one group feels 'put upon' by another. But the staff were also in receipt of projected aspects of Sarah's inner world. These were pushed into the staff by the 'projective imperative' originating in this girl's multiple early traumas. The staff could not help but feel the power of these projections together with the invitation to retaliate. This has affinity with the process described earlier in this chapter in the case of Samantha, who pushed into me the utter helplessness of the traumatic suicide of her father. It is through providing individual and organisational contexts that can provide space for and bear to think about these experiences in the countertransference that help can be mobilized for people traumatised by suicidality.

Conclusion

In this chapter I have discussed the impact of suicide and suicidal behaviour on family members and professionals. I follow Hale (Chapter 1, this volume) in not making a clear distinction between completed suicide and suicide attempts. These differ in that completed suicides do not permit reparation towards the individual, but there are important similarities in the ways that others are enlisted to play a part in the emotional dynamics of the suicidal acts. In the discussion and the examples chosen to illustrate this, I have shown the importance of understanding the role of the hypercritical, abnormal superego, projecting or pointing out blame and criticism. Those affected by suicide, in families and organisations, are thus placed under terrific emotional pressure to enact a cruel, critical or stigmatising relationship or role. Postvention, described thus, requires thoughtful psychotherapeutic help in order to work through the effects of traumatic experiences, and to thus prevent future mental ill health and increased suicidal risks in the 'survivors'.

Note

1 This line from the play was used by Fiedler and Lindner (1999) and I thank them for initially drawing my attention to this.
2 Interpretative Phenomenological Analysis.

References

Barlow, C. and Morrison, H. (2002) 'Survivors of suicide: emerging counseling strategies', *Journal of Psychosocial Nursing and Mental Health Services* 40: 28–39.
Berman, A., Jobes, D. and Silverman, M. (2006) *Adolescent Suicide: Assessment and Intervention*, 2nd edn, Washington, DC: American Psychological Association.
Bowley, J. (1996) 'Survival at the front: a study of the work of the nursing staff in an adolescent psychiatric unit', MA dissertation, Tavistock Clinic/University of East London.
Briggs, S., Maltsberger, J., Goldblatt, M., Lindner, R. and Fiedler, G. (2006) 'Assessing and engaging suicidal teenagers in psychoanalytic psychotherapy', *Archives for Suicide Research* 10, 4: 1–15.
Clark, S. and Goldney, R. (2000) 'The impact of suicide on relatives and friends', in K. Hawton and I. van Heeringen (eds) *The International Handbook of Suicide and Attempted Suicide*, New York: John Wiley and Sons.
Fiedler, G. and Lindner, R. (eds) (1999) *So hab ich doch was in mir, das Gefahr bringt: Perspektiven suizidalen Erlebnis*. [Yet have I in me something dangerous: perspectives on suicidal experience], Gottingen: Vandenhoek & Ruprecht.
Freud, S. (1917) 'Mourning and melancholia', in J. Strachey (ed.) *The Standard Edition of the Works of Sigmund Freud, XIV* (pp. 237–258), London: Hogarth.
Freud, S. (1923) 'The Ego and the Id', in J. Strachey (ed.) *The Standard Edition of the Works of Sigmund Freud, XIX* (pp. 1–66), London: Hogarth.
Garland, C. (2004) 'Traumatic events and their impact on symbolic functioning', in S. Levy and A. Lemma (eds) *The Perversion of Loss: Psychoanalytic Perspectives on Trauma*, London: Whurr.
Gibb, E. (1998) 'Dreaming after a traumatic bereavement: mourning or its avoidance?', in C. Garland (ed.) *Understanding Trauma: A Psychoanalytic Approach*, London: Duckworth/Tavistock Clinic Series.
Hollway, W. and Jefferson, T. (2000) *Doing Qualitative Research Differently*, London: Sage.
Jacques, E. (1965) 'Death and the mid life crisis', *International Journal of Psychoanalysis* 46: 502–514.
Jobes, D., Luoma, J., Husted, L. and Mann, M. (2000) 'In the wake of suicide: survivorship and postvention', in R. Maris (ed.) *Textbook of Suicidology and Suicide Prevention*, New York: Guilford Press.

Jordan, J. and McMenemy, J. (2004) 'Interventions for suicide survivors: a review of the literature', *Suicide and Life Threatening Behaviour* 34, 4: 337–349.

Levy, S. and Lemma, A. (2004) *The Perversion of Loss: Psychoanalytic Perspectives on Trauma*, London: Whurr.

Meltzer, D. and Harris, M. (1986) 'Family patterns and cultural educability', in D. Meltzer *Studies in Extended Metapsychology: Clinical Applications of Bion's Ideas*, Strathtay, Perthshire: Clunie Press.

Menzies Lyth, I. (1988) 'The functioning of social systems as a defence against anxiety', in I. Menzies Lyth *Containing Anxiety in Institutions: Selected Essays*, London: Free Association Books.

National Institute for Mental Health in England (2002) National Suicide Prevention Strategy for England. http://www.nimhe.gov.uk

NICE (2004) 'Self-harm: the short-term physical and psychological management and secondary prevention of self-harm in primary and secondary care. http://guidance.nice.org.uk/CG16

O'Shaughnessy, E. (1999) 'Relating to the superego', *International Journal of Psychoanalysis* 80: 861–870.

Rutherford, T. (2005) 'An exploration by interview of the feelings of mothers of adolescent children who have attempted suicide', MA dissertation, Tavistock Clinic/University of East London.

Shakespeare, W. (1607/1997) *Hamlet*, ed. H. Jenkins, *The Arden Shakespeare*, Walton-on-Thames: Thomas Nelson and Sons Ltd.

Shneidman, E. (1980) 'Suicide', in E. Shneidman (ed.) *Death: Current Perspectives*, Palo Alto, CA: Mayfield Publishing.

Shneidman, E. (2001) *Comprehending Suicide: Landmarks in 20th Century Suicidology*, Washington, DC: American Psychological Association.

Steiner, J. (1993) *Psychic Retreats*, London: Routledge.

Stekel, W. (1910/1967) 'Symposium on suicide', in P. Friedman (ed.) (1967) *On Suicide* (pp. 33–141), New York: International Universities Press.

Thrift, O. and Coyle, A. (2005) 'An interpretative phenomenological analysis of maternal identity following child suicide', *Counselling Psychology Review* 20, 2: 18–23.

Williams, G. (1997) *Internal Landscapes and Foreign Bodies: Eating Disorders and Other Pathologies*, London: Duckworth/Tavistock Clinic Series.

Wright, J., Briggs, S. and Behringer, J. (2005) 'Attachment and the body in suicidal adolescents', *Journal of Clinical and Consulting Child Psychology* 10, 4: 477–491.

Name index

Subject index

acting out xxii, 6, 15, 35, 116, 123, 134. 135, 141, 177, 179, 180, 181–85, 188, 192, 218; *see also* enactment

adolescents xvii, xxii, 5, 35, 41, 49, 50, 61–71, 72–9, 80, 81, 88, 96–7, 102, 109–27, 129, 130, 158, 176, 180, 187, 207–8, 226–35

aggression 43, 82, 89, 95, 97, 103, 106, 124, 135, 171, 177, 185, 193; archaic 135; associated with suicide 95, 96; *see also* suicide, suicidal; infant projections of 116; destructive 106; directed at ego 38, 39; *see also* ego; family 97–8; internal 95, 96; *see also* internal; neutralized 40; parental 115; projected 122, 226; turned against self 3, 95, 130

anger 21, 97, 104, 124, 129, 131, 134, 176, 180, 182, 192, 193, 232; turned against self 17, 95; projected 116

antidepressant medication xvii, xix, xx, 104, 165

anxiety 5, 26, 27, 31, 32, 35, 41, 44, 47, 49, 52, 55–8, 65, 67, 69, 77, 81, 91, 104, 116, 136, 141, 150, 178, 179–86, 188, 202, 223, 233, 234, 237; depressive 30; *see also* depressive; disorder 16; paranoid 194; persecutory 5, 59; primitive 26, 69, 115, 116; realistic 177; traumatic 38, 43; *see also* trauma; unconscious 31, 194; *see also* unconscious; 'useful' 179–84

anguish 21, 38–43, 81, 82, 83, 169

body xvii, xxi, 7, 14, 35, 39, 40, 42, 44, 49, 67, 68, 90, 91, 123, 126, 128, 130, 131, 132, 134, 216; adolescent phantasies of 64; *see also* phantasy; adult 67; attacks on 4, 15, 19, 41, 50, 63, 68, 80, 82, 89, 136, 158, 199, 216; barrier 18–19; damaged 146; destructive relatedness to 5, 14, 15, 20, 25, 26, 113, 216; *see also* destructive; female 50, 135; hated 50; identified with bad object 48, 49, 51, 56, 158; *see also* object; identified with mother 33, 70; image 40, 65; in old age 187; killing 5, 20, 26, 31, 32, 50, 109; magical repair of 51; piercing 99; representation 40, 43; sexual 50, 56, 67, 77; suicidal 80, 87–8, 89, 90 see also suicidal); use of 128–137

borderline: patients 42, 65; personality disorder xvii, xix, 16,69, 100, 166, 222; welfare 222

containment 8, 9, 66, 72–3, 76, 77–9, 116, 140, 159, 202, 203, 205, 207, 212–18, 219, 221, 227, 232

core complex 4, 5, 17–19, 136

countertransference xvii, xxi, 6, 9, 25, 29–31, 36, 37, 58, 59, 97, 98, 99, 107, 110, 111, 115, 123, 124, 140, 150, 155, 157, 171, 175, 179–84, 189, 191, 192, 195, 196, 205, 207, 208, 209, 220, 221, 235

cutting *see* self-harm

death xvi, 41–2, 54, 69, 73, 78, 80, 113, 115, 117, 118, 129, 133, 143, 151, 156, 167, 177, 178, 181, 190, 192, 195, 212, 225, 226, 230; *see also* suicide; accidental 224; by

Lightning Source UK Ltd.
Milton Keynes UK
UKOW06f0118120815

256739UK00005B/78/P